The Restoration
of Perfection

The
Restoration
of Perfection

❧

Labor and Technology
in Medieval Culture

❧

George Ovitt, Jr.

RUTGERS UNIVERSITY PRESS

NEW BRUNSWICK AND LONDON

The author gratefully acknowledges permission to reprint
the following material:

Chapter 3 appeared in a different form in *Viator*.
©1986 by the Regents of the University of California.
Reprinted from *Viator*, vol. 16 (1986) pp. 1–18, by permission of The Regents.

Portions of Chapter 4 appeared in *Viator*.
©1983 by the Regents of the University of California
Reprinted from *Viator*, vol. 14 (1983) pp. 89–101, by permission of The Regents.

Library of Congress Cataloging-in-Publication Data

Ovitt, George, 1948–
The restoration of perfection.

Bibliography: p.
Includes index.
1. Technology—Religious aspects—Christianity—History.
2. Work—Religious aspects—Christianity—History of doctrines—Middle
Ages, 600–1500. I. Title.
BR115.T42095 1987   306'.36'0902   86-27998
ISBN 0-8135-1235-2

British Cataloguing-in-Publication information available

for Kathy and Alexis

Contents

Contents

Preface

Being convinced that the human intellect makes its own difficulties, not using the true helps which are at man's disposal soberly and judiciously; whence follows manifold ignorance of things, and by reason of that ignorance mischiefs innumerable; he thought all trial should be made, whether that commerce between the mind of man and the nature of things, which is more precious than anything on earth, or at least than anything that is of the earth, might by any means be restored to its perfect and original condition, or if that may not be, yet reduced to a better condition than that in which it now is.
—Francis Bacon, *Proemium* to *The Great Instauration*

WHEN Francis Bacon wrote of "the commerce between the mind of man and the nature of things" and expressed the hope that the reconciliation of the intellect with the world could be accomplished through the mediation of "true helps," he was setting out a program that he hoped would assist human beings in recovering the lost perfection of a once perfect world. The most practical of utopians, Bacon knew that the blessed island could only be reached after a long voyage and that those who would make the journey would need to be well grounded in natural philosophy, mathematics, and the mechanical arts in order to arrive safely. For Bacon, the history of human relations with the earth was a history of lost opportunity: the human mind had chosen to lose itself in pointless abstractions ("there is only a whirling round about") and to ignore the assistance offered by natural philosophy and technology. In order to effect the reconciliation of human nature with the nature of things, human beings would first have to understand the ends for which their talents were shaped; then they would need to apply these talents to reasserting human domination over a perfectible world.

Of course, Bacon could have had no idea of the direction the restoration of perfection would take. I cannot help but doubt that he would have agreed with the means we have employed to subdue the earth, or that he would think we have acted "soberly and judiciously" in applying our knowledge of nature to the more practical project of rendering the world habitable. Baconian empiricism may have rejected the abstractions and logic chopping of Aristotelianism, but Bacon did cling to the faith that the human mind could invent those tools—both rational and material— capable of reconciling human needs with the hidden powers that animate the earth. Yet Bacon is sometimes blamed for creating the empty pragmatism that has come to serve as our version of the commerce between the "mind of man and the nature of things." We have found in his writings a distinction between facts and values that has provided an efficient means of getting things done; but, unlike Bacon, we have failed to discover the ends for which we do them.

In one sense, this book is offered as an extended commentary on this short passage from Bacon. I would like to explore in some detail Bacon's suggestion that the human intellect, materially assisted by manual labor and the mechanical arts, might restore the earth to its "perfect and original condition." Although this book is a study of texts written before 1400, it originates from a concern with problems that are modern and compelling. I would like to understand, first of all, what cultural imperatives existed in support of the labor of human beings, labor that would, in due course, transform European and eventually global life. I would also like to explore Bacon's suggestion that a failure of imagination had caused the previous age to neglect the reconciliation of the "mind of man and the nature of things." Did medieval Christianity offer an intellectual and spiritual framework within which the economic and technological transformation of Europe could occur? Did monks and friars help create a set of attitudes that made the domination of the earth the morally acceptable imperative of human beings? Did monasteries serve as models of economic and technological efficiency, microcosms of the capitalist and entrepreneurial worlds to come? Was work holy, a form of prayer, or was it a source of pain? Above all, what did those who looked at labor and its products have to say about them; what did the theoreticians of culture—who were primarily religious men—think about the project of restoring the earth to its original perfection through the work of the hands?

As I have said, this is a book that describes the contents of other books. It is not a history of technology or of economics; neither is it as concerned with practice as it is with theory. This is a book about what people thought, or at least what they wrote about their thoughts. I am in search of the same elusive answer Bacon sought in that I would like to know what impediments the human intellect has placed in the way of understanding the physical world as well as the reasons why we have chosen to use the earth in the ways we have. While I have written a book that discusses manual labor and technology, my real subjects are ideas, attitudes, and "cultural climates."[1]

I am by no means the first to consider these questions, and I have commented not only on the writings of medieval theoreticians of culture but also on the writings of the scholars who have helped to shape our perceptions of the medieval contribution to technology. Like my predecessors, I too have tried to recreate the intellectual history of the Middle Ages on the basis of materials that are often inadequate. The types of texts I have chosen to examine—commentaries on the first chapters of Genesis, monastic rules and commentaries on these rules, treatises on the classification of learning, a handful of treatises written by craftsmen—reveal both the vitality and the numbing repetitions of medieval thought. One reads, for example, dozens of paraphrases of Genesis that are drawn from common authorities and which draw common conclusions in order to locate the single variant treatment that expands the possibilities of interpretation. While the contents of these texts allow us to draw certain conclusions about what a particular group of writers thought, they fail to help us reconstruct the mental lives of the "people without history."[2] The kinds of texts I have studied provide ample instances of attitudes prevalent in the class of men who wrote them, but they leave only traces of the lives of the men and women whose labor was in fact responsible for building the world we inhabit. Although I have looked a little at these hidden lives (in chapter 6) this study remains incomplete, a guide to some consistently expressed attitudes toward the labor and technology that shaped the physical and mental world of the Middle Ages, but by no means a full exploration of the contours of that world.

Thanks to a brilliant essay by Jacques Le Goff that describes "the several Middle Ages of Jules Michelet," those of us who look backward in order to see more clearly what is before our eyes can be aware of the dangers involved in such reconstructions. While I have by no means avoided the temptation to extract historical generalizations from the texts I discuss, I have done so in full awareness of the risks—the biases, the limitations of evidence, the ideological preconceptions, and so forth—that such a reconstruction entails. Like my medieval authorities, I have willingly blurred the distinction between books and life, and I have assumed that evidence gathered from the former has bearing on the latter.

Preface

I WOULD LIKE to express my gratitude to the staff of the Van Pelt Library of the University of Pennsylvania for allowing me to use their collections; most of this book was written in their hospitable institution. Thomas Canavan and Bernard Sagik of Drexel University provided material and moral support. I am deeply grateful to Bert Hall and John Staudenmeier for reading the manuscript and supplying me with detailed and helpful criticisms; the errors and judgments that remain are my responsibility. Lynn White, Jr., to whose learned books and articles I often refer, first stirred my interest in medieval technology; indeed, most of what I have written begins as a reflection on his ideas. I thank him for his generous support of my work. David Lindberg's books have taught me a great deal about medieval science; in addition to his scholarship, I appreciate his kind personal support. Karen Reeds of Rutgers University Press has been a supportive, patient, and thoroughly professional editor. Abigail Bok's editorial skills have improved this book considerably; I thank her for her care and thoroughness. I owe a special debt to my friends Edward Reed and David F. Noble for discussing many of the ideas in this book with me, for reading various drafts, for lending me books, and, above all, for teaching me so much through their own work. My colleagues in the University Seminar for Feminist Inquiry at Drexel helped me to work out my arguments in chapter 6. Special thanks to Mary Ann O'Connor, Julia Epstein, Woon-Ping Holaday, Pat Cooper, Julie Mostov, Mary Hazard, and Ellen Rose. I want to thank my friends Jack and Jesse Connor for teaching me about the natural world, from Halley's Comet to the Hudson Canyon. Kathy Hart has discussed every idea in this book with me over the last five years, and her editorial skills have helped me to shape the presentation of my arguments; she has also provided the best possible audience by sharing my hope for, if not a perfect world, at least an equitable one. As for Alexis, I hope that someday she will approve of what I have written.

IN PARAPHRASING medieval texts, I have retained their consistent references to "man" and "mankind," as well as their use of masculine pronouns. Likewise, when reconstructing medieval ideas in my own words I have retained patriarchal usage so as not to distort the biases of the period. In writing in my own voice, I have used genderless words like "people," "humankind," and "human beings."

The use of the present tense in referring to texts written in the Middle Ages is a recognition of their status as "living" documents; shifts to the past tense in referring to the authors of these texts is a recognition of the fact that, while their words may not pass away, they have.

In the body of the text, I have quoted my sources in English translations; in many cases, original Latin texts may be found in the notes. I have given English titles for Latin texts readily available in translation (*City of God,* for example), and left in Latin the titles of other, more obscure texts (*De scientiis*).

Unless otherwise indicated, I am responsible for all translations.

The Restoration
of Perfection

Introduction

THIS BOOK began with the self-evident observation that the physical world we encounter in the late twentieth century might look very differently than it does. From the vantage point of an old and worn-out Eastern city, a city ringed with clogged highways, sulfurous oil refineries, and obsolescent industries, anyone might reasonably wonder what chain of causes, what convictions and cultural values, led human hands to construct this particular world out of all the worlds that were theoretically possible. Why, in particular, have the technological choices we have made over the course of many centuries left us in overheated glass towers rather than in geodesic domes or subterranean cities; why is it the automobile—that icon of modernity—and not the bicycle that transports us to our cities; why have we chosen to base our economies on finite resources rather than on replenishable ones; why have we created structures of labor that demand so much time for so little effect; or, in a more complex vein, why did the sublime tools of modern medicine, or the terrifying tools of modern warfare, come into our hands long before we were capable of understanding the implications of their use? The furnishings of the physical world seem to have a rootedness and inevitability about them, and we are almost grateful that technological determinism can free us from having to decipher the reasons we have filled our lives with objects that delight, perplex, and all too often threaten us. Yet, if we are willing to acknowledge that both the world's physical appearance and the social realities underlying that appearance are the product of conscious human choices, then we are bound to be interested in understanding the ideas and actions that lie behind what we see.

The first step, of course, is to concede that the human will operates in the world with a certain autonomy, and that even the constraints we inherit were created out of a freely chosen desire to have the world look just so. If we can accept human freedom, then we can legitimately ask ourselves why human beings have used the power of their minds and the dexterity of their hands to create this particular world; we can also ask what ideas have helped shape the technological choices human beings have made. Both of these questions imply that technology is the material means through which we give shape to our ideas about the proper form of the physical world; I assume, therefore, that "technology" must be broadly understood to include not only objects and techniques but also systems of thought and the language in which these thoughts are expressed. If we grant that the world we inhabit is in large measure a consequence of a particular way of thinking—ignoring for now the issue of *whose* thinking—the obvious question to ask is this: where did the intellectual predisposition to create this particular world come from?

A number of modern historians have argued that the technologies that dominate our world did not appear suddenly in the nineteenth century but were created over the long course of global history.[1] These historians have shown that the impetus to support some technologies rather than others grew out of a process of inventing and adapting objects to human needs, but that ideas and social constraints, even more than objects, have created the technology that shapes the world we inhabit. While historians in the past have written about inventions as though they had a life of their own (see chapter 1), most now agree that technology, like science, is essentially a social enterprise and that the decision to adopt a particular invention involves more than an evaluation of design characteristics, efficiency, or mechanistic elegance. Beginning with Karl Marx's discussion of technology in the first volume of *Capital* and extending through the writings of Max Weber, Lewis Mumford, Brooke Hindle, Langdon Winner, Merritt Roe Smith, David F. Noble, and others, there have been descriptions of the interwoven web of social forces and material conditions that lead to the creation of what we might wish to call, with Winner, "autonomous technology." Since it is hardly self-evident that technological development is dependent on social forces, on the history of ideas, and on the shifting self-perceptions of interrelated cultures, a summary of some key ideas found in three of these writers will furnish a vocabulary and provide models for investigating the origins of the systems of thought that lie behind the shape of our world.

In his analysis of the significance of labor, Marx notes that work is the means through which man "regulates and controls the material reactions between himself and Nature."[2] For Marx, human labor is performed in opposition to nature in the sense that human beings must appropriate nature's own production "in a form adaptable to [human] wants." By laboring at nature's expense, people come to change themselves as well, and one of these changes involves the cultivation of the human will in a struggle with a recalcitrant natural world. In depicting the struggle with nature, Marx provides a model for the exploitation of labor that he could then use to explain the relation between the creators of surplus value and the dominant capitalist class.[3]

Marx's analysis of the origins of labor is complemented by Engels's analysis (in the *Dialectics of Nature*) of the role played by labor in the evolution of human culture. Engels argues that human labor is unique in using tools to transform the natural world—a contention that has been cast into doubt by recent studies of tool use by primates[4]—and, indeed, Engels insists that the purposeful deployment of the instruments of labor is the most salient characteristic of *Homo sapiens*.[5] In making his case, Engels argues that tool use led to the development of human speech by placing early hominids into associative roles in which communication was a necessary part of communal labor. While the relation between tool use and human speech has been shown to be more complex than Engels supposed, current anthropological opinion does support his view that the ability to visualize the use of a tool and the ability to use one tool as a model for the creation of another do contribute to the process of symbolization that lies behind the invention of language systems. As one recent writer has put it, "both tool-making and speech represent indirect or mediated interventions in the natural and social world."[6]

If one accepts the centrality of labor and the use of tools to the formation of social relations, one can turn to the first volume of *Capital* for a description of the role that technology played in the creation of capitalist society. Before doing so, I should anticipate the specter of Marx's alleged technological determinism.[7] Those who have argued that Marx was a determinist usually cite his preface to *A Contribution to the Critique of Political Economy:*

> In the social production of their existence, men inevitably enter into definite relations, which are independent of their will, namely relations of production appropriate to a given stage in the development of their material forces of production. The totality of these relations of production constitutes the economic structure of society, the real foundation, on which arises a legal and political superstructure and to which correspond definite forms of social consciousness. The mode of production of material life conditions the general process of social, political, and intellectual life. It is not the consciousness of men that determines their existence, but their social existence that determines their consciousness.[8]

While this argument seems to evoke technological determinism, the reader must be careful not to equate "productive forces" with "technology" as though machinery was the only constituent of material change deployed by human beings. For Marx, technology includes all the products of human industry. Thus railroads, telegraphs, and machines in general "are organs of the human brain, created by the human hand; the power of knowledge objectified." However, technology is also the embodiment of human values. Marx writes in *The German Ideology* that "As individuals express their life, so they are. What they are, therefore, coincides with their production, both with *what* they produce and *how* they produce" (Marx's emphasis). The individual human self is expressed in labor, and one of the causes of workers' alienation is capitalism's separation of what a human being is from what he or she produces.[9] Marx recognized that human labor was conscious and purposeful ("we are architects, not bees"), and he argues that while the scope of human free will is restricted by the social and material relations of human life, it is by no means negated by these relations.[10] Furthermore, as Raymond Williams reminds us, the German verb *bestimmen*, which the English translators of Marx's works usually render "to determine," actually means "to set limits" rather than "to fix" or "to render inevitable." With this linguistic nuance in mind, Williams quotes Engels's remark that "We make our history ourselves, but, in the first place, under very definite assumptions and conditions" and then Williams plausibly suggests that Marxist "determinism" must be described in terms that distinguish between internal and external "laws." To observe that there are limitations on human autonomy is a far cry from asserting that productive forces create external and ironclad conditions that inexorably shape human consciousness.[11]

When one turns to Marx's discussion of machinery and large-scale industry in the first volume of *Capital,* one finds him asserting that "Technology reveals the active relation of man to nature, the direct process of the production of his life, and thereby it also lays bare the process of the production of the social relations of his life, and of the *mental conceptions that flow from these relations.*"[12] In this chapter, Marx does not equate "productive forces" with technology but makes a distinction between tools as the "instruments of labor" in manufacturing and machines as the "instruments of labor" in large-scale industry. Technology is the mechanized extension of the tools that were once the mode of production in small-scale handicraft industries; machines are mechanisms that perform the same operations once performed by workers using their tools. The function of the machine is to displace direct worker involvement in the process of production, and one by-product of technology is the alienation of labor. The worker becomes, at most, "merely the motive power of the machine" if he or she is not displaced altogether. The effect of deploying technology on labor, as Marx argues in the empirical studies that fill chapter 15, is the "appropriation of supplementary labor," that is, the hiring of women and children; the lengthening of the work day as a means of increasing the production of capital; and the intensification of labor. The introduction of technology into the factory system leads not to the diminution of labor but to its increase and dehumanization. The explanation of this paradox is contained in Marx's observation that machines are extensions of simpler tools and that they are developed as a means of replacing individual workers in the interests of enhancing capital. Technology becomes a powerful instrument in the exercise of social domination by one class over another; that which might reasonably be supposed to ease the burdens of labor and enhance the human potential to control nature becomes instead a means of exploitation, which, ironically, has human beings performing the functions once served by natural forces.

Unlike Marx, Max Weber saw technology as an attempt to deal with what he calls the "organic limitations of human labor." Weber's analysis of the rise of technology and industry is primarily a search for the sources of production's "rationalization." In a virtuoso style that substitutes brilliant and provocative generalizations for the methodical exposition characteristic of Marx, Weber investigates what he takes to be the material and cultural causes for the systematizing of production, labor, and consumption. He finds the impetus toward capitalism in the creation of mass-market demand, which came into being only when the goals of production shifted from satisfying the narrow desires of the upper classes to satisfying the broader needs of both the population as a whole and those specialized groups—like armies and bureaucracies—that arose in the fifteenth century.[13] The desire to lower prices in relation to costs, not for the purpose of amassing capital but for the purpose of meeting broadened demands, led to significant technological innovations.

Weber recognized, however, that technology considered by itself was not sufficient to account for the productive successes of the West. Thus

7

his analysis of the conditions that permitted the rise of capitalism includes discussions of the following factors: the rational organization of labor, the influence of religious and ethical systems on both entrepreneurs and laborers, the establishment of a legal system based on the concept of citizenry, and the foundation of a professional class of administrators whose function was not to produce goods but to rationalize the social environment in which they were produced.[14]

In reading through Weber's *General Economic History,* one is struck by the characterization of technology and industrialization not as *causes* of capitalism but as *symptoms* of cultural changes that were the real motive force behind its origins. This sense is strengthened in his recurrent forays into comparative history throughout the work. Here one finds, for example, Weber's speculations on the impediment to technological development presented by magic. Since, in Weber's view, magic resists "rationalization"—and by this he means that magic impedes the objectification of reality by assuming that spirit is one with matter—it stands in the way of the development of technology and productive labor. One also finds Weber's view of changing attitudes toward material gain, attitudes that had to be transformed in order for capitalist forces to be integrated into traditional societies:

> Originally, two opposite attitudes toward the pursuit of gain exist in combination. Internally, there is attachment to tradition and to the pietistic relations of fellow members of tribe, clan, and house-community, with the exclusion of the unrestricted quest of gain within the circle of those bound together by religious ties; externally, there is absolutely unrestricted play of the gain spirit in economic relations, every foreigner being originally an enemy in relation to whom no ethical restrictions apply; that is, the ethics of internal and external relations are categorically distinct. The course of development involves on the one hand the bringing in of calculation into the traditional brotherhood, displacing the old religious relationship. As soon as accountability is established with the family community, and economic relations are no longer strictly communistic, there is an end of the naive piety and its repression of the economic impulse. This side of the development is especially characteristic in the west.[15]

Weber's analysis of the means through which this characteristically Western alteration occurs is well known from *The Protestant Ethic and the*

Spirit of Capitalism. While medieval Catholicism, in the form of Benedictine monasticism, foreshadowed the rational system of productivity central to capitalism, it was not until Calvinism's concept of the "calling" had sanctioned the pursuit of gain and merged the contradictory impulses of asceticism with material achievement that Western capitalism received its decisive form.[16] According to Weber, other religions and other areas of the world—he takes his examples from India and China in particular—were never able to formulate an ethic receptive to economic gain. In India, the caste system retained the vestiges of magic in its purifications and pollutions, while Buddhism failed to develop a sufficiently binding personal ethic.[17] For Weber, the "rational mode of living" created by Protestantism was unique because it revealed a means of reconciling cultural norms and social organization with the acceptance of technological innovation and material productivity. Weber's account of the relation between piety and profits is useful for understanding changes that occurred in medieval Europe during the twelfth and thirteenth centuries, when agricultural and commercial productivity forced the Christian church to confront the effects of labor and technology on religious ideology.

Lewis Mumford has examined the relation between technology and human culture in a number of his books, beginning in 1922 with *The Story of Utopias* and extending through the two-volume study entitled *The Myth of the Machine,* published in 1967 and 1970. Although fifty years separate these works, Mumford has maintained a remarkably consistent attitude toward the place of technology in the development of human culture, and over the years he has extended his analyses to include such issues as the relation between art and technology and the role of technology in the establishment of cities.

At the heart of Mumford's analysis is the view that "cultural work"— that is, the development of the "symbolic forms" of human language, rituals, and arts—and not "manual work" is central to the nature of *Homo sapiens.* Mumford believes that the Greek concept of *techne* makes no distinction between industrial production and "symbolic production," and that it was only with the modern split between what human beings are and what they produce, between "life" on the one hand and "labor" on the other, that technology has come to have a narrow meaning centering on productivity as a thing considered apart from culture. As Mumford has put it, "I submit that at every stage man's inventions and transformations were less for the purpose of increasing the food supply or controlling nature than for utilizing his own immense organic resources and expressing his latent potentialities, in order to fulfill more adequately his superorganic demands and aspirations."[18]

Unlike Marx, Mumford sees the work of the hands, and the tools created to extend their power, primarily as servants of a highly developed and creative intelligence; labor does not create consciousness, but consciousness directs labor toward the end of establishing human cultural systems within nature. Tools are not the "main operative agent" in the creation of culture but rather subsidiary instruments. At the heart of developing human culture was ritual—"a mode of order man was forced to develop, in self-protection, so as to control the tremendous overcharge of psychal energy that his large brain placed at his disposal."[19] Language is an important product of the symbolizing tendencies that underlay this ritualistic mode of living, but by no means the only one. Like mechanical tools, language was part of a life that was fully integrated into the natural world until the modern age. Neither language nor tools had the mechanical domination of nature as their primary function; rather, they were needed to create an environment capable of subsuming the enormous creative energies of the overheated human brain. However, once in place, "technics" tended to support and enlarge the capacities of human beings and to act as a "timely corrective" to those inordinate powers of mind that always threatened to inflate the human ego. Because of human beings' power to symbolize through language and ritual, the danger always existed that the energy of the mind would become mired in the unproductive pursuits that Mumford identified with magic; tools and technology channeled this energy into "efficacious work," which, in turn, further enhanced human potential.

If Marx presents an anthropology and Weber a sociology of labor, Mumford's account presents a psychology of labor, one that stresses that work and its amelioration through technology is but one of many means human beings employ to create an environment hospitable to consciousness. In view of his perception that tools and technology are extensions of the mind, perhaps it was inevitable that Mumford would see handicrafts and small-scale technologies as more natural than the "megatechnics" of the modern industrial state.[20] What happaned to technology over the course of the ages was that from Sumeria and Pharaonic Egypt to modern Europe and America, machines became the allies of the dominance seekers. Tools that at the dawn of humanity were the natural extension of human powers became instead instruments of the power one group wielded over another. For Mumford, the coming of the "megamachine" meant the creation of a social existence that used technology to wrest power away from individuals and to invest it in a centralized authority. While for Marx the dehumanized purpose of technology is the amassing of capital, in Mumford technology is a source of domination rather than of production.

Mumford's case studies in the history of technology and labor are painted with a rather broad brush—they lack the precision and the documentation of Marx's—but they have great intuitive appeal. For example, Mumford observes that Benedictine monasticism supplied the West with an idealized community in which labor and handicraft technologies were united with moral purpose to create a balance "more favorable to a diversified and humane life than anything that earlier technics had ever before achieved."[21] Mumford suggests that the Benedictines provide an example of Weber's Protestant Ethic long before Calvin, and he argues for a continuity in attitudes toward technology between the time of the monastic establishments and the rise of medieval guilds. However, in Mumford's view, this near-synthesis of work, technology, and culture within the moral framework of the Middle Ages failed to create a fully integrated environment for human activity because of the Christian church's proclivities toward "the forces specializing in power—absolutism, militarism, and capitalism." The human mind was prevented from creating an organic society—a society in which labor and its tools serve rational social purposes—by the greed and ambition of a dominant institution. This is the troubling story that Mumford tells over and over in the two volumes of *The Myth of the Machine;* in some respects at least, it is a story that I will be retelling in this book.

These summaries of the views of Marx, Weber, and Mumford on the shaping on technological change do not exhaust either the thought of these three writers or the range of possible arguments on this subject. Many other writers have discussed the place of technology in the definition of human culture.[22] But from the analyses of Marx, Weber, and Mumford I would like to extract three observations concerning the history of labor and technology that will be useful in my own discussion of the Middle Ages.

First of all, I take from Marx and Engels the observations that tool use has shaped human culture and that labor expresses human lives, as well as the conviction that work "is the everlasting nature-imposed condition of human existence."

Second, as Weber states, the creation of technology is one part of the general process of "rationalizing" society that lies at the heart of Western history. By "rationalizing society," I take Weber to be referring to the construction of ideology—that is, to the construction of ideas and values that sustain one group's (or class's or order's) domination of others.

Finally, I will build on Mumford's claims that "organic" and "integrated" social forms, incorporating technology and labor within a moral and intellectual system, existed potentially in the Middle Ages within the Christian church and, in particular, within the Benedictine tradition.

MEDIEVAL TECHNOLOGY

The analyses of Marx, Weber, and Mumford also confirm the observation that within the context of an urbanized and economically expansive society the effects of technology are mediated by social, economic, and cultural factors. In the interest of clarifying what these cultural factors were in the Middle Ages, I would like to summarize the views of three contemporary writers who have dealt with the question of technology's place in the life of the Middle Ages. Like the more general accounts of Marx, Weber, and Mumford, these discussions of medieval technology attempt to fit machines and labor into an enlarged cultural context.

The history of medieval technology is a relatively new subject. In the nineteenth century, and through the first two decades of the twentieth, most historians denied that the Middle Ages had any technology (or science) worthy of the name (see chapter 1). When the first accounts of medieval technology appeared in the studies of Richard Lefebvre des Nottes, Franz Feldhaus, Marc Bloch, Lynn Thorndike, and Lynn White, Jr., they were revolutionary because they introduced evidence for the centrality of the Middle Ages to the rest of Western technological history. Like all revolutions, this one had its radical, expansive phase (beginning, as Lynn White has noted, in 1931), followed by a long and fruitful phase of consolidation and lateral exploration.[23] Once the history of inventions was clarified and, thanks to Joseph Needham, once the technological dependence of the West on China became clear, the question remained of how the age of Augustine and Aquinas could have produced such important technological innovations. That is, how could the theology of the

medieval church, with its insistence on strict orthodoxy and its apparent
otherworldliness, countenance not only mechanical inventions, but also
the creation of a productive economic system and a well-organized tradition of manual labor and craftsmanship? What became increasingly clear
as a second generation of historians took up these questions was the fact
that not only had the Middle Ages created a subsistence agriculture that
was productive enough to sustain a complex economy, but its contribution to economic history had touched the modern world by creating
many of the institutions most closely associated with the "rise of capitalism" in the sixteenth century. At the heart of these studies remained the
paradox of an otherworldly Christian culture influencing technological
and economic development. How was one to reconcile technological
achievement with asceticism and Scholasticism? Implicit in this question
was a larger and possibly more interesting question about the cultural
conditions that favor technological development.

One of the most provocative studies of the cultural variables that affected technological change in the Middle Ages is found in the work of
the theologian Ernst Benz.[24] Benz argues that there is a causal connection
between the creation of Western technology and "the specifically Christian premises of our Western culture." In Benz's view, the medieval image
of God as artificer sanctified not only the earth and the creatures that
inhabit it but also the labor through which God fashioned all that exists.
God has created the world for human use, and he has provided a paradigm of productive labor that human beings should take as their model
for activity in the world. Furthermore, as technology grew more sophisticated, the conception of the Creator shifted form. God the Potter gradually became God the Master Builder, and the primal matter used to
fashion Adam was replaced by the compasses used to measure the human
habitation. Finally, Benz argues that the other great world religions, in
lacking the image of a personal creator, lack a basis upon which to
sanctify technology.

The characterization of God as Creator and Architect of the universe
provides Benz with the first part of his explanation for Western technological success. The second part of his discussion entails the identification
of human beings with God and assumes that human domination of the
creation has been divinely ordained. Benz cites Genesis 1:27 and 9:6 in
support of his contention that "compared to all other creatures [human
beings are] understood to be the 'image of God.' " This notion of "natu-

ral" human domination over the rest of creation has often been cited as a key factor in the history of Western technological mastery; the assumption of this dominance has also been cited as the key to the impending Western technological disasters (see chapter 2).

Benz's third point centers on the contribution to Western technological progress derived from the Christian conception of time.[25] The use of the word "progress" implies the existence of a linear conception of time and the sense that events are both unique and connected to one another through chains of cause and effect. Add to this the Christian expectation of a proximate eschatological event, and a theory of meaningful action and of technological progress seems compelling. "We must work . . . while it is day," writes St. John, and we must do so in order to "redeem the time." Benz anticipates the obvious objection to an argument for technological progress based on the anticipation of an end of time when he notes that one will certainly ask why the "work" of preparing for the dissolution of the world should be physical rather than spiritual. Benz answers that, for the Christian of the Middle Ages, no sharp distinction was maintained between spiritual and material labor. Labor was a form of worship, and the material and technological products of labor were manifestations of a devotion that prepared the Christian for the dissolution of time. The incentive to shape the physical world after human ideas was reinforced both by the sense of urgency that accompanies the belief in finite time and by the sense that work itself may be offered to God as a prayer.

Lynn White, Jr. has developed some of Benz's suggestions into a persuasive argument for the influence of medieval Christian theology on the creation of a "cultural climate" hospitable to the growth of Western technology. White argues that the medieval Christian conception of human dominance has provided the intellectual and moral background against which the growth of technology must be understood.[26] In White's view, "Man shares God's transcendence of nature. Christianity, in absolute contrast to ancient paganism and Asia's religions (except, perhaps, Zoroastrianism), not only established a dualism of man and nature but also insisted that it is God's will that man exploit nature for his proper ends."[27] In studies of iconographic and literary evidence, White argues that, beginning in the eleventh century, a consensus was created among theologians in support of the exploitation of nature and of technological innovations that reduced the onerous burden of physical work. To lessen the burden of manual labor was seen to be part of Christian charity, and the use of wind and water power, as well as the invention of specific tools drawing on these sources of motive force, was supported by the scholars whose views created the cultural climate of the Middle Ages.[28]

A representative example of White's method of cultural analysis may be found in his essay "The Iconography of *Temperantia* and the Virtuousness of Technology," first published in 1969.[29] Here he uses the medieval tendency to "identify advanced technology with high morality" to show that over the course of the tenth through fourteenth centuries the virtue of Temperance was elevated to the status of the "preeminent Virtue," and that its symbol—the clock—was chosen in recognition of the fact that "action in measure" is the primary characteristic of Temperance. White's detailed argument concludes, "The new icon of Temperance tells us that in Europe, below the level of verbal expression, machinery, mechanical power, and salutary devices were taking on an aura of 'virtuousness' such as they have never enjoyed in any culture save the Western."[30] An emerging capitalism received the "moral sanction" of the medieval Christian church, and this sanction not only reflected the power of a particular economic system (and the technology that made it possible), it also helped to insure that this system would come to dominate European life.

Jacques Le Goff provides an alternative view of the role played by Christianity in supporting technological change, one that sees theology adjusting in response to the changing material conditions of Europe rather than creating these conditions. Le Goff argues that until the twelfth century, the medieval church viewed labor and craftsmanship as forms of penance and therefore of little value in themselves.[31] As penance, labor was not regarded by churchmen as a means of subduing the physical world but rather as a form of personal self-discipline. Beginning in the twelfth century, a new theory of labor and craftsmanship emerged from the attempt to redefine the mutual obligations of feudal society. For Le Goff, technology was not a means of easing the burdens of labor (as White has asserted) or a means of reflecting the creative power of God in human terms (as Benz supposed), but the outgrowth of changing material and social conditions. Le Goff's argument is that technology developed as a consequence of economic forces and that the medieval church responded to the whole range of these forces by creating a new theology, one receptive to the idea that human beings should dominate the physical world through mechanical means. Beginning in the ninth century, Le

Goff writes, labor "developed a new meaning, centered on the idea of acquisition, profit, and conquest, primarily in the rural context, where the word [*conlaboratus*] was connected with pioneering." Le Goff contends that the reevaluation of manual labor was part of an ideological struggle to increase worker productivity, but he also acknowledges that "worker pressure" helped to enhance the value of labor among those who formulated the "mentalities" of the age.

In the chapters that follow, I will examine more closely the claims of Benz, White, and Le Goff for the relation between medieval "mentalities" and the practice of medieval labor and technology. My purpose is to describe the role played by the medieval church in the creation of Western technology and in the creation of the ideology that supported it. My evidence comes primarily from theologians, for it was a hierarchy of literate men who defined the "mentalities" and "cultural climate" of the age. Nonetheless, I hope that my account of these ideas is not mistaken for a complete description of medieval intellectual life. If ideology is defined as the set of ideas that describes and supports a particular social order, then my purpose is to recreate the ideology of the medieval church as it related to manual labor and technology.

In chapter 1 I begin by looking at the views of those writers who, beginning in the seventeenth century, denied that the Scholastic age could have produced any science or technology because of the incompatibility of religion with any rational or productive enterprise. The goal of this exercise in historiographic criticism is to clarify the grounds on which it is proper to speak of technological progress in the Middle Ages; it also creates a context in which to reconsider the definitions of "technology" and "progress."

Chapter 2 takes up some of the interpretations of medieval technology discussed here, namely Benz's idea that the medieval Creator God supplied the West with a model for human craftsmanship and White's idea that the medieval church sanctioned exploitative technologies in the interest of fulfilling human needs. My argument is that a close reading of the hexaemeral literature suggests that the views of both Benz and White need to be revised. In particular, any interpretation of medieval theology that finds in it a justification for the exploitation of nature needs to define carefully the limits and purposes of this exploitation.

In chapter 3 I examine the claims of Max Weber and Lewis Mumford for the influence of monasticism on the formulation of rationalistic capitalism. In rereading the literature surrounding the foundation of the monastic tradition in the East and in looking again at the monastic rules of the West, I attempt to show that the Weberian model of protocapitalistic monastic enterprise misstates the true thrust of monasticism as articulated by its major theoreticians.

In chapter 4 I argue that the status of the mechanical arts in the Middle Ages was determined by the needs of theologians rather than by an interest in the evaluation of all forms of learning. I argue further that because of the assumptions of the medieval classificatory system itself, there was little chance that technology could have been evaluated in terms of its contributions to the material culture of Europe.

In chapter 5, I look at twelfth-century attitudes toward labor and technology in order to test Le Goff's view of the importance of social forces on the creation of medieval attitudes toward labor and craftsmanship and to show how the economic and technological expansion of twelfth-century Europe affected the church. In particular, I examine the secularization of labor that occurred when twelfth-century theoreticians reconsidered the proper functions of the various orders or classes of medieval society.

Finally, in chapter 6, I turn to an investigation of the status of those whose labor sustained medieval society—the "people without history"— the men and women whose silence must not lead us to underestimate their presence or importance. The recreation of medieval working people's elusive history has yet to be undertaken. My comments are intended to erect a bridge between the theoretical discussions of labor and technology carried out in learned texts and the harsh realities of daily labor that have been the burden of most men and women throughout history.

In my conclusion I argue that Bacon's dream of the restoration of the earth to its original perfection was surrendered during the later Middle Ages when the ideal of morally ordered, nonexploitative, cooperative labor was abandoned by the men who defined the ideology of the Christian church. In its place, the theoreticians of medieval culture turned to matters of personal transcendence and left the work of the world to social managers, merchants, and capitalists. As it turns out, world making is still the business of these men, and the perplexing technological choices with which I began this chapter have originated in their view of the way the world should be used. By documenting the history of the idea of labor in the Middle Ages and by showing the connections of this history to religious, social, and cultural convictions, I hope to suggest that the project of restoring the world might have been approached differently and might have had different results. What is more, it seems to me that the world might still be restored, but only if we base its restoration on a thoughtful assessment of the bonds that unite the human mind with what Bacon called "the nature of things."

CHAPTER I

Progress and Providence
in the Middle Ages

FEW ASPECTS of the history of ideas have been as richly contested as the history of progress, for few subjects are as reflective of a historian's personal and cultural biases. The identification of what is valued by a particular society helps determine the historian's perception of the amount of progress within that society. In the West, most histories of progress have been tied to the history of science and technology, and "progress" has most often meant the gradually increasing hegemony of man over nature. Likewise, the "idea of Progress" has had as one of its chief components the configuration of beliefs that supports those actions intended to dominate the physical environment.

According to most historians, progress was born during the seventeenth century, for it was only then that the otherworldliness and spiritual passivity of the medieval period was undercut by a newfound commitment to the cultivation of reason, the observation of nature, and the creation of those technologies which, in a memorable phrase of Freud's, acted like a mighty prosthesis in extending the power of man over his world. Likewise, most histories of the idea of progress stress the incommensurability of religion and science; in view of this bias, it comes as no surprise that the medieval period has been excluded.

The history of the idea of progress is a *Geisteskraft,* a celebration of the spirit of understanding and control that has gradually pushed back the dark edges of religious superstition while affording mankind increasing domination over the forces of nature. Progress itself has been seen as open-ended, a force for change that has infused Western culture since the seventeenth century and has ridden the arrow of time out of the darkness and into the bright light of understanding.

In this chapter, I will sample some representative accounts of the fanciful and ideologically charged history of progress, paying particular attention to the role played in it by the Middle Ages, and then abstract the principal assumptions on which the view of medieval attitudes toward progress has been founded. The purpose of thus reconstructing a surprisingly consistent set of attitudes is to create a context in which an alternative approach to the history of medieval technology can be advanced. Technology—in the form of manual labor and the mechanical arts that formalized this labor—was indeed subordinated by the theoreticians of medieval culture to the salvationary purposes of theological science, but this subordination did not preclude the possibility of technological change. The dismissal of the fact, or even the possibility, of technological progress in the Middle Ages has had more to do with a too-narrow definition of the term than with the attitudes or accomplishments of the Middle Ages in technological enterprises.

THE HISTORY OF PROGRESS

SEVENTEENTH-CENTURY VIEWS OF PROGRESS. The history of the idea of progress usually begins with the ideas of Francis Bacon, for it is within the Baconian account of the past failures and projected triumphs of science and technology that historians have discerned a characteristically modern attitude toward the understanding and use of nature. At least through the nineteenth century, this history generally neglected the existence of the idea of progress in classical antiquity, and recent scholarship has clarified the extent to which this oversight has distorted Greco-Roman thought.[1]

Another oversight of the history of progress is that it has not been balanced by a complementary history of the antagonism to progressive thought. A consequence of this one-sidedness has been to render even more inevitable and invulnerable the "rise" and "growth" of scientific and technological progress. While a historian like William Whewell reaches back into the thirteenth century to discover in Roger Bacon a precursor of progressivist thinking, few historians discuss anomalous writers such as Cornelius Agrippa, whose sixteenth-century *On the Uncertainty of . . . All Sciences* maintains that the sciences offer nothing but untrustworthy opinions, "doubtful and full of error," and argues that technology leads "mankinde to ruine."[2] Another obscure figure, William Ames (1576–1631), declared the mechanical arts to be "sordid, lucrative, and ignobile," while a great many other writers, operating within a vital tradition defined by hermeticism and natural magic, created a "radical Enlightenment," opposed to scientific rationalism, which has yet to be fully explored.[3]

The neglect of seemingly anomalous writers like Agrippa and Ames by historians of progress is in keeping with the assumption that a progressivist ideology was born in the seventeenth century and that, once born, its ontogeny determined that it develop in one direction only. An alternative view, one that sees the Western progressivist tradition as a particular ideology, has been explored by some writers,[4] while others have resisted progressivism by citing specific cases of continuity in the histories of science and technology or by showing progressive thought to be based on a complex process of transforming deeply ingrained ways of thinking about the relations between human beings and the physical world.[5]

These exceptions aside, most histories of progress written from the seventeenth century to the present preserve assumptions about the "birth," "growth," and "maturity" of the scientific and technological enterprises. And, to linger with this metaphorical language a moment longer, the father of these histories (and the enormously profligate father of much else in the world of ideas as well) is Francis Bacon, whose preface to the *Great Instauration* summarized the failures of science as it had been studied in "ages past." Such science was, in Bacon's view, full of empty disputations, dependent on the contributions of isolated individuals, and not grounded in the observation of nature: "For those who before me have applied themselves to the invention of arts have but cast a glance or two upon facts and examples and experience, and straightaway proceeded, as if invention were nothing more than an exercise of thought."[6] Bacon believed that while the mechanical arts had progressed to a certain extent, the sciences had stood still, and that they would continue to do so until a method was applied to the understanding of the physical world which would allow for the consistent movement from nature and specific fact toward theory and generalization—from what Bacon calls "experiments of Fruit" to "experiments of Light." This new method would not be steeped, as was the Scholastic-Aristotelian methodology, in syllogisms, in propositions that constitute mere "tokens and signs of notions." Instead, Bacon proposes to "sink the foundations of the sciences deeper and deeper" by creating a methodology that would move inductively from observation to axiom, and from axiom to axiom, so that the general views reached at the end of the process would be solidly based on specific empirical evidence and controlled inferences. While it is true, as Bacon freely admits, that the senses may deceive us, they also provide us with the surest means of perceiving and unraveling this deception, a mode of evaluation far more reliable than any offered within the closed system of syllogistic logic. "For God forbid," Bacon writes, "that we should give out a dream of our own imagination for a pattern of the world; rather may he graciously grant to us to write an apocalypse or true vision of the footsteps of the Creator imprinted on his creatures." For Bacon, the dreamers were the followers of Aristotle, in whose science one sees only the words of logic, not the facts of experience. Until this methodological shift is accomplished, progress in the sciences will be impossible.

Bacon's writings call for nothing less than a revolutionary restructuring of the sciences. At the same time, he believed that, independently of his hoped-for intellectual and scientific revolution, the mechanical arts would continue to progress as long as groups of individuals discovered devices capable of extending human control over nature. Bacon's acknowledgment of progress in technology has often been overlooked by later writers who have chosen to focus on his critique of the failures of Scholastic science. At the heart of the Baconian view of the mechanical arts was the perception that the purpose of thought was not the contemplation of the world but its improvement: "Knowledge and human power are synonymous, since the ignorance of the cause frustrates the effect. For nature is subdued by submission, and that which in contemplative philosophy corresponds with the cause, in practical science becomes the rules."[7] Understanding these rules of the practical sciences is a part of the instauration that must occur in human thought and action "if we do not wish to revolve forever in a circle, making only some slight and contemptible progress."[8]

Bacon was not alone in discussing the progress of the mechanical arts. Giordano Bruno, in the *Expulsion of the Triumphant Beast,* celebrated the progress of the mechanical arts and saw in their advance a continuation of the union between thought and action that lies at the heart of the Christian conception of man as a creature combining mind with body.[9] Like Bacon and Bruno, Robert Norman, Juan Luis Vives, and Bernard Palissy presented arguments in support of the intrinsic value of the mechanical arts.[10]

Bacon thought that the way to avoid circularity and "contemptible progress" is to separate matters pertaining to natural philosophy from matters pertaining to theology—the "absurd mixture of matters divine and human."[11] In describing a project for writing natural history, Bacon considers the value of the mechanical arts as instruments whereby the investigator may "control, alter, and prepare natural bodies," as in agriculture, chemistry, cookery, dyeing, and manufacture. At the same time, Bacon notes that the mechanical arts provide the student of nature with opportunities to study scientific questions, as when, in boiling a lobster, the cook incidentally investigates the scientific basis of "redness."[12] At the same time, Bacon repeats the charge—found in medieval classifications of the sciences—that the mechanical arts may be a source of danger ("for [the] mechanical arts are of ambiguous use, serving as well for hurt as for remedy"), and that while he also calls them "illiberal," he dismisses this term of abuse as "arrogant."[13]

It was Bacon's critique of Scholastic science—and his emphasis on the weaknesses of the deductive method, his insistence on enhanced opportunities for observation, and his utilitarianism—that had the greatest influence on seventeenth-century views of the history of science and technology. One typical account growing out of the Baconian tradition is Joseph Glanville's *Plus Ultra, or The Progress and Advancement of Knowledge Since the Days of Aristotle,* published in 1668. When Glanville wrote, the formation of societies for the support of research and the establishment of formal networks for the publication of research results had made the issues raised by Bacon seem more pressing. Scientists like Galileo, Kepler, and Tycho Brahe, as well as craftsmen like Robert Norman, Vannuccio Biringuccio, and Agostino Ramelli, had written in defense of their work and in order to describe the proper methods whereby discoveries in both science and technology could be made.[14] Glanville's ostensible subject was the Royal Society, but he was also moved to defend the moderns against the ancients and, in particular, to defend the practitioners of the "empirick school" against the "School of Talking" represented by Aristotelianism.

Glanville argued, first of all, that Aristotle, as the champion of syllogistic reasoning, was the clear opponent of all experimental science, and Glanville grouped "arts, instruments, observations, experiments, inventions, and improvements" together as developing out of the same set of interests and the same methodology. This dismantling of the distinction between arts, sciences, and techniques is in keeping with the Baconian program of unifying the pursuit of useful knowledge on the basis of a common method and may be found in the writings of Thomas Sprat and Robert Boyle as well as in the charter of the Royal Society.[15] Citing

Bacon, Glanville asserts that only useful knowledge is worthy of the name. Unfortunately, he failed to clarify exactly how he understood the word "useful": "For neither can Nature be well known without a resolution of it into beginnings, which certainly may be best of all done by Chemical Methods. And in those vexatious analyses of Things, wonderful discoveries are made of their Natures, and Experiments are found out, which are not only full of pleasant surprise and information, but of valuable use."[16] Unlike Bacon, whose parable of the ants, spiders, and bees demonstrated the extent to which true science combines data gathering (the work of the mechanical ants) and theory formation (the work of philosophical spiders and bees), Glanville failed to show how the true "empirick" science would mingle what Bacon called "gross observations" with the formation of theories that could then become the basis for interpreting data and deriving useful inventions.[17]

In 1667, one year before Glanville's *Plus ultra*, Thomas Sprat produced his *History of the Royal Society*, the first part of which describes some of the methodological changes that made the experiments performed by members of the society (described in the second part of the *History*) possible. Sprat's avowed purpose was to describe "the Progress which [members of the Royal Society] have already made" in the advancement of knowledge "for the Benefit of humane life."[18] Sprat's emphasis is rigorously utilitarian; he takes great pains to show both the usefulness of specific discoveries and the applicability of the methods through which these discoveries were made to other intellectual problems. Thus, in tracing the history of natural philosophy, Sprat makes the clever suggestion that the downfall of Scholasticism was initiated by the fact that the argumentative tools that had been so useful against heretics were turned inward, so that religion, once "fitted for the benefit of humane Society," was "miserably divided into a thousand intricate questions."[19] The age of contention passed into a quieter time, a time as "quiet as the dark of the night," the dark age of the Roman church. Under the bishops of Rome the world slept a long sleep, ignorance was profound and universal, curiosity was dead. This situation lasted until some of the monks, "in the idle course of life," lighted upon the opinions of Aristotle. Sprat naturally found a perfect fit between these idle monks and the talkative emptiness of the "Peripatetick opinions," and he surmises that there was a political reason for the Scholastic cultivation of a loquacious latinity—the laity was kept ignorant and all things depended on the "lips of the Roman clergy."[20] Thus the history of medieval thought from the rediscovery of Aristotle onward was one of misperception: its axiomatic method could not lead to truth in the physical world but only to disputations in theology; medieval men did not observe nature, and as a consequence, they created no useful knowledge. Aside from their admirable defense of religion, the Scholastics were worthless as guides to thought; though vestiges of their dogmatic philosophy survive, the modern critical philosophy has largely superseded them. For Sprat, the towering symbol of the new "enterprize" of critical reasoning and productive natural philosophy was "one great Man"—Lord Bacon.[21]

Other seventeenth-century writers provided similar analyses of the history of natural philosophy and argued that the accumulation of scientific knowledge was evidence for mankind's general progress. These discussions were in part subsumed by the bilious literary quarrel over the relative merits of the ancients and moderns. While the defenders of classical oratory and rhetoric cited the superiority of Greek and Roman literary accomplishments, when it came to discussing the comparative values of ancient and modern scientific achievements the argument was generally one-sided: "it cannot be a matter of controversie, who have been the greatest geometers, arithmeticians, astronomers, musicians, chymists, botanists, or the like," argued William Wotton in 1694, for the moderns have outstripped the ancients in all fields of useful learning.[22] Echoing Bacon, Glanville, and Sprat, Wotton, whose spirited defense of progressivist views sprang from his desire to demonstrate that the world could not be eternal—a curiously Scholastic intention—expended some efforts beyond the praise of the moderns in searching for the cause of their remarkable achievements in science and technology. Why, he wondered, has mankind been at a "full stop for 1500 years" in all areas of human enterprise except ethics? His answer is important: "This great difference has arisen from the desire which every man has, who believes that he can do greater things than his neighbors, of letting them see how much he does excel them."[23] It is competition among men and among nations that has spurred on progress and awakened Europe from its moral, but unproductive, sleep. Anticipating Toynbee's theory of challenge and response, Wotton opines that it is only when their superiority is in dispute that men begin to accomplish great things. The enemy of science has been complacency, its catalyst the "New Philosophy" with its promise of reactivating the slothful human will.[24] As Paolo Rossi has noted, it was not only the defenders of the Royal Society like Glanville, and of the New Philosophy like Wotton, who argued for the progressive perfection of the arts, crafts, and sciences; theologians of the seventeenth century also noted the great accomplishments in these areas, and they praised inventions and progress as part of a general advancement in learning that centered on the increasing knowledge of God's world.[25]

THE EIGHTEENTH CENTURY: TURGOT AND CONDORCET. The most detailed proponent of progressive thought in the eighteenth century was Turgot (1727–1781). He developed the analysis of the Baconian tradition and strongly influenced nineteenth-century discussions of progress. He also added important modifications to the arguments of Bacon, Glanville, Sprat, and Wotton. In 1750, the brilliant "founding philosopher of progress" presented his "Philosophical Review of the Successive Advances of the Human Mind" in a public lecture at the Sorbonne. One of Turgot's first contributions was to find the impetus to progress in the developing mind of humanity as a whole: "The human race, considered over the period since its origin, appears to the eye of the philosopher as one vast whole, which itself, like each individual, has its infancy and its advancement."[26]

Turgot did not, however, advocate a simple model of linear progress; the sciences grow, but they are also retarded in their growth by societal and individual weaknesses. Yet the mind and its products, upon reemerging from one of these periods of stagnation, is more developed and continues its slow but inexorable movement toward perfection. For Turgot, it was the discovery of writing that enabled humanity to advance because the preservation of memories, opinions, and discoveries served as a foundation for successive contributions to the arts and sciences. The method of progress as envisioned by Turgot combined the rationalism of Descartes with the empiricism of Bacon: the mind confronts the facts of nature "as it is" with an inherent ability to assemble and organize ideas, an ability best represented by the deductions of mathematics. "The natural philosopher erects hypotheses" on the basis of his observations, and then "follows them through to their consequences, and brings them to bear upon the enigma of nature. . . . Time, research, and chance result in the accumulation of observations, and unveil the hidden connections which link a number of phenomena together."[27]

Turgot's guiding metaphor in this account of the history of progress is the single developing human being. The species learns clumsily, like a child, and gradually grows toward mature understanding. The teleological assumption built into this metaphor dictates that the earliest stages of thought are the most awkward, a "slow progression of opinions and errors." The reliance on supernatural causes that characterized the first attempts at understanding were ridiculous and absurd, "sad monuments to the weakness of the human mind." Shifting metaphors, Turgot likens this early stage of error to the first tentative shoots of a plant—flowerless, but containing the potential to bear fruit. Turgot's choice of metaphors was in keeping with the preferences of his age: biologists and geologists had come to favor progressivist explanations for the origins of the earth's topography and for the diversification of life forms, and it is perfectly reasonable to see in Turgot's developmental description of progress the same commitment to growth-by-design that one finds in such writers as John Ray, Charles Bonnet, and Jean-Baptiste Robinet.[28]

Turgot was original enough, however, to add his own touches to the progressivist theory. For example, in explaining why some societies had advanced to a certain point and then found themselves intellectually immobile, Turgot suggests that the ignorance of the first philosophers tended to create in them the dogmatism natural to those who know little—"because the less one has discovered, the less one sees what remains to be discovered." This, Turgot wrote, had been the case in Egypt, in India, and in despotic China ("held back forever in mediocrity").

A worse fate was to befall Europe with the collapse of the Roman Empire. A certain level of perfection in the arts and sciences was attained by the Greeks and Romans, but with the coming of the barbarians the fire of reason was fully put out, and the human race (that is, the Europeans), gravely wounded, required centuries to heal itself. Although Charlemagne tried to stir the ashes of extinguished reason, he failed, and Europe was covered with a new darkness. "The Kings were without authority, the nobles without any constraint, the peoples enslaved . . . all commerce and communication were cut off; the towns inhabited by poor artisans enjoying no leisure. . . . An unhappy picture—but one which was only too true of Europe for several centuries!"[29] Interestingly enough, Turgot's view that progress is as continuous and inevitable as the growth of an organism commits him to the seemingly contradictory view that, despite the dismal picture of society from the ninth to the fifteenth centuries, progress was "imperceptibly taking place and preparing for the brilliant achievements of later centuries." Here the metaphor of the plant is especially useful: though the flowers and shoots are blasted, the roots, unseen, continue to grow, so that one day, when the plant is rejuvenated, its reappearance will not be a miraculous event but only the culmination of a process that has been going on invisibly for a long time. For Turgot, progress in the arts and sciences is obviously an independent force in history, its existence dependent only on the passage of time and not at all on the wills of individuals or on the circumstances of intellectual or political life. The mechanical arts are perfected over the course of the dark centuries "by virtue of the simple fact that time was passing" and because, whatever the general decline of culture, a few extraordinary individuals always exist whose labors sustain the forward motion of an otherwise inhibited progress. Turgot acknowledges that a host of inventions unknown to the classical age grew out of the age of barbarity, and he lists musical notation, paper, windmills, clocks, eyeglasses, gunpowder, and the magnetic needle among these contributions. These achievements in the mechanical arts, which use the forces of nature and are the result of a "succession of physical experiments," reveal that progress, like a subterranean river, can disappear for a time and still move forward "swollen by all the waters which have seeped through the earth." Like other historians of progress, Turgot was forced to acknowledge the technological progress that occurred during the "dark ages" of European history.

Turgot's analysis of the history of progress was generous; not only did he admit the contributions of unknown medieval artisans and mechanics, he also recognized the impact that other civilizations have had on the development of European ways of thinking about nature. His was not a theory of revolutionary change but rather a theory of inexorable progress that had come in his own lifetime—the "Century of Louis, century of great men"—to a crescendo. Although the forces of history have often conspired to impede the free development of the arts and sciences, they have nonetheless continued to grow, just as an individual, or the species as a whole, continues to grow and to develop. The final passages of Turgot's remarkable oration praise the role played by religion in this history of progress, for whatever the changing fortunes of human invention and human reason, the stability of belief preserves the values that provide the context within which all change occurs. Indeed, the force of belief may be identified with the force of progressivism, for both remain essentially unchanged throughout history and provide a standard against which attainments in other areas may be measured. Turgot began with this theme in the first discourse of his unfinished "Universal History." He observes, first of all, the inescapable evidence for a Supreme Being— "everywhere we see the print of the hand of God." Then he remarks that while the force that drives mankind toward greater perfection is progress, the hidden cause of all things must be found in the providential nature of creation. G. K. Chesterton once remarked that progress implies a goal; for Turgot, the definition of progress equates human advancement with the subtle but ubiquitous force of Providence, the invisible net cast by the Creator over his creation.[30] Remarkably, Turgot's location of a providence within progress precisely reflects the medieval view of history, as I shall argue subsequently.

Turgot's disciple Condorcet did not share this view of the providential nature of human progress. Indeed, Condorcet's writings on progress, including the influential *Equisse d'un tableau historique de progrès de l'esprit humain,* while accepting Turgot's view that progress is an inevitable force in the history of humanity, argued that only when mankind is freed from the superstitions of religion and the influence of churches can true advances be possible in the sciences and technology.[31] Condorcet also accepted the centrality of writing to this history, and, like Turgot, argued that the collective experience of mankind over time is what constitutes the vehicle through which the sometimes hidden, sometimes visible force of progress accomplishes its work. Yet progress, while inevitable when the proper conditions for its propagation are insured, may nonetheless be impeded by superstition and metaphysics—two sides of the same coin for Condorcet. Thus, during the sixth age of mankind, from the fall of Rome to the invention of printing, priests and aristocrats conspired to subject society to a tyranny that was both political and intellectual. Bodies and minds were enslaved, the light of reason was extinguished in Europe and burned only fitfully among those "Arab" scholars who studied and translated Aristotle and who made discoveries in astronomy, optics, and medicine.[32] Yet despite the bleakness of the centuries dominated by corrupt priests, intellectual advances did occur, slowly and silently. Though degraded by tyranny, progress returned to bring mankind back into the light—in the seventeenth century.

If progress is aligned in silent partnership with providential theology in Turgot's writings, it is aligned in Condorcet's with antiauthoritarian political sentiments. Progress is a symptom of intellectual curiosity in Turgot and of an impatience with tyranny in Condorcet; science and technology are irresistible evolutionary forces in Turgot and equally irresistible revolutionary forces for his disciple. These two treatments of the history of progress, with their shared continuo of disdain for medieval accomplishments, continue to play out their themes and variations in the nineteenth and twentieth centuries.

THE NINETEENTH CENTURY. In his *History of the Inductive Sciences* (1857), William Whewell narrated the history of progress as a component in the development of empirical methodologies in natural philosophy. Whewell, professor of mineralogy at Cambridge and active participant in the midcentury disputes over the mechanisms of geological change and the origin of species, wrote in his history of the sciences that there have been two periods of "School philosophy"—one was during the Golden Age of Greece, the other during the dark age of the Middle Ages ("the period of the first waking of science, and that of its mid-day slumber").[33] Like Bacon, Whewell thought that the growth of science encompasses a twofold process of movement toward a greater interest in the natural world and away from the "mysticism" that substitutes extraphysical or unknowable causes for perceptible material ones. Thus, in his discussion of "the mysticism of the Middle Ages," Whewell notes that during the Middle Ages, "men attempted to reduce [events in the natural world] under spiritual and supersensual relations and dependencies; they referred them to superior intelligences, to theological conditions, to past and future events in the moral world, to states of mind and feelings, to the creatures of an imaginary mythology or demonology," to anything, that is, but to the material causes that were their true source of being.[34] Magic, alchemy, and astrology dominated human thought during the Middle Ages and "delayed and impeded the progress of true science."[35]

Summarizing his criticism of medieval "School philosophy," Whewell cites both the tendency to refer to "remote causes," which are neither material nor capable of being generalized, and the "enthusiastic" emotional state of those who thus misconstrue the true causes of natural phenomena. Induction, the source of all reliable knowledge about the physical world, began with Copernicus, and Whewell, like other internalist historians of science, moves from Copernicus to those other key figures whose work revealed more of the "true nature" of the physical world.

Whewell also notes that the work of craftsmen did not significantly contribute to the discovery of the laws governing nature because craftsmen, in manipulating objects toward particular ends, do not use inductive reasoning to formulate statements of the laws that govern natural phenomena. Technology is a form of problem solving and is therefore incapable of passing from a particular invention to the crucial stage of identifying the general causes that make this technique operative. The sciences begin with "common observations of facts"—that is, with observations devoid of motive or structure. In the succeeding stages of theory formulation, the observer hones this raw observation toward the selection of certain kinds of facts. Here is Whewell's critical point: one may observe the world forever without creating any science and without initiating the forces of progress unless one uses accumulated observations to formulate a method that will shape raw data into theories of cause and effect. Technology, like the untutored observation of natural phenomena, does not lead to the perception of causes or to the extrapolation of the general principles that constitute inductive science. In Whewell's view, methodology and science are inseparable; put another way, only a scientific state of mind can create science, and the Middle Ages, lacking both method and theory, could offer no more than unstructured observation superstitiously explained by mystical doctrine. Whewell concludes that "the inventions of the middle ages . . . though at the present day they may be portions of our sciences, are no evidence that the sciences then existed; but only that those powers of practical observation and practical skill were at work, which prepare the way for theoretical views and scientific discoveries."[36] Even Whewell's rhetoric contributes to his critique: "practical observation and practical skill" are reified into advance scouts for theoretical science; no one in particular did these things in the Middle Ages, but the supposition that they existed, in some primitive form, helps to explain the otherwise confusing fact that certain medieval inventions are still in use today. For Whewell, no scientific progress existed during the Middle Ages, little noteworthy technological progress occurred, and, indeed, there was a slumber of such profundity that only the tenacity of a handful of revolutionary figures could awaken reason to the unfinished business of discovering the causes of things.

Whewell's analysis of medieval progress was by no means unique. In his *Sketch of the Progress of Physical Science* (1843), written as a part of the series "Useful Works for the People," Thomas Thompson, Regis Professor of Chemistry at the University of Glasgow, writes that "It was not to be expected that mankind should at first make any rapid progress in investigating the laws which regulate the changes that take place in the material world." At first, "there are to be found only accounts of prodigies and wonders, while the regular operations of nature scarcely attracted attention." In the classical world, only Archimedes and Hipparchus used observation and experiment to investigate nature. Their solitary contributions stand alone until "the revival of letters" in the sixteenth century, when "a spirit of observation and inquiry awoke." Thompson cites Francis Bacon as the first to describe a scientific methodology and as the first to make progressive thought possible. "When Europe began to awake from the lethargy of the dark ages": these images of a benighted sleep dominate Thompson's account of the vast sea of time separating a few enlightened Greek thinkers from modern Europe. According to his view, two obstacles stood between the dark ages and progress: a lack of interest in natural phenomena, and, what would seem to follow necessarily from this, the failure to develop a method of observation and experiment. Thompson avoids matters of religion and morals except to point to the restrictiveness of a "mysticism" that he clearly sees as a form of enthusiastic popularism unworthy of comparison with the rational theology of the nineteenth century.[37]

John Tyndall's inaugural address presented to the British Association for the Advancement of Science in 1874 is more informative on the subject of nineteenth-century attitudes toward medieval progress. After giving an unusually sympathetic account of ancient Greek science and concluding with the grateful observation that the Greeks had "shaken free" from that brand of fruitless inquiry which "had vainly sought to transcend experience and reach a knowledge of ultimate causes," Tyndall wondered what had managed to stop the victorious advance of learning.[38] Why, he wondered, did the "scientific intellect, like an exhausted soil, . . . lie fallow for nearly two millenniums before it could regather the elements necessary to its fertility and strength"? The answers to these questions are found, Tyndall thought, in Bacon and Whewell. The early Christians came to "scorn the earth" and to find their only science in the

Bible. Citing Boniface and Augustine on the impossibility of human life at the Antipodes, Tyndall concluded that such restrictive ways of thinking are not conducive to the free inquiry that makes intellectual progress possible. The spirit of the Middle Ages was "menial," and "the seekers after natural knowledge had forsaken that fountain of living waters, the direct appeal to nature by observation and experiment."[39] Scholasticism, which followed Neoplatonism and its "mysticism" as the dominant mode of thought in the Middle Ages, used only the "least mature" elements of Aristotelianism—presumably Tyndall meant the *Prior* and *Posterior Analytics.*

By the end of the nineteenth century, Tynall's view of the regressive tendencies of the medieval period was typical; the rekindling of interest in ancient science merely lowered the value of the "bizarre, monstrous, amazingly artificial state which was that of the Middle Ages."[40] As amazing, perhaps, was the fact that this bizarre age, already so maligned, with scarcely an advocate in sight, had yet to be definitively examined for antiprogressive tendencies. The final blow was to come in the early years of the twentieth century.

THE TWENTIETH CENTURY. In 1920, J. B. Bury wrote *The Idea of Progress,* a book that has a profound impact on discussions of progress to the present day. Bury's analysis of the Middle Ages exemplified a preoccupation with autonomous facts and set the tone for a whole series of discussions of medieval progress. "The idea of the universe which prevailed throughout the Middle Ages," Bury writes, "and the general orientation of men's thoughts were incompatible with some of the fundamental assumptions which are required by the idea of Progress."[41] This "Progress," seen as a force moving silently through modern history, cannot exist where its preconditions are not met, and no culture concerned with happiness in another world can be interested in the "gradual amelioration of society or the increase of knowledge." This was Bury's reading of Augustine, the principal author on whom he bases his argument. Only a writer who is able to put aside the pressures of otherworldliness, a writer like Roger Bacon ("who stands alone on an isolated pinnacle"), can possibly glimpse the forward thrust of the progressive spirit. Bury equated progress with curiosity and knowledge of the natural world—that is, with science, rather than with technology or with economic development. Only in the Renaissance, when men freed themselves from the tyranny of otherworldliness and developed self-confidence, was a theory of progress possible.

Bury's insistence on the incompatibility of progress with religion became a major theme of twentieth-century reconstructions of the history of science and technology. For example, in his book *The Ascent of Humanity* (1929), Gerald Heard writes of "The Arrest of Individuality: The Monastic Age" and notes the failure of the Middle Ages to develop either a theory of progress or, what was even more significant, a theory of the value of the individual within a progressive society.[42] Similarly, Carl Becker's *Progress and Power* (1936) concentrates on the scientific and technological rather than the political, but reaches virtually the same conclusions: there was neither progress nor a theory of progress in Europe until the seventeenth century.[43]

Michael Postan's article of 1951, "Why Was Science Backward in the Middle Ages?" argues that Scholasticism was incompatible with scientific and technological progress because it eschewed the observation of facts and an adequate interest in the natural world. Postan denies that the Middle Ages possessed any "scientific incentive" to understand nature or any practical incentives to control it. Scientific understanding, even when it did exist, could not advance toward modernity because technological improvements were so few. For this backwardness, Postan blames medieval economic policy, which he describes as having thrown numerous obstacles in the way of innovation. Vast structures of bylaws impeded free economic development and were based on a technological state of the art that had long been frozen at a low level of sophistication. Postan concludes by stating a characteristic view of medieval progress: "What [the Middle Ages] achieved in advancing the practical arts of humanity . . . they did in so far and so long as they were not typically medieval."[44]

Often a dismissive critique of medieval scientific and technological progress is broadened to include the assertion that progress in all areas of life was nonexistent during this period—a suggestion resisted by most commentators in the nineteenth century because of the contributions of medieval theology to the dominant moral viewpoint of the West. However, as the idea of progress was detached from specific areas of change and developed an autonomous existence—as progress became Progress—the recognition of distinctions between technological advance and moral or spiritual sophistication broke down. Thus, Sidney Pollard in *The Idea of Progress* (1968) defined progress as the belief in a "pattern of change . . . in one direction only, and that . . . direction is toward improvement from a 'less to a more desirable state of affairs.' "[45] This last phrase, borrowed by Pollard from Charles Van Doren's *The Idea of Progress* (1967), introduced a new way of evaluating a particular society's contribution to progressive ideas. For the most part, historians had looked at the products of medieval culture and judged them to be insufficient to warrant inclusion in the history of progress (which was really the history of emerging modernity); what Pollard did was to judge medieval culture as a potential source of progressivism and find it wanting. The Middle Ages did not simply fail to progress, it lacked the intellectual and cultural means to do so. All cultures that move forward possess a relatively fixed idea of what constitutes "a more desirable state of affairs," and this a priori set of assumptions is the necessary precondition for any advances a culture may experience.

Pollard's critique is far more provocative than any that focuses on achievements alone. In response to the historians who deny the existence of medieval progress one may adduce a considerable body of contrary evidence. However, in response to the charge that the Middle Ages lacked even the potential to develop a progressivist ideology, the historian must look at attitudes—toward nature, history, innovative thinking, and so forth—in order to construct a refutation. Since this book is concerned with examining these attitudes, I will not take up the challenge of Pollard's analysis here, except to note one obvious fact, namely, the retrospective bias built into any analysis of the history of progress, which presumes there to be "a more desirable state of affairs" for a particular culture. A common tactic in the histories of progress I have examined is to assess the importance of the past by discovering in it those attitudes that seem to foreshadow the present. An obvious response to this analysis is to evoke the logic of progressivism itself: if the current level of scientific or technological progress is estimable, and if the history of this progress presupposes "irreversible change in one direction only," then every antecedent culture has contributed to the current state of affairs, was equally necessary, and therefore equally valuable. In a sense, this is what Turgot meant when he described the "silent growth" of progress. Of course, any counterargument must be more complex than this, for what Pollard and others have argued is that the movement toward modernity could not begin until the Middle Ages ended because the *will* to progress did not

exist until the seventeenth century. It is this lack of a "will" to progress—
a lack, that is, of a cultural consensus supportive of those activities which
extend human domination over nature—that has proved most difficult
for historians to characterize. I shall return to this issue later in this
chapter.

Other questions raised by twentieth-century evaluations of medieval
progress are equally difficult to answer because of the persistence of
certain forms of analysis and the endurance of Baconian assumptions
about the structure of science and technology. For example, one assumption has been that no one in the Middle Ages was capable of organizing
sense data, so that the development of science and technology were fatally impeded. L. Houllevigue wrote in a popular text called *The Evolution of the Sciences* (1910) that "[The Middle Ages was] a long chaotic
period, during which the data of observation float[ed] without order or
connection in the mass of human knowledge, the whole forming, as it
were, a great nebula, which, when the time comes, condenses round
separate nuclei."[46] Only in the Renaissance did specific data, and scientific disciplines, "crystallise out" of this unwieldy mass of intellectual
flotsam, and only then did a method arise that made the use of this data
possible.

The failure of methodology is a common theme in twentieth-century
histories of science and technology. Ernest Brown's *Development of the
Sciences* (1923) makes the point that "certain inhibitions" (left unspeci-
fied, but having something to do with metaphysical concerns) prevented
Greek, Roman, and medieval thinkers from developing an experimental
methodology.[47] W. T. Sedgwick and his collaborators' volume entitled *A
Short History of Science,* a popular textbook first published in 1938 and
reprinted seven times through 1958 (and one which this author recalls
using in high school), makes the same point about the failure of medieval
thought and goes on to deny that the "Schoolmen" ever bothered to
observe the natural world. However, with the "dawn of the Renaissance . . . a new spirit is arising in Europe . . . a zeal for knowledge which
hadn't been known for centuries"—the jarring shift to the present tense
merely underscores the sense of continuity between the Renaissance and
the modern world and of discontinuity with the Middle Ages.[48]

Neither are these assumptions about the history of progress confined to
the first half of the twentieth century. A recent book, Thomas Goldstein's
Dawn of Modern Science (1980), shares with its predecessors a strong

commitment to the organic theory of progress, suggesting that it was the gradual "nourishing" of the scientific spirit that led to the "dawn" of the Renaissance. During the Middle Ages there were, at best, a few false steps on the road to this evolution: "around the middle of the twelfth century, a handful of men were consciously striving to launch the evolution of Western science, and undertook every major step that was needed to achieve that end."[49] The factor of intentionality introduces a new muddle into the arguments against medieval ideas of progress. Medieval preconceptions and failures of observation held back a heroic effort to create a protomodern science in the twelfth century; yet, like Turgot, Goldstein finds below the surface of this resistance, "the connecting tissues" forming the body of modern thought.

A more carefully argued and documented view than any of those cited thus far was Edgar Zilsel's, whose articles written during the 1940s presented a comprehensive theory of the origins and development of the concept of scientific progress. Although Zilsel's arguments were derived to a considerable extent from the tradition of thought that stretches back through Bury, Whewell, and Condorcet to Francis Bacon, he did write with the benefit of considerably enhanced access to manuscript sources, and he did assume a far greater degree of continuity in the history of scientific progress than did his predecessors.[50] Nonetheless, Zilsel thought that no theory of scientific progress existed before Francis Bacon, and he established a clear-cut set of criteria whereby the historian may judge if this view is correct. He maintained that the idea of progress includes the "insight that scientific knowledge is brought about step by step through contributions of generations of explorers building upon and gradually amending the findings of their predecessors." According to Zilsel, the idea of progress also assumes the belief that making a contribution to progress is the goal of every scientist who works to unravel the mysteries of nature. Yet even before these assumptions about what constitutes the nature of progress may be applied to the history of a particular culture, Zilsel contended that one additional set of preconditions need be met, namely, that the "unrestricted authority of Scripture, of the church fathers and the scholastics, and of Aristotle and classical antiquity" give way to the model of free inquiry described by Francis Bacon. Zilsel denied that there existed any theory of scientific advance in antiquity because "a characteristic combination of metaphysics and rhetoric was the backbone of higher education" in that period. Likewise, even though the classical period and the Middle

Ages achieved certain successes in the mechanical arts, these achievements were not dependent on a scientific methodology and did not lead to any substantial material benefits for society as a whole. Zilsel's further remarks are unsurprising: "For obvious reasons the ideal of the progress of knowledge was foreign to the medieval schoolman"—obvious because all thought was subsumed under theological concerns and all labor was antiprogressive in being either solitary (as with the monks) or stagnant (as in the guilds). Gradually, however, the individual genius of the entrepreneur-inventor developed as economic incentives to technological innovation were created. It was out of this economic situation that the Renaissance craftsmen emerged. Once a scientific methodology and a habit of observing nature were common, the craftsman was in a position to begin the process of discovery and cooperation that resulted in the creation of a distinctive modern science and technology.

THE CASE AGAINST MEDIEVAL PROGRESSIVISM. In looking back over the literature that treats the history of progress, a number of arguments against the existence of a progressivist ideology in the Middle Ages may be abstracted. The strongest argument, presented often in the late nineteenth and early twentieth centuries, was that there was a total cessation of scientific and technological progress during the Middle Ages. The weaker version of this argument is that there was some progress during the period and that isolated geniuses, like Roger Bacon, struggled within a vast emptiness to invent modernity.

The most persistent argument, dating from Francis Bacon, has been that medieval progress, especially in scientific fields, was fatally impeded by a slavish dependence on Aristotle. Apart from dependence on Aristotle, the impediment to progress most often evoked has been the alleged medieval lack of interest in, and failure to observe, the phenomena of the natural world. Implicit in most of the accounts of medieval progress is the assumption that a preoccupation with theological issues is inimical to the investigation of the natural world.

Historians of progress have also tended to discount the existence of interchanges of ideas and methods between those working in the craft traditions and those concerned with natural philosophy; the existence of networks of collaborative investigation is presumed to be a feature of seventeenth-century science missing in the Middle Ages.

A more subtle assumption involves the methodology of the historians themselves. Most of those who have written on the history of progress have taken an internalist view; that is, they have seen the history of progress in science and invention as a history of notable contributions made by notable men, and they have tended to ignore both the importance of cultural forces in shaping the ideas of these men and the vast number of anonymous (and often female) contributors to this history.

Underlying these accounts is the equation of progress with an evolutionary gradualism punctuated by revolutionary leaps in understanding. The idea of progress has tended to be viewed as a history of organic development, with the arrow of time propelling discovery inexorably forward, creating more complex scientific theories and technological artifacts from simpler ones.

If one accepts these arguments and assumptions, the history of medieval failures to contribute to the progress of the West becomes plausible; indeed, the "Middle Ages," taken as a vast entity and a homogenized culture, may very well be guilty of each of the antiprogressivist sins outlined here. Patterns of economic, scientific, and technological development were by no means uniform across the millennium and more that constituted the "middle age," nor did the peasants of Lombardy look at the world in the same way as the monks of Bury St. Edmunds. Yet fine distinctions have not been the preoccupation of those historians whose views I have recounted here, and one must be careful not to fall into the attractive traps of cultural relativity ("every culture attains optimum progress") or rigid continuity ("medieval science/technology was continuous with modern science/technology") in refuting them.

What I want to do instead is to make things less simple by advancing three related sets of claims. First of all, each of the assumptions that I have abstracted from these historians of the idea of progress invites a bit of probing and amending; while it would take another whole book to critique each of these points, I can offer some brief observations in the interest of finding the cracks and fissures inevitable in such a disturbingly uniform portrayal of medieval (non-, anti-) progressivism. Second, it needs to be argued—though again, only briefly—that an altogether different account of the meaning of "progress" is conceivable so that the arguments carefully made by the writers discussed here can be shown to amount to the proposition "the Middle Ages did not possess the *modern* theory of progress." And finally, I shall argue that, in any case, theories of progress are merely ex post facto reconstructions of events that occur for altogether different reasons, and that these events, which have their source in the attempt to solve problems deeply embedded within every culture, evoke a variety of psychological and material responses having nothing to do with what we call "science" or "technology." To put this third point more directly: the history of progress has been written as a narrative description of the material consequences of human action, which is altogether too narrow a way of viewing what this history purports to describe. First, however, my comments on the assumptions I have listed.

The first position—the nonexistence of scientific and technological achievement during the period A.D. 500 to 1400—is seldom advanced any longer, though many textbooks still ignore the contributions of medieval science and technology or relegate them to a paragraph at the beginning of the discussion of "the Scientific Revolution." The medievalist merely needs to cite the scholarly studies of Marc Bloch, Bertrand Gille, Friederich Klemm, and Lynn White, Jr.; of Pierre Duhem, Anneliese Maier, Marshall Clagett, Edward Grant, and David Lindberg; of Georges Duby, Jacques Le Goff, R. S. Lopez, and E. L. Jones, and then submit that the strong version of the "dark ages" argument has been untenable for some time.[51] The history of invention presented in most modern texts does include mention of the medieval discovery, or adoption, of such things as mechanical clocks, efficient plows and harnesses, siege weapons, eyeglasses, astrolabes, water mills, lateen sails, double-entry bookkeeping, and water-powered trip hammers and saws. Indeed, the alleged slumber of the dark ages must often have been interrupted by the din of labor, so much so that, in response to the weak version of this argument, I would merely cite the clear-cut ecological evidence that there existed an ethic of appropriation throughout the whole period. The persistent effort required to deforest Europe and to extend the range of cultivated land involved generations of laborers as well as a social commitment to the primacy of human habitation.[52]

While it is true that many of the most important medieval inventions were clustered around the period of the eleventh through fourteenth centuries, it is demonstrably not true that only a few isolated individuals contributed to the development of these inventions. By examining the history of a particular industry—for example, the cotton industry—and tracing the combination of mechanical and organizational innovations that made it successful, one can demonstrate the limitations of the "isolated genius" view of medieval technological progress.[53] Furthermore, one must not assume because those who labor have little to say about the writing of history that their contributions should be invisible. Did white plantation owners single-handedly create the economy of the antebellum South? Could modern medicine have been created without the silent contributions of the women and men who work in menial jobs as lab technicians? Although we may never know their names, we should know that technological progress is the work of the masses of men and women and not only of the isolated few whose names survive.

The argument that medieval thought demonstrates a dependence on Aristotle is more problematical, for it is true.[54] However, ever since Francis Bacon launched his attack on Scholasticism in the *Novum organum* the nature of this dependence has been largely misrepresented. First of all, the introduction of the Aristotelian corpus into European intellectual life in the twelfth century was anything but intellectually stifling, especially if one compares the commentaries written on these texts to the typical products of the encyclopedic writers of an earlier period. Second, the presumption in much of the criticism of Scholasticism has been that the commentators slavishly defended Aristotelian suppositions, even when, as in the case of questions involving the eternity of the world, the free fall of bodies, and the concept of "natural place," Aristotle's views were contradicted by experience or reason. Careful scrutiny of specific commentaries reveals that this notion of uncritical acceptance does not hold up. While it is true that Aquinas's commentaries exerted a considerable effort on Aristotle's behalf, those of other writers were often critical, and, in the case of a question like that involving violent motion and impressed force, it was precisely this critical attitude that led to significant gains in conceptual understanding.[55]

Finally, it must be noted that Aristotelianism did not end with the Middle Ages. The persistence of Scholasticism in the universities was precisely what troubled Francis Bacon; however, recent historical scholarship has indicated the extent to which those who were in the forefront of scientific developments during the sixteenth and seventeenth centuries were themselves immersed in traditions of thought that were distinctly Aristotelian.[56] Thus, in matters pertaining to the influence of Aristotle, I would suggest that the proper historical perspective is to look for a continuity of thought and a gradual transformation of long-lived influences growing out of a vital, multicultural tradition, rather than for a simple dialectic of reaction by a newborn empirical spirit against a stagnant, Scholastic conservatism.[57]

The alleged lack of interest on the part of medieval men and women in nature and their failure to observe natural phenomena is another of the assumptions that has been central to the historiography of the Middle Ages. Again, the source of this criticism lies in the Baconian critique. Since data gathering constitutes the first stage of scientific progress, the failure to develop an empirical temper precludes scientific progress. No doubt Bacon was partly right about this; early medieval writers like Isidore of Seville, Bede, and Johannes Scottus Eriugena (John the Scot) display a predisposition toward ignoring the facts of the material world in favor of the traditions of favorite textual sources. Yet Bacon himself acknowledged the accomplishments of medieval artisans, whose manipulations of the materials of their crafts constitute the purest form of empiricism. On a more general level, it seems obvious that a rural, agrarian society could not possibly be uninterested in the facts of the natural world, and there is a considerable body of evidence in the visual arts to suggest that careful observation of nature was commonplace by the twelfth century.[58] Perhaps what one can reasonably conclude is that questions of method, analysis of propositions, and proof through logical demonstration did dominate medieval natural philosophy (which one modern writer calls "natural science without nature"), but that the Middle Ages as a whole exhibited a considerable interest in nature—witness the writings on agronomy, medicine, navigation, animals real and imagined, as well as the herbals, artist's and craftsmen's "recipe" books, the collections of guild lore, the literature of secrets, and so forth.[59]

The history of collaborative exchanges between craftsmen and scholars during the Middle Ages has yet to be written. Central to this history was the truly revolutionary effect of the introduction of printing in the fifteenth century, an event that succeeded in broadening the basis of contacts between scholars and artisans.[60] But the increasingly significant role played by craftsmen-scholars in the thirteenth and fourteenth centuries should be emphasized: men like Giovanni de' Dondi, Richard of Wallingford, Konrad Kyeser, Jacopo da Siena (called Taccola), Jean Fusoris, Bernard Palissy—to name just a few—illustrate the extent to which the boundaries between these two roles, which had often been rigidly defined during the earlier Middle Ages, began to break down.[61] In the twelfth and thirteenth centuries, scholarly accounts of the mechanical arts were more appreciative of the value of practical disciplines, but they nonetheless continued to assign a lesser function to techniques as opposed to speculation (see chapter 4). In specific fields like medicine, there were often heated rivalries between theoreticians and practitioners.[62] Yet, by the thirteenth century these intraprofessional conflicts in medicine abated at the same time that medical practitioners moved toward a greater concern with questions of natural philosophy.[63]

Yet these generalizations are subject to a cautionary note. For one thing, we have evidence for the scholars' attitudes toward craftsmanship but very little evidence for the feelings of craftsmen toward scholars— theory is well documented while practice is not. Few craftsmen wrote anything at all. In one of the craftsman's "handbooks" we do have, Theophilus's *De diversis artibus,* there is a clear mingling of practical with scholarly interests (see chapter 6). Theophilus, an unidentified thirteenth-century Benedictine monk, defends his interest in the creation of beautiful objects by asserting that such interest is a form of worship, much as Abbot Suger had before him.[64] Likewise several "theoreticians," among them Gerbert of Aurillac, Roger Bacon, and Albertus Magnus, were associated in medieval legend with the creation of mechanical devices of a quasi-magical nature. Roger Bacon's reputation as a scholar-craftsman was enhanced by his specific statements on the power of the mechanical arts as well as by his visionary description of what technology promised in the future.[65] A later writer, Konrad Kyeser (born 1366), illustrates in a concrete fashion the blurring of the earlier distinction between theoretical and mechanical knowledge. His *Bellifortis* (1405) describes weapons of war within the context of a wide-ranging and often bizarre description of astrology and magic.[66] Indeed, William Eamon's work suggests that there is a sense in which the magical arts provided a middle ground between the theoretical work of theologians and the practical labors of craftsmen; magic was the shadow discipline in which physicians, theologians, and craftsmen brought their knowledge to bear on a wide range of practical and scientific problems.[67]

It is also worth noting that even though most craftsmen were silent during the Middle Ages, and even though many theoreticians continued to look askance at the products of the mechanical arts, neither of these considerations changes in the least the simple fact that from the tenth century onward, technology touched every aspect of European life. Such a paradox seems endemic to societies that utilize technologies in areas like food production, the building trades, and the military arts, perhaps because it is the existence of such technologies that makes meaningful debate about social and cultural values occur in the first place. At Clairvaux in the twelfth century one notes the uneasy coexistence of St. Bernard's ascetic ideals with an equal commitment to an economic self-sufficiency founded on the technologies of water power.[68] Would there have been any debate about the proper function of a monastic establishment if mechanical and organizational technologies had not lessened the burden of labor prescribed by the Benedictine Rule? Indeed, how often in the history of technology has a quiet, seemingly autonomous "revolution" presented an unprepared society with ethical and political choices it was ill-equipped to make?[69] The largely invisible technological revolutions of the Middle Ages—in agriculture, in the adaptation of water power, in labor organization, in manufacture—had to be adapted to a set of values that was, at least until the twelfth century, relatively static and unreceptive to change. Instead of seeing the resistance to these changes and the simmering antagonisms between scholars and craftsmen as symptomatic of medieval backwardness, we might do well to consider such resistance and such antagonisms as a typical model of the painful adjustments necessitated by technological change.

That science and theology are to be seen as perched on opposite sides of a balance beam, the ascent of one determining the decline of the other, has been a pervasive assumption of the histories of progress since the eighteenth century. Condorcet made this antagonism a central assumption in his account. In particular, the advent of modern science and technology has been tied to the devaluation of theological speculation and to the discovery of rational modes of inquiry that substitute causal laws for divine Providence. Theology did not, of course, disappear in the seventeenth century, nor did it in the nineteenth. What changed was the emphasis given to theological propositions relative to propositions in natural philosophy. If Aquinas used the truth of his faith to demonstrate the lesser truths of the natural world, and if endless numbers of theologians used the medium of the commentary on Peter Lombard's *Sentences* to consider the relation between the truths of theology and the truths of science, then Descartes used a method of thinking designed to consider the natural world as a means of demonstrating the truths of his faith. The *scientia* of the Middle Ages was theology, but theology was understood to include not only the nature of God and of moral laws, but also the nature of the world created by God. The science of the seventeenth century looked first of all at the laws governing the operations of the natural world; nonetheless, behind these laws the natural philosopher often found the handiwork of God and justification for the truths of his faith.

Robert Boyle, the embodiment of the experimental spirit in the new mechanical philosophy, was able to write in his work "Of the Usefulness of Experimental Philosophy" that the two advantages of "a real acquaintance with nature" are the instruction of our understanding and the cherishing of our devotion.[70] In this work Boyle presents an argument that was repeated throughout the nineteenth century, that it is in the perfection of the world and the discovery of physical laws that the hand of the Creator is seen. Boyle uses the metaphor of the clockmaker and asserts that the Creator has infused his creation with the means of functioning and his creatures with the means of inquiring into the mechanisms of this function. Nature, Boyle writes, is the "grand instrument" of Providence, and it is precisely this view that is proposed most often during the course of the seventeenth, eighteenth, and nineteenth centuries.

All of which is not to say that the interests, methods, and discoveries of the twelfth and seventeenth centuries were equivalent, or that the medieval preoccupation with theology did not curtail original work in natural philosophy. But clear-cut differences in interests and methods have often obscured similarities and continuities between medieval and early modern modes of thought. It is easy enough to maintain a broad distinction between medieval and modern ways of looking at the world and to see the former as antiprogressive and the latter as embodying the true spirit of progress. But to take a single idea, like the plurality of worlds or the genesis of geological change, and trace its history—as Steven Dick and Paolo Rossi have done—is to see not radical discontinuities in thought, and certainly not persistent conflicts between religion and science, but instead a long-lived tradition of asking similar questions, often of the same texts, and deriving answers that sometimes differ radically and sometimes differ not at all.[71] The desire to extract a linear and upward-surging arrow of progress plotted against the two simple variables of "technological (or scientific) change" and "time" has tempted some of the scholars discussed here to overlook continuities of thought in favor of radical discontinuities. A likelier graph depicting the history of progress, plotted in many dimensions and including a multitude of variables, would record short bursts of change, long spans of stagnation, and counterbalanced simultaneous "regressions."[72]

I would like to group the final two assumptions together, for the history of the idea of progress has linked the internalist approach to history with a view favoring evolutionary gradualism to create a model for understanding the scientific and technological mastery of the world. If the history of progress is taken to be the history of individuals' discovery of laws and devices, then—accepting the existence of linear time (a "discovery" of the Judaeo-Christian tradition)—it must follow that later ages are necessarily more advanced than earlier ages, irrespective of any constraining economic or social factors. While particular periods may be barren of discovery, and while particular discoveries may prove incorrect, still, within the evolutionary model it must be the case that over the course of time progress will be made in science and technology.

No historian of progress has been willing to offer the alternative views that there is no optimum amount or normatively more "correct" kind of science or technology and that each culture creates for itself the view of the natural world most suited to its needs. Neither does the history of the idea of progress offer examples of the view that social "needs" might be collectively defined to include, for example, a custodial rather than an exploitative attitude toward nature or an emphasis on sciences other than physics and biology. Any such alternative description of the history of progress is subject to severe criticisms—surely, the pure progressivist argues, it would be absurd to deny that advances in technology are good in themselves and desirable from the point of view of any imaginable culture. What I would like to argue, however, is that the idea of progress has been too narrowly defined by those writers whose views have been surveyed here and that a tendency to reify progress has led to the undervaluation of the those cultures and epochs, like the Middle Ages, whose direct contribution to a modern ideal of scientific and technological mastery is difficult to measure.

An example may clarify the difficulty we face in confronting a culture that has failed to experience the kind of progress that counts. Jack Goody has shown that during the period known in the West as the Middle Ages, large portions of Africa had economies that were at a stage of development comparable to Europe's. East Africans traded with Europeans, used coinage, and established productive relations that were in most ways analogous to those established in the West. Yet Africans had a wholly different system of land tenure and a far less productive system of agriculture, partly because of the comparative poverty of the soil and partly because of their failure to invent the heavy plough. Likewise, the capability of harnessing wind and water power, capabilities so richly exploited in Western Europe, were not realized in Africa because they neither invented nor imported the wheel. The reasons for these technological failures in an otherwise analogous economy are complex, if not inscrutable. It is clear that the materials existed for these inventions, and it is clear too that in other areas, like metalworking, innovation was acceptable. Did Africans simply not understand what constituted "progress"? Or did a complex group of forces—environmental, social, attitudinal—preclude the discovery of a few "breakthrough" technologies? Whatever the answer to this question might be, it is clear that the road of progress is neither straight nor headed toward a single destination.[73] What is needed, it seems to me, is both a reconsideration of what "progress" entails, and detailed studies of the cultural contexts within which particular technologies have developed.

THE AMBIGUITY OF PROGRESS

As we have seen, beginning in the seventeenth century the literature describing the history of progress has been primarily concerned with science and technology, and "progress" has been most often defined as the related histories of discovery and invention, assuming, perhaps quite reasonably, that the description of theoretical and practical innovations constitutes the history of progress. However, there is another way of looking at the history of technology, one that is based on Marx's view of the relation between technology and culture. If technology is not the collection of inventions used to master nature but a collection of ideas and objects that mediate human commerce with nature by extending human capabilities, then the history of technology must be written in a different fashion: it becomes the history of tools.[74]

Arnold Pacey offers an example of this way of viewing technology in his book *The Culture of Technology*. Pacey argues that the traditional way of viewing progress has been to look at the development of specific machines or techniques and to measure the extent to which these machines or techniques have been improved. Thus, for example, the history of timekeeping is a history of improvements in the accuracy of clocks. But such a history is one-dimensional because it neglects the obvious fact that machines are extensions of human beings and that any discussion of technological progress must consider the relations between human beings and their machines. So in looking at the history of the development of the lathe, one might, in the tradition of most historians of progress, look solely at the mechanical improvements made in the design and operation of the machine itself. By plotting such improvements on a graph, the historian can obtain the satisfying upward-sloping curve that is the result of quantifying the changes made in virtually any area of mechanical invention. Yet what remains unclear is the impact of technical improvements on the workers whose job it is to use such machines. Pacey cites Ian Crockett's opinion that the counterpart of the history of lathe improvement is the history of the deskilling of the labor force using the machines. "As lathes became more nearly automatic they displaced not only muscular and manual skills, but the operator's judgment as well."[75] David F. Noble has demonstrated the same phenomenon in his study of the automation of the machine-tool industry, and he has argued further that technological "progress" often reflects alignments of social and political power rather than advances in machine or process design.[76] Other historians have assumed that attenuating the burden of labor has always been technology's purpose and that one of Christianity's contributions was to make the onerous tasks of manual labor more bearable.[77] Yet at the same time, the easing of labor through technological innovation has had an undeniable impact on the level of laborers' skills, an impact not measured in graphs showing technological development but a factor in the history of technology nonetheless.

One may find similar examples in nonmechanical areas of technological development as well. The processes of growing grain have enabled harvest yields to increase, but, as Pacey shows, the yield per unit of energy consumed on farms has actually decreased. Again, the view of technology that focuses on results—on levels of efficiency, the improvement of techniques, and enhanced mechanization—measures progress in terms of two variables only—in terms of machines and their productivity. This sort of account reflects the interests of those who manage and control technology. The missing variable, the impact of technology on the human worker or on the inhabitant of a culture or ecosystem, has seldom been considered.

A human- or worker-centered approach to technology not only suggests another way of measuring progress, it also suggests another way of evaluating the contributions other cultures have made to the history of progress. Instead of focusing on the hardware of technological history—on machines and productivity—we might look instead at technology's "software"—at the values that stimulate or impede innovations, at the social purposes fulfilled or thwarted by particular technologies, at the effects of technological choices on individual workers or communities of workers. We must also be willing to acknowledge that standards of efficiency and productivity vary from culture to culture, and that resistance to technological innovations might reflect disparate social values rather than backwardness. For example, the first great cathedrals built in the Île de France were constructed very inefficiently by modern standards. They took decades to complete; stones were transported over great distances at the expense of human and animal labor and without the aid of anything more than the simplest machines.[78] Yet, as products of technology, these structures had no peer in Europe until the nineteenth century. The resolution of this paradox is possible only if we broaden the way we understand the word "technology." Measured solely in terms of the machines used—wheelbarrows, manual or water-driven saws, animal- or human-powered lifting devices—the cathedrals are products of a backward technology; measured instead in terms of organizational skills, of pure (machineless) engineering, of long-term communal involvement, of aesthetics and structural durability, these same buildings are technological marvels. If technology is the organization of human effort and the deployment of tools in order to make manifest human ideas about the use of the natural world, and not merely the history of disembodied mechanisms, then the notion of what constitutes technological progress must be reexamined.

If medieval technology is relocated in the social, intellectual, and religious context from which it has been severed by historians of progress, its accomplishments can be evaluated more accurately. In the chapters that follow I will attempt to recreate some portion of this larger context as it touched on labor and technology. In looking at this history, I should like to keep in mind the idea that technological change is not the history of machines but the whole history of human beings adapting, and adapting to, the natural world. Before turning to the formulation of early medieval attitudes toward creation and the natural world, I would like to outline briefly an alternative theory of progress, the one within which the technological changes of the Middle Ages occurred. In surveying post-Baconian attitudes toward the Middle Ages, I have established a collection of assumptions which, when laid aside, makes the reperception of medieval accomplishments possible. But perception, unlike creation, is never begun ex nihilo, and the medieval writers who considered the role of labor and technology in the life of their culture also possessed a set of assumptions about the meaning of progress.

PROGRESS: A MEDIEVAL PERSPECTIVE

It seemed self-evident to the first generations of Christian apologists that the existence of their religion was evidence of an essential improvement in the course of history. Tertullian remarks in his *Apology* that the world has improved in all respects since the coming of Christianity, especially in moral terms.[79] Eusebius quotes a letter of Melito of Sardis to Emperor Antoninus in which the bishop reminds the emperor that the power of Rome has grown great since the coming of Christianity and that this power will continue to increase only if the Christian faith is preserved and allowed to grow to full stature.[80] Lactantius's *Divine Institutions* repeats the conviction of its author that Christianity represents both a moral and a social improvement over paganism.[81] In book 6, Lactantius writes that human progress may take two forms, the way of virtue and the way of vice, and that Christianity represents the strongest form of virtuous progress—a point that suggests the paradoxical conclusion that the Christian idea of progress was itself responsible for ending the history of progress.

The fourth-century historian Paulus Orosius, whose *History Against the Pagans* influenced Augustine's *City of God,* likewise argues for the superiority of Christianity over paganism and for the rejuvenation of the world within the new, bright light of Christian faith.[82] Indeed, on the issue of Christianity as an innovative movement, one finds numerous examples of Christian writers answering charges to this effect leveled by pagan writers. In Tertullian's *Apology,* the rebuttal is made to pagan charges that it is not only the Christians who have introduced "novelties" into the world.[83] Precisely the same point is made by Arnobius in *Against the Nations,* a work written early in the fourth century: "When you [the pagans] say that we [the Christians] have abandoned [the customs] of earlier centuries, you should look more carefully, and not charge us with abandonment but note in what we have followed [custom] . . . if it is a crime to abandon an opinion and to leave behind ancient institutions for customs that are new, then this charge can also be leveled against you who have often changed your way of life."[84] In a late fourth-century controvery with Symmachus concerning the restoration of the Altar of Victory in the Roman Senate, St. Ambrose was incited to write, in the voice of Rome herself, that conversion to Christianity represented a step forward for mankind, a restoration of morals, and an acknowledgment that "there is nothing shameful in passing to better things" (*nullus pudor est ad meliora transire*).[85] In another letter to Symmachus on the same subject, Ambrose reminds the senator that the preservation of old ways represents a denial of the possibility of progress, and he cites the creation of the world from chaos as an example of how the world can be seen to change, and improve, with time. It is this theme of the moral amelioration of mankind, when joined to the Hebraic concept of linear time, which gave medieval Christianity its conception of historical progress.[86]

Tertullian made an even more explicit argument for progressivism in his *On the Soul* when he wrote that "If you look at the world as a whole, you cannot deny that it has grown progressively more cultivated and more populated . . . farms have replaced wastelands, cultivated land has subdued the forests, cattle have put to flight the wild beast, barren lands have become fertile, rocks have become soil, swamps have been drained, and the number of cities exceeds the number of poor huts found in former times . . . everywhere there are people, communities—everywhere there is human life!"[87] This hymn in praise of human energy and initiative, of the progress made by man in controlling and using the natural world, is balanced in Tertullian by an acknowledgment of the problems that can accompany progress of this kind. In this same passage, for example, Tertullian goes on to note that man "has now become a burden to the earth" through the expansion of population, and in Malthusian fashion, that the earth is hardly capable of sustaining the numbers of individuals who now inhabit it. He even suggests that natural disasters have the positive consequence of diminishing a population that would otherwise overwhelm the earth's resources. Tertullian goes farther here than any other early Christian writer in indicating the progressive nature of human history and in insisting, as did Origen and others as well, on the lineality of time.[88]

Augustine's ideas on the nature of progress contain themes found in many of the writers already mentioned; his contribution was to place the idea of progress in the broader context of Christian history as a whole. The formulation of a theory of linear time was the most important general contribution he made to the Christian theory of progress. On the personal level, Augustine considered the meaning of the ineluctable "now" in the *Confessions,* and, in particular, he demonstrated that the sense of the passage of time is dependent on the observation of changes in the physical world: "if nothing passed there would be no past time; if nothing were to happen, there would be no future time; and if nothing were, there would be no present time."[89] He writes specifically of the movement of bodies as a measure of time; furthermore, he insists that the passage of time measures purposeful change, that is, movement toward a goal or destination.[90]

This temporality in which Augustine places the purposeful progress made by the individual soul toward God—for it is God who is the goal of Augustinian time—is extended to Christian history as a whole in the *City of God.* In the twelfth book, Augustine explicitly denies the pagan philosophers' belief that time revolves and that there is to be a repetition of events that will go on forever.[91] He also argues for the applicability of the same view of linear time to history as a whole that he has argued for in the individual Christian life: "But if the soul goes from misery to happiness, nevermore to return, then there is some new state of affairs in time, which will never have an end in time. If so, why cannot the same be true of the world? And of man, created in the world?" Each event in history is unique, and, in Augustine's historiography, charged with a meaning through its relationship to one of the three principal events of linear history—Creation, Incarnation, or Judgment. Indeed, the structure of *City of God* itself, with its systematic treatment of the Creation (books 11–14), of human history (books 15–18), and of the Last Judgment (books 19–22), shows the relation between historical events and the encompassing salvationary history that gives them meaning. Within the confines of his historical discussions, Augustine shows the *excursus* or "development" of mankind to consist in a spiritual progress that proceeds through stages characterized symbolically by the six ages of man.[92] Linear history contains the record of mankind's alternating triumphs and failures in securing moral perfection. With the coming of Christ, the moral history of mankind becomes relentlessly progressive, while material history remains only haltingly so. The realization of worldly desires may be accomplished—through labor, invention, statecraft, and other means—but only as a by-product of a moral development that remains dependent on God:

> The experience of mankind in general, as far as God's people is concerned, is comparable to the experience of the individual man. There is a process of education, through the epoch of a people's history, as through the successive stages of a man's life, designed to raise them from the temporal and the visible to an apprehension of the eternal and the invisible. . . . For all things which men can receive at the hands of either angels or men, are in the power of the Omnipotent—and anyone who does not admit this is insane.[93]

While it is fitting that mankind should hope to have some of the "inferior goods of this world, which, though essential for this transitory life, are to be despised in comparison with the eternal blessing of that other life," still, any success mankind has in obtaining material goods must be seen as a gift of Providence and as incidental to the true purposes of both the individual human life and salvation history as a whole. But the attainment of such material benefits—through the labor of the hands and the inventiveness of the mind—is in no way precluded by this view of history, nor is there any doubt that progress is an acceptable by-product of the process of spiritual development that is the principal occupation of both individuals and Christian societies. Providence, which is the working out of God's intentions for man within the framework of history, uses mechanisms of all sorts in achieving its goal of mankind's spiritual regeneration; Augustinian history has ample scope for material change, for technology and invention, insofar as these activities retain their proper providential significance:

> Who can adequately describe, or even imagine, the work of the Almighty? There is, first, this capacity for the good life, the ability to attain eternal felicity, by those arts which are called virtues, which are given solely by the grace of God in Christ to the children of the promise and of the kingdom. And besides this there are all the important arts discovered and developed by human genius, some for necessary uses, others simply for pleasure. . . . Think of those wonderful inventions of clothing and building, the astounding achievements of human industry! Think of man's progress in agriculture and naviga-

tion; of the variety, in conception and accomplishment, man has shown in pottery, in sculpture, in painting; the marvels in theatrical spectacles, in which man's contrivances in design and production have excited wonder in the spectators and incredulity in the minds of those who heard of them; all his ingenious devices for the capturing, killing, or taming of wild animals. Then there are all the weapons against his fellow man . . . all the medical resources for preserving health. . . . Consider the multitudinous variety of the means of information and persuasion. . . . Consider man's skill in geometry and arithmetic, his intelligence shown in plotting the positions and courses of the stars. How abundant is man's stock of knowledge of natural phenomena! . . . It must be remembered that we are now speaking of the natural abilities of the human mind, the chief ornament of this mortal life, without reference to faith or to the way of truth, by which man attains to the life eternal.[94]

This hymn to human capabilities and to human progress is echoed in the writings of Tertullian, Gregory of Nyssa, and in Ambrose; in John the Scot, in Hugh of Saint Victor, and others. Note, however, the care with which Augustine places technological and intellectual achievements in a moral context. The next portion of book 22, chapter 24 of *City of God*—from which this long passage is taken—considers the impact of original sin, the weakness of the body, and the resultant proof of the existence of a divine Providence that has turned weakness to strength by making the substandard body servant to a rational soul. The various arts and inventions act as a kind of adjunct to the soul and add grace and power to man's feeble body. "Then there is the beauty and utility of the natural creation, which the divine generosity has bestowed on man, for him to behold and to take into use, even though mankind has been condemned and cast out from paradise into the hardships and miseries of this life." Progress, which is the material form of Augustinian Providence, has given man both the prosthesis of technology and a bountiful nature subject to the human will. Even in his fallen condition, man can savor some of the lost pleasures of paradise through the exercise of his sovereignty over nature; and, more to the point, he can also anticipate the greater, unlimited pleasure of his postmortem existence.

Augustine's presentation of the role played by human progress in providential history strikes the major themes that animate Christian theories of progress as a whole. Of course, debates over the specific role played by particular innovations continued to occur throughout the Middle Ages. In particular, twelfth-century writers discussed what sorts of "modern" innovations were acceptable in theology, natural philosophy, social policy, and technology.[95] Nor was universal agreement given to the Augustinian concept of providential history, though the uniqueness of each human life, and therefore of the overall experience of mankind, remained canonical. The restraints on innovation in the natural sciences and technology that existed during the Middle Ages—restraints felt, for example, by Adelard of Bath—cannot be ignored, but neither should they have become a priori components of any reconstruction of the history of science and technology.[96]

That early Christian writers could see a connection between material and moral progress, between human sovereignty over nature and the striving for sovereignty over the more intractable self, suggests the direction in which one should look for the place of progress in medieval culture. The themes they explored—such as the relationship of human beings to nature, the role of labor in the religious life, the acceptability of material change, the status of disciplines whose function was the creation of such change—suggest that even in denying the contributions of the Middle Ages to the history of technology, students of this history cannot ignore the debates that provided the intellectual context within which their "progress" occurred.[97] Indeed, "progress" has itself been an impediment to understanding—not just the Middle Ages, but the material and intellectual contributions of other cultures as well. I have tried to suggest that when progress is measured only in terms of machines and products, rather than in terms of products and their relationships with human beings, a distorted view of the history of technology emerges. Likewise, "technology" must be understood in a broader way if a descriptive history of anything other than post-fifteenth-century Western European history is to be written.

For example, the pervasive assumption that the development of science and technology stands opposed to religious values is a creation of the European Enlightenment and hardly a self-evident truth. It might be asserted, on the contrary, that theology and technology are both systems through which human beings exercise control over their environment or, following Max Weber, that theology provided a model of what such a system might aspire to achieve.[98] Neither is it self-evident that technological progress in the absence of cultural consensus, or in the interests of a repressive political, economic, or social system is really "progress" at all. One need not be a Luddite to question the value of a particular technology, or a reactionary to wonder if material progress that occurs in a moral vacuum is desirable.[99]

An openness to alternate versions of the history of progress is a great help in reconstructing the attitudes of medieval writers to the constellation of questions that forms the background to medieval technology. One can no doubt feel a certain sympathy for those nienteenth- and twentieth-century champions of industrial technology, hearty Yankee or Yorkshire capitalism, and unsentimental theology when reading through those generic Schoolmen who puzzled at great length over such questions as the meaning of human domination or the place of hard work in a Christian life. The willingness of a materially successful monastic establishment to question the efficacy of labor and the hair splitting over "just price" must surely have compelled men who lived in the midst of a seemingly benign progressivism to darken even more the "long night of the Middle Ages." Like all complex ages, the middle millennium has provided a mirror superbly fitted to reflect the predispositions of all sorts of scholars. Although I shall no doubt fall prey to the same temptation, I shall also attempt in what follows to reconstruct the attitudes of medieval writers toward nature, labor, and technology in order to discover what a culture committed to the idea of progress as a form of Providence contributed to the history of technology.

CHAPTER 2

God as Craftsman and Man
as Custodian: The Hexaemeral
Literature

G OD, "WHO CREATED all things in number, weight, and measure," (Wisdom 11:21) was often portrayed in the Middle Ages as the archetypal craftsman, the master artisan who shaped the raw material of the universe into the harmonious and infinitely diverse contents of the physical world.[1] A significant portion of the intellectual effort of medieval scholars was dedicated to analyzing the mechanisms through which the creation of the world was accomplished. The commentaries on the six days of creation—the hexaemeral literature—sought to demonstrate the purposefulness of the physical world, its union with the nature of God, and the goodness inherent in its system of carefully related physical phenomena. Like the creation stories of other cultures, the narrative of Genesis addresses the cosmological and theological question of how the world came to exist. Like many of these other stories, it also locates within the idealized form of the created world the place of disharmony and evil.

The commentaries on the first chapters of Genesis—which begin with Philo Judaeus's De opificio mundi (ca. A.D. 40), extend through Robert Grosseteste's thirteenth-century Hexaemeron, and culminate in Milton's Paradise Lost—describe the physical and spiritual mechanisms according to which the world operates. They do so in a variety of formats, including paraphrases, allegorical interpretations, and straightforward, literal exegesis. Like Plato's Timaeus, which provided an influential model for the earliest writers of hexaemeral commentaries, discussions of the meaning of the creative acts recounted in Genesis take place within an intellectual and moral framework that rests on the assumption that the world is imbued with a spiritual purpose.[2] Beginning with Basil of Caesarea's Homilies on the Hexaemeron, however, the medieval commentaries on Genesis also examine in detail the physical processes through which this spiritual purpose is achieved. The hexaemeral literature is therefore one of the richest sources available for reconstructing the scientific views of early Christian writers.

The hexaemeral commentaries also provide us with a great deal of information that is not directly concerned with the spiritual purposes and physical mechanisms of creation. In the course of retelling or clarifying the meaning of the first three chapters of Genesis, commentators often took up questions that had a bearing on the development of medieval attitudes toward labor; they also considered the question of the proper relation between human beings and the natural world, as well as questions about the material consequences of the fall. Although it would be useful to have a comprehensive account of the content of the hexaemeral literature, that project is beyond the scope of this study. Instead, this chapter will present a description and analysis of a number of hexaemeral texts as they bear on two specific questions. First, how is the creative action of God represented, and how does this representation change between the time of Basil and that of Thomas Aquinas? And second, how do medieval commentators understand the seemingly paradoxical charges given to Adam both to "subdue" and to "dress and keep" the natural world (Genesis 1:28 and 2:15)?[3] Each of these questions is informed, in turn, by a precise purpose. In the first instance, I would like to discover if the portrayal of God as the primal craftsman can in any way be seen to provide a sanction for the inherent value of craftsmanship (thereby supporting a contention made by Ernst Benz). In the second, I would like to clarify the issue of whether the Christian ethos, as presented in hexaemeral texts, justifies the exploitation of nature for the satisfaction of human needs. This analysis will make it possible to describe a portion of the intellectual context from which medieval labor and technology emerged.

GOD AS CRAFTSMAN

In the fifth-century frescoes of San Paolo fuori le Mura in Rome, which are now available for study only through a set of drawings made in the seventeenth century, God the Father is depicted in the act of separating light from darkness; his upper body is depicted within a half-circle whose interior is adorned with stars, his right hand is slightly outstretched in a gesture of benediction; personifications of light and darkness float above the barren landscape, a landscape as yet unformed into the bountiful

Earth, watched over by the light of the sun and the darkness of the moon.[4] Likewise, in the sixth-century Cotton Genesis, as in the thirteenth-century mosaics at San Marco in Venice that are based on this manuscript, one may see the Creator depicted as a figure placed apart from the sphere of the universe, standing among his angels and gesturing in an understated way toward the object of his creative power.[5]

Seven centuries later, in a thirteenth-century French manuscript, God is portrayed as a craftsman who uses the tools of the architect: he measures out the perfect proportions of the universe with a compass and the practiced eye of a master mason.[6] It is perhaps largely an accident of evidence that has made the image of the Creator as architect dominate the image of God as the detached director of generative forces. Still, an examination of the literary evidence in the hexaemeral commentaries suggests that the figure of God as detached creator was just as common during the first twelve centuries of the Christian era, and that, therefore, Ernst Benz's speculation that human craftsmanship was sanctified by the model of divine craftsmanship should be reconsidered.

Philo Judaeus believed that created things represent the combination of an active cause and a passive object. God, whom Philo compared directly to a "man with skill in architecture," first planned out the city of the world in his mind and then proceeded to build it according to this model. Although the creation of the universe took place over the course of six days—and Philo understands the six days as a perfect representation of the male and female principles (the number two [female] times three [male] equals six)—he shows that the passage of time was unnecessary because God created instantaneously through his reason: "[After the first day] the incorporeal world was already completed, located in the Divine Mind, and the physical world was made on the model of it."[7] The biblical convention of the "days of creation" is a means of showing how the structure of the world was given a perfectly harmonious arrangement perceptible to human senses. Philo was deeply influenced by Plato, especially the *Timaeus,* and his description of how the world was made as "an image of an image" taken from the mind of God recalls very clearly the Platonic creation story.[8] God created the world because he wished others to share in his goodness—the same motive is given by Plato in the *Timaeus* (29e)—and he created the world by giving form to a preexistent chaotic matter rather than by creating matter itself from nothing. Yet matter retains its imperfections even after being touched by the shaping images of the divine mind; therefore, man was created by God and *others:* "Let us make man after our image, and in our likeness" (Genesis 1:26). Philo uses God's assistants to free himself from the difficulty of explaining how God could have been the author of human evil: "Moses says . . . 'Let *us* make man,' which assumes other beings as assistants so that God, the ruler of all things, might have the innocent actions of man . . . and his assistants [man's] contrary actions."⁹ While Philo uses the metaphor of the builder to explain the means through which the divine image of the world is given substantial form, he does not explain the physical mechanism through which this process occurs. Like Plato, he thought the creative will of God had merely to focus on an act in order for the act to be done: "[Moses] sets before us the incorporeal ideas perceptible to the intellect that are the seals of the perceptible works, perceptible to the senses."

The *Homilies on the Hexaemeron* of Basil of Caesarea (died 379) is one of the two most influential hexaemeral commentaries—Augustine's *De Genesi ad litteram* is the other. Basil's Greek text, translated into Latin and disseminated through the writings of Ambrose, introduced detailed physical questions into commentaries on Genesis. In the first of his homilies on the Hexaemeron, Basil begins by chiding those who would attribute a material cause to the origin of the universe. God, "through his will alone," was able to create the world, and in doing so he used only a small portion of his power—an even greater universe is imaginable. Like the potter who makes a vase, God did not need to exhaust his potential creativity in order to make this world because even if the single work embodies the essence of his craft, no single work necessarily preempts the craftsman's ability to realize this essence in another form.¹⁰

According to Basil, the world and time were created together, and someday they will end together. Just as the parts that compose the world are corruptible, so too is the whole world corruptible and impermanent. The "vain arts" of geometry, arithmetic, "the study of solids," and astronomy exist as a recognition of the finitude—the measurability—of the created world.¹¹ Like Philo, Basil attacks those who believed the world to be eternal, and he expresses disdain for those who would attempt to comprehend the precise mechanism through which the world came into being. In the "time" before the creation, God perfected his art by creating the angels, and then he created the world as a place where the souls of human beings could be trained.[12]

Basil next remarks that the material objects created by human beings are, like the world itself, marked by the transitory nature of time, by its flux and elusiveness. He writes that the arts that have been created by human beings in order to shape the world are divisible into the creative, the practical, and the speculative. Basil notes that while the products of the practical and the theoretical arts pass away quickly, the products of the creative arts—of architecture, woodworking, metalworking, weaving, and so forth—are more durable; and in this durability, the mark of their creator is felt even if he is not physically present. It can be said that the world itself is the work of art through which human beings may contemplate the wisdom and power of the craftsman-creator, God himself. Indeed, Moses, as the author of Genesis, has described a Craftsman whose invisble but pervasive presence gives substance and harmony to the universe.[13]

At this point, Basil steps back from his analysis of the Creation and warns the reader that speculations on the origins of the world are not as fruitful as the simple act of contemplating God's power in creating the perfection that we see in the product of his labor. "Set a limit to your thoughts" is Basil's advice, for even if we could understand natural phenomena like the movement of the heavenly bodies, our understanding can only serve the useful purpose of exciting greater admiration for the divine Craftsman.

In evaluating the use of the metaphor of God as artisan in Basil's *Homilies,* it is important to recognize the extent to which this metaphor is employed to evoke images of inscrutable power and aesthetic perfection rather than workmanlike skill or mechanical harmony. Basil's Creator is an artist who inspires awe for the perfect beauty of his work; we are invited to contemplate this beauty but are warned that it is futile to try to understand the mechanism through which it was created. Furthermore, the real miracle of God's creative power is not the shaping of matter but its creation. Human art is the fabrication of formless material, while divine art, of an immeasurably higher order, consists of creating the material out of which all objects, and the acts which beget them, have their origins.[14] God "at one and the same time" created the forms and matter from which all objects are constituted. To each portion of the creation he assigned an appropriate nature, and he bound the whole world together through a natural affinity that acts through a continuous bond of mutual attraction. God is by no means just an inventor of shapes, and the comparison of God with the human artisan is valid only insofar as it recognizes that the divine artisanship is primarily concerned with the infusion of matter with meaning as well as with material form. Further undercutting the image of God as craftsman is the fact that the mechanism of the divine creation was not the manipulation of matter but the utterance of words—"Act and Word were one" is how Basil describes the process of creation.[15]

Yet, however misleading it may be to think of God as a divine craftsman or artisan, subsequent hexaemeral commentators continued to use this analogy, perhaps out of deference to Basil's influence and perhaps because no other human image could approximate so well the combination of thought and action that the commentators wished to convey in their description of the Creation. However, the exact use to which the metaphor of the Creator as craftsman was put varied considerably within the hexaemeral literature, and, in many instances, the metaphor was deliberately undercut in the interest of calling attention to the rational rather than the manual aspect of the Creation.

For example, Ambrose, who diffused Basil's ideas in the Latin West, wrote that God created the world and time together through the power of his will and his word.[16] God did not merely create a model or an Idea and then allow matter itself to generate the world after this model, as the Platonists maintained. Furthermore, Ambrose asserted that the created world was wholly good and that evil was introduced as a consequence of the adversary within human beings.[17]

In chapter 5 of his first homily on the Hexaemeron, Ambrose considers the extent to which the created world is a model of the handiwork of God, and he asserts that it is through the work that we know the Worker. Some of man's arts are practical and have to do with physical or verbal acts; their products are transitory and do not survive the act that initially creates them. Other arts are theoretical or rational; their products endure, as in the case of a building. This world is an example of a theoretical creation: it is the product of wisdom of God, it instantiates this wisdom, and therefore it endures. Ambrose's intentions are not difficult to perceive—the object of human admiration must be deflected away from the material world and toward its maker.[18] This admiration must be rational so that it is directed toward the wisdom of the world's creator rather than the beauty of his creation. Ambrose points to the endurance of ideas and the illusiveness of actions: the divine Craftsman is admired for the perfection of his idea rather than for the skill of his craft. God creates the world much as the philosopher "creates" his wisest thoughts, and Ambrose implicitly draws the reader away from seeing the Creation as a physical process and directs him toward seeing it as the product of an unbounded will: "God is not merely an artist, but one who is omnipotent."[19]

Augustine's commentary on the literal sense of Genesis departs from Basil and Ambrose in its shift of emphasis away from the "physical" details of creation toward its metaphysical and salvationary implications. The God of Augustine's *De Genesi ad litteram* is the tranquil and sustaining center of the universe, and this image of God dominated medieval descriptions of the creator's role once the act of creation was completed.[20] Augustine's God creates through the Word, and questions dealing with matters such as the relations of the Trinity in the act of creation, the meaning of specific words, the meaning of "God's rest," and the nature of angelic knowledge occupy Augustine a great deal.[21] The reader of Augustine's *Confessions* (books 11 and 12 in particular) will be familiar with the extent to which the nature of creation was related in Augustine's mind to the nature of time. A complex problem for Augustine was the issue of why and how an eternal God should create a temporally bounded world. Augustine's placement of the motives for creation and the true sense of time's meaning within the Divine Will eliminated some of the more difficult questions raised by his account. The Augustinian God created for the same reason as the Demiurge of the *Timaeus*, because he was not envious and was wholly good; or, as Bernardus Silvestris maintained in the *Cosmographia*, God created the world so as to allow that which existed in chaotic potential to become as perfect as its actualized nature would allow.[22]

Augustine's God creates through the Word in a single act, and Augustine takes the notion of the "six days" to be a metaphor for the sense of process that God's method of creation engenders in human observers. In the beginning—even before time itself existed—God created undifferentiated matter and "forms" (*rationes*), some of which were immediately embodied in preexistent matter, though to use the word "preexistent" is to use language loosely; in reality there was no delay between the creation of unformed matter and of the forms that were embodied within it. Other of the forms waited, as seeds, to be embodied in matter at the proper time. The creation was not a series of interrelated acts spread out over six "days" but a single act of will, which either actualized or created the potential for the existence of every object or being that will ever exist.[23] Like the tree, the fruits of the Creation appear slowly but inevitably in the course of time. Augustine's Creator is a detached and imperious sovereign who sets an enormous process into motion with a few words; he is not to be imagined as measuring out the heavens with a compass or, worse yet, molding the human form from the mud of Eden. Neither is Augustine any more interested in the physical details of creation than his Creator: though he does describe the creation of the heavens and the firmament, Augustine avoids a detailed description of their construction by citing the impossibility of understanding that which must simply be believed on the authority of Scripture.[24] God's role in the world after the moment the creation was completed was to maintain that which had been made.

A creator who exists at an even greater remove from his creation is found in the ninth-century *Periphyseon* of John the Scot (Johannes Scottus Eriugena).[25] Eriugena's Neoplatonic discussion of the organization of the natural forces that created and sustain the universe sees God as the unbounded first Cause, "the Cause beyond causality and the Goodness beyond being, by participation in Whom all principles and all causes of all things subsist, while He Himself participates in none because he has no principle at all . . . that is not coessential with Him."[26] God is the stable central point of the universe, and language that refers to such things as the "beginning," "middle," or "end" of this universe reflects divisions created by the human intellect rather than any perturbation in the unchanging essence of the Creator.[27] Thus, in his small-scale hexaemeral treatise, which is incorporated into book 3 of the *Periphyseon,* Eriugena speaks of how, in the beginning, the reality of heaven and earth were hidden in the Divine Will, unknowable, until they "flowed forth into forms and species."[28]

Eriugena thinks that the creation consists of a series of "processions" of forms: the internal nature of God generates the idealized model of all things; from this model emerge generic types and species. All things that exist are a part of God; therefore, he is drawn to deny the doctrine of creation ex nihilo. The act of creation is an act of the divine will, which affirms a certain set of forms; once affirmed, these forms grow from the very essence of God. Like Augustine, Eriugena denies that it took six "days" for the Creation to occur. The number six is symbolic in its perfection, but the creation itself was a process set in motion according to logical relations built into the divisions of nature. When God said, "Let there be light," he was really saying "Let the primordial causes proceed into forms and species manifest to those who contemplate them"—language and will manifest what existed potentially "within" God.[29]

Indeed, the use and understanding of language is at the heart of Eriguena's version of the creation, and his God is aptly characterized as a rhetorician rather than a craftsman. When God said, "Let the earth bring forth flourishing vegetation," it was as if God had said—and Eriugena supplies the expanded readings of God's aphoristic commands—"Let the seminal force of crops and trees, which is causally created in the inward reasons of substances, proceed through generation into sensible forms and species." And it was done.[30] Likewise, just as God uses words to set in action the generation of species out of ideal forms, so too do the commentators struggle with language as a means of rendering these acts comprehensible to those who would understand the Creation. Eriugena points out that as we "grope in the darkness of our ignorance" in attempting to behold the light of truth, we use words in simple patterns that are comprehensible to the human intellect but which do not necessarily reflect the realities of God's actions. Thus, Eriugena says, St. Basil wrote a narrative about the Creation, and described it as taking place over the course of six days, because words cannot express ideas instantaneously but must succeed temporally: "For every art which in the mind of the wise man is formed as a whole can be communicated to the ears of his hearers only by being divided into parts and ordered in words and syllables and sentences which follow one another in temporal succession."[31] Language, which both sets into motion and makes (reasonably) comprehensible the act of creation, reflects the divisions of the world by being divided itself. Words represent the actions of the Word, which "all at once" created all things and formed them into genera and species "like a ball which rolls down a slope and does not stop until it comes, as it were, to rest at the end of the universe."[32] Eriugena's Creator is a shaper of divine intentions into language, and he is not depicted as a laborer or craftsman because what he creates are the seeds that evolve into the objects that fill the world.

Eriugena, like many other hexaemeral writers influenced by Augustine, accepted the idea that the creation of the world was instanteous and that God cannot be compared to a human worker whose labor occurs within a temporal framework.[33] Alcuin, for example, wrote that God creates through four "modes": through his Word he creates all that is; through "infused matter" he creates specific corporeal things; through the specific generations of the six days he separates and distinguishes between species and forms; and through the "primal seeds" he continues the creative process over time.[34]

Eriguena's "divisions of nature" were to have a long life, both within and outside the hexaemeral tradition. In fact, the discussion of the relation between instanteous creation and the leisurely unfolding of potential forms continues to occupy an important place in scientific and pseudo-scientific writings today, as the arguments between evolutionists and creationists demonstrate.[35] The Augustinian concept of seminal forms, as developed into the formal system of successive divisions by Eriugena, provided a means of meshing the manifestation of divine power inherent in the original creation with the manifestation of divine Providence that is revealed in the continuing creativity inherent in the natural world. As I have already suggested, the conviction that the physical world has inherent in it the material and moral mechanisms of divine Providence was what defined the medieval Christian idea of progress.

From its original Neoplatonic sources, through Augustine and Eriugena, one may trace the ideas of continuing creation and latent forms into such works as the *Clavis physicae* of Honorius Augustodunensis. Honorius writes of God as the "uncreated Creator" who forms the primordial causes generated in time and space, and who, as the "uncreator," also brings to a close the forms and objects manifested through his Providence.[36] Raymond Lull also utilizes this scheme in the *Ars brevis* and the *Ars magna,* and he offers a taxonomy of human knowledge based on an understanding of God's unfolding potency in the *Arbor scientiae.*[37]

The longevity of the idea of continuing creation may be seen in its adoption by the seventeenth-century Platonist Ralph Cudworth in his dispute with the proponents of the "mechanical laws." In "The Digression Concerning the Plastick Life of Nature," which is part of his *True Intellectual System of the Universe* (1678), Cudworth argues that "since neither all things are produced Fortuitously, or by the Unguided Mechanism of Matter, nor God himself may reasonably be thought to do all things Immediately and Miraculously; it may well be concluded, that there is a *Plastik Nature* under him, which as an Inferior and Subordinate Instrument, doth Drudgingly Execute that Part of his Providence, which consists in the Regular and Orderly Motion of Matter."[38] God, the seventeenth-century mystic Jacob Boehme thought, places "a signature on all things," and this signature is the mark not of continuing intervention but of the activity of a created, and controllable, intermediary. Although she does not accept Cudworth's "Plastik Nature" and holds instead that the Creation was instantaneous, Anne Conway accepts the existence of "seeds" or primary principles from which the succession of creatures would grow in the course of time. She writes in her *Principia philosophiae* (1690) that while God's will and his word act at once in creating the world, his word also creates the "universals, seeds, and principles" of all things, which are the springs and foundations from which created things flow in the course of time.[39] The "detached" God who creates all at once and then oversees the ongoing temporal process of providential and natural history helped generations of scholars, philosophers, and exegetes to reconcile the immediacy of the creation and the power of God with the unfolding of creatures and divine Providence.

In the twelfth-century *De operibus sex dierum* of Arnold of Bonneval, God exists as a will and as the potential to act, as a great binding force whose power reconciles all contradictions inherent within matter. God creates through the Word in a single act of will, but the world grows from its foundations according to the laws inherent in creation from the first moment of time.[40] Likewise, Bernardus Silvestris's *Cosmographia* describes the Creation of the world by the divine Mind as the imposition of order on chaos and as the continuing emanation of forms out of the "formless chaos."[41] The image of an "unfolding" creation is also found in Thierry of Chartres's *De sex dierum operibus* as well as in his commentary on the *De trinitate* of Boethius.[42] Thierry was profoundly influenced by Eriugena, and he argues that unity or oneness is God's essential nature; therefore, all that exists participates in this unity in some way.

A different tradition of hexaemeral interpretation, at least concerning God's role in the creation and maintenance of the world, grew out of the *Hexaemeron* of Bede. Unlike Augustine and those influenced by him, Bede held that the "days" of the Creation were clearly delineated periods of time during which the primordial matter of the first "moment" of creation was differentiated into the various species of created objects.[43] Bede's break with Augustine over the matter of the *rationes seminales* (seminal reasons) committed him to the controversial view that Creation consisted of the disposition of matter into the visible multitude of created things.[44] The Creator depicted in Bede's *Hexaemeron* is, therefore, an active force whose work is ongoing, and this view of God's role coexists with the Augustianian view in twelfth- and thirteenth-century hexaemeral commentaries.

Hugh of Saint Victor, like Bede, was opposed to the Augustinian view of an unfolding creation, and he took the six days of creation to refer to a literal expanse of time by arguing that God could be conceived of as having done his work over the course of time without detracting from his power.[45] Likewise, Peter Abelard's *Expositio in Hexaemeron* describes the Creation as an act of divine will, but acknowledges the existence of ongoing natural causes that operate autonomously, and reflect divine Providence, but do not demand God's direct intervention.[46] William of Conches makes the same point—that nature operates independently after the Creation—in the *Philosophia mundi*. For William, as for Abelard, the natural laws according to which the divine power is manifested are a mechanism that is not in competition with God and whose existence does not detract from God's power—only from the extent to which the workings of the world are "natural" as opposed to "miraculous."[47]

This shift toward more literal readings of the act of creation in Bede and in some twelfth-century writers reflected an attempt to redefine God's relation to the world. The work of the six days was extended, through the medium of natural laws, into the present and future; while the emanationists like Augustine and Eriugena describe the Creation as essentially complete with the first division of the divine nature, the literalists portray God as building laws into the structure of the world that continue to operate over time. These laws are themselves observable, or at least neither so inaccessible nor so sacred as to be beyond the intellectual and moral powers of the curious seeker. If the mysterious emanations of divine being led to the mystical poetry of Bernardus Silvestris or Alan of Lille, or to the cryptic diagrams of Lull and the opaque descriptions of Eriguena, then the natural causes fixed in the web of creation by the divine Workman may legitimately be sought in natural philosophy and in mathematics.[48]

Each of these possible interpretations of the mechanism of creation is represented in the comments of Aquinas on the Creation. In the *Summa theologiae*, Aquinas describes God as the creator of "primary matter" and the first cause of all that exists. God inscribes forms on indeterminate matter; these forms reside in the mind of God in the way that the form of a house resides in the mind of an architect.[49] In question 45, Aquinas considers the physical means whereby this inscription of form occurs. Creation is the emanation of being out of nonbeing and takes place without any movement or change of state on God's part. Creation is a relationship between God and a creature based on an act of the divine will rather than on any physical change. In considering the creation of matter prior to the imposition of form, Aquinas cites the disagreement between Augustine (in *De Genesi* 1, 15), who did not believe that matter was formless before the Creation, and Basil and Ambrose, who did believe in the precedence of amorphous matter. Aquinas occupies a middle ground in this dispute: he believes that primary matter was neither formless nor formed in a particular way before the Creation; instead, he proposes that primary matter existed "under distinct forms" as in the way that potency precedes act.[50] In the *Summa contra gentiles,* however, Aquinas insists that creation was ex nihilo and that it did not involve any succession of forms. Aquinas uses an example from the study of the intensity and remission of forms to show that any event that proceeds by succession takes time, and that the creation could not have taken time because the "becoming" that would have preceded a creation in time could have no substance (since before it occurred, nothing existed). Thus, with Basil (*Homilies* 1, 5) and Aristotle (*Physics* 6, 3), Aquinas holds that the Creation took place instantaneously in the first moment of time.[51]

We have seen that the creation of the world is understood in a variety of ways by medieval writers commenting on Genesis. God is often compared to a laborer or artisan in the hexaemeral literature, but this metaphor is undercut by an equally common insistence on the detachment of the Creator from his creation. The visible world is primarily a manifestation of divine power, its maintenance a manifestation of divine intentions, and its development a manifestation of divine Providence. In Basil, Ambrose, Augustine, and Bede—the most important hexaemeral commentators—there are disagreements about the mechanisms of creation, but a consistent view of the transcendent power of the Creator. In one sense, the descriptions of God as Craftsman reflect a perennial question about the relations between artisans and the objects they create: to what extent does the maker continue to be responsible for that which he or she makes? The fallen world must be seen to bear the marks of its divine origin and the imprint of a continuing Providence, without impugning the skills or judgment of the Master Craftsman. If, as Ernst Benz supposes, the hexaemeral literature supports a divine sanction for craftsmanship, it does so very gingerly, in full awareness of the terrible fact that created objects may not be able to sustain the good intentions for which they were made.

MAN AS CUSTODIAN

The second issue raised by the hexaemeral literature centers on the relationship between human beings and the natural world. Are Ernst Benz and Lynn White correct in ascribing to Christianity an exploitative attitude toward nature? Is it possible to construct an alternative set of attitudes on the basis of medieval commentaries on Genesis?

In an article that first appeared in 1967, "The Historical Roots of Our Ecological Crisis," White developed Benz's view that the Judaeo-Christian tradition is the source of the conviction that the natural world exists to be exploited by human beings. Christianity, as the "most anthropocentric religion the world has seen," provides in its conception of the Creation and its identification of man with the creator a rationale for the subordination of the earth and the earth's creations to the human will.[52] White sees the crux of the Western view of nature in the Christian displacement of "pagan animism," with its respect for the spiritual life inherent in nature. Once the spirituality of the natural world was negated by a concern for the well-being of human beings, the way was opened for the development of science and technology, enterprises that seek to understand and control the world for human ends.

In other essays, White has cited the comparative technological backwardness of other areas of the world as evidence for the contribution of Christian theology to the creation of conditions favoring the development of technology. In particular, he cites the cases of China and India, whose "passive" religious ethic either stalled the development of technology (as in China) or forestalled the initiation of sophisticated technology (as in India). White also contrasts the contemplative theology of the Eastern church with the active theology of the Western in order to present additional evidence for his central argument—that the theology developed during the first centuries of the Christian era sanctioned the creation of a view of nature and of its use that fostered the growth of technology.[53]

White's views have not gone unchallenged. John Passmore has objected to White's contention that an exploitative view of nature is inherent in the Old Testament, and he has cited a considerable body of textual evidence in support of his claim that a custodial view of nature can be derived from the Judaeo-Christian tradition. Passmore does agree, however, that the language of the Old Testament freed humankind from the obligation to regard itself as bound to nature by moral constraints.[54] Other writers have gone further in their criticisms of White's analysis. F. B. Welbourn cites texts from Deutero-Isaiah (41:17–20) and Leviticus (19: 23–26) to support his argument that nature was not regarded by biblical writers as an object for exploitation; he also doubts that the Bible supersedes the animistic conviction that nature is infused with a sacrosanct life.[55] Other critics of White, including William Coleman, have questioned both the idea that Christianity has been unique in creating a theology that supports the exploitation of nature and the centrality of the medieval period in the history of such an idea's formulation. Coleman believes that it was only in the seventeenth and eighteenth centuries that Christian writers came closest to creating the kind of theology that favored the domination of nature and the rise of technology. Coleman also cites the close connection between Christianity and capitalism during this later period as a likely source of the ethic of domination.[56]

In a more fundamental analysis, Lewis Moncrief questions the influence that religious beliefs have on the creation of a consensus that nature exists to be exploited. Moncrief wonders if the connection between Christianity and domination is any more plausible than the connection between Christianity and capitalism.[57] Recently, Robin Attfield has provided a comprehensive critique of White's views and has argued effectively that "the biblical position, which makes people responsible to God for the uses to which the natural environment is put, has never been entirely lost to view."[58] Attfield's argument for an ethic of stewardship as opposed to an ethic of domination offers an alternative to White's theory of the influence of Judaeo-Christian culture; it does not, however, approach the larger question—which is really at the heart of White's analysis—of the contribution made by medieval Christianity to creating conditions under which a uniquely effective technology could arise.

In reviewing this literature, several issues emerge. The first is that it is probably impossible to reconstruct the medieval attitude toward the natural world solely through reference to passages in the Old Testament. The existence of the science, and, one might also say, the industry of biblical interpretation during the Middle Ages makes it imperative that one look at commentaries on the Bible as well. This has been done, though to only a limited extent, by White himself, by some of his critics, and by other scholars.[59] The second point is that Coleman, Moncrief, and others are no doubt quite correct in reminding us that neither religion in general, nor Christianity in particular, can be understood to operate alone in shaping the conditions under which an ethic of domination or a consensus favoring technological innovation were created.

Certainly one might plausibly suggest that in the case of the "Protestant Ethic and the spirit of capitalism" theological arguments that seem to have catalyzed economic initiatives, manufacture, and trade were attempts to rationalize events that had occurred for reasons having nothing whatever to do with theology or ethics.[60] While a clarification of the religious context within which Western attitudes toward nature have arisen can be a valuable aid to understanding the history of technology, such a clarification cannot be a substitute for the detailed study of particular innovations within the broadest possible context. In looking for the source of the medieval attitude toward the use of nature, one should examine religious views not with an eye toward finding the cause of a particular kind of behavior, but in order to recreate the context within which this behavior occurred. By the twelfth century of the Christian era a complex economy had been created in Europe that applied a variety of technologies and significantly altered the environment. Did the interpretation of the Bible create an intellectual and moral context within which the domination of nature through work and invention could proceed? The hexaemeral literature will help us to answer this question.

To begin with, Philo Judaeus sees in Adam's prelapsarian role the clearest possible statement of human hegemony over the created world. Since man was created in God's image and as an epitome of all the rest of creation (man is like every other kind of animal at once in that he can inhabit the realms proper to birds, fish, mammals, and angels), it was proper for him to share in the work of creation by exercising the power of naming and using lesser creatures. "And as was very natural, the power of domination was excessive in that first created man, whom God formed with great care and thought worthy of the second rank in the creation, making him his own viceroy and the ruler of all other creatures."[61] As time has passed since the Creation, and as mankind has lost some of the power of reason it once possessed, so too has the natural domination of human beings over the "irrational beasts" lessened, though a spark of it still survives. In view of the first man's perfection—the fact that he was created after no model but from an image of the divine mind itself—it follows from Philo's view that this perfect man should dominate the rest of creation. However, this domination should be based on moral superiority ("[man] is superior to all of these [other] animals in regard of his soul"), and should be characterized by "correctness of judgment" rather than by any arbitrary or irresponsible exercise of power.[62]

In his fifth homily on the Hexaemeron, Basil of Caesarea observes that in creating the vegetation that adorns the earth, the Creator was preparing food for the cattle and horses "who furnish wealth and enjoyment for [mankind]."[63] Furthermore, some of these plants are food for human beings, and Basil makes a distinction between those plants which are "useful" to men and those which, like hemlock and mandrake, are harmful. That these plants were created before man does not detract from their function, "and every created plant has a certain particular reason for its creation." Basil continues this line of argument by reminding his teachers that just because some things are poisonous does not mean that they do not have other uses: the bull, for example, whose blood poisons a human being, nonetheless was created to provide a strength "necessary for many things."[64] Likewise, those creatures which are good to use in their natural state may be improved through husbandry. Basil also ties this theme of an improved nature to the complementary theme of nature's perfection when it existed in its newly created state. Even after the commission of the sin that caused man to "eat [his] bread in the sweat of [his] brow," the earth remained fertile; though sin modified nature, causing the thorn to appear on the rose, sin did not affect nature's fecundity or usefulness to mankind.[65] The fertile and richly diverse natural world is also a symbol of the human relationship to God. Just as farming can alter particular plants, so too can moral husbandry alter the weaknesses of the sinner's soul. Still, nature is not useful merely as a source of food or a repository of symbols. The primary benefit derived from the use of nature is the reminder of God's power and solicitude for mankind. Nature is to be used and admired; its relation to mankind is one of both physical and spiritual sustenance. Everything in nature attests to the foresight of God, provisions that he "provided for us from the beginning."[66] The "wise Craftsman" has provided human beings with the fruits of the natural world to assist them in their movement toward spiritual perfection. One sees in Basil's homilies a natural world that is useful, but "useful" in the sense of nurtured and studied, not in the sense of exploited or dominated.

The extent to which the natural world is a repository of moral lessons rather than a kingdom to be exploited is clear from Basil's seventh homily, which deals with the creation of the creatures of the sea (Genesis 1:20). Basil argues that by regarding the habits of the animals who live in or near the sea—the "deceitful" octopus, the acquisitive crab, the prescient sea urchin—a human being can better learn his duty toward God. If creatures who lack reason can fulfill their function in the creation so successfully, why should creatures who have an innate understanding of good and evil squander their lives in unreasoning pleasure?[67] How can a wife leave her abusive husband when even the sea lamprey remains united to the poisonous serpent? And should the brutal husband not reciprocate the wife's sacrifice by discharging his venom? The book of nature teaches the Christian his or her moral duty; while the creation helps to sustain the bodily life of mankind, it fulfills a more important duty by sustaining mankind's spiritual life. Basil asks, "Why does the earth bring forth living creatures?"—so that human beings may learn the difference between the souls of beasts and the souls of men.[68] The plenitude of nature gives human beings cause to worship God; the creatures of the earth "ornament" the world, and the proper duty of the Christian is to be moved to virtue by the creation. The earth serves God: it spontaneously generates grasshoppers and eels, mice and frogs; it creates creatures after their own kind, from generation to generation, without any change or alteration ("time does not alter the characteristics of animals").[69] In his desire to find lessons for mankind in nature, Basil grants animals a variety of values, including a primitive moral consciousness, that makes any discussion of their exploitation by mankind impossible. Some animals seem to have a sense of time insofar as they prepare for the future (like ants and cattle); others, while they lack reason, have instincts that are akin to reason (the dog). Yet, whatever the virtues of animals, whatever their lessons for human beings, they have been created to be subject to the human will "because we have been created in the image of God."[70] In summary, then, Basil's *Homilies on the Hexaemeron* pictures a relation between human beings and the natural world that is based on the physical and moral benefits derivable from plants and animals, but which suggests that human domination is not to be exploitative but based on a moral superiority that assumes responsible behavior.

Ambrose clearly used Basil's account of the origins and purposes of the various "ornaments" of creation—the creatures of the sea, the air, and the land—in his account. He also adds material that has bearing on the reconstruction of Christian attitudes toward the domination of nature. For example, in discussing Genesis 1:20—"Let the waters abound with life and above the earth let winged creatures fly below the firmament of the heavens"—Ambrose points out that in creating a variety of animals before creating Adam, God prepared for man both "nourishment" and temptation. Human beings are inclined to see the riches of the earth as personal possessions, but Ambrose argues that all things were to be used in common. The earth gives freely of its fruits, but man makes the mistake of thinking that these gifts belong to him alone—avarice was born in nature's plenitude.[71]

Ambrose follows Basil in drawing moral lessons from his (bookish) observation of natural phenomena. Like Basil, he points to the fact that those fish which prey upon smaller creatures are themselves the food of still larger fish—the fellowship of the eater and the eaten. The lesson to be drawn from this unseemly fact is that while irrational creatures may be forgiven their appetites, human beings, whose tastes should be governed by reason, cannot be excused for violence to their fellows. When Ambrose writes that the creatures of the sea were given to man for his use, he means that they were given to nourish both the body and the soul: "they represent a pattern of the sins we observe in society."[72] Indeed, from the simplicity of fishes' lives the Christian can draw one of the surest lessons about human nature, namely, mankind's inability to be contented with the physical restraints placed upon it. Human beings have explored the sea and broken the barriers between the oceans and the land in search of a means to quiet an irrepressible restlessness. In praising the willingness of earth's simpler creatures to be contented with natural boundaries, Ambrose testifies to the restlessness of mankind that creates and sustains technology: "The earth alone is insufficient. . . . Men claim the sea through rights of property and brag that they have made fishes their slaves; like kings, men divide the elements among themselves."[73]

The moral lessons of nature are further extended by Ambrose in his discussion of birds. He describes a primitive communism in which birds take turns leading their flight, having for a brief time the advantages of preference and then voluntarily taking their place among the flock so that another may soar (and labor) at the head of the group. Ambrose extends this example in order to point out that, originally, human communal organization was based on natural models, and that everyone in this form of "primitive community" had a clearly defined set of duties and privileges. An advantage of the natural system of rotating responsibilities that is germane to this discussion is that, under such a system, manual labor is made less onerous because it is finite; every servant labors in the knowledge that he will at some point become a master—though, in truth, there are no masters or servants in such cooperative communities.[74] Other moral and social lessons may be learned from the birds with whom mankind shares the creation—lessons regarding filial piety, devotion to progeny, loyalty to spouse, and responsibility to the community.

In the ninth homily, Ambrose takes up the meaning of what occurred on the sixth day of Creation. He discusses, first of all, the common perception that the beasts of the earth (Genesis 1:20–24) are taken to be symbolic manifestations of various sorts of human folly—stupidity, cupidity, wickedness, and so on.[75] Ambrose states his lack of interest in the "science" of creation ("What does the measure of the circumference of the earth mean to me?"). His true interest lies, he asserts, in the concrete reality of those things—beasts and human beings—which inhabit the world, thereby denying the importance of the symbolic readings of creation he has been pursuing.

In the case of the "beasts and crawling creatures," Ambrose notes that these terrestrial creatures are spawned from the earth itself, "according to a fixed law."[76] The productivity of like from like is a form of homage the earth pays to its Creator. Are these creatures to be used for the profit of mankind? If so, Ambrose argues, it makes no sense to deny their natural being—presumably he means their literal as opposed to their anagogic being—but then he returns at once to a consideration of the moral meaning of bestial nature. "Do not bend over like cattle—do not physically bend, nor morally." The bestiary that follows in the ninth homily covers well-known ground: Ambrose reads the moral natures of dogs (dumb but seemingly rational, like men who think that they have discovered some complex truth), lambs, leopards, lions, and so on. More to the point is Ambrose's observation that every animal was created in the form most appropriate to its role in the environment. Adaptation is not an issue in this ecology, since each animal's morphology meshes perfectly with its habitat and eating habits: what Ambrose actually says is that "carnivores do not need long necks [because] they bend down in the act of feeding," while, on the other hand, camels have a long neck and therefore feed on large plants. In other words, creatures and environment are in perfect balance, and each species was created in a particular form precisely to preserve this balance.[77]

The human place in this scheme is exalted because of the "likeness" of man to God. But the similarity of a human being to God resides not in the form of the flesh but in the being of the soul—in our imaginative and reflective selves.[78] This language, which Ambrose uses in chapter 8, leads anticlimactically to a condemnation of women's use of makeup—the marring of a naturally perfect work of art.[79]

It also leads to an affirmation of the natural conditions of human life and to the observation that the physical and spiritual greatness of mankind should not be allowed to become a temptation. Ambrose's moral lesson is that human beings should learn from the perfection of the body and the rational structure of nature to avoid the unnatural temptations of worldly wealth and power; to learn to face death bravely; to perform one's spiritual and social duties conscientiously. Nature exists to be used by human beings because they are the pinnacle of the creation, but the relationship that Ambrose describes in the ninth homily is by no means exploitative or one-sided. The offspring of Adam have a great deal to learn from the behavior of animals, and while men may domesticate and consume beasts and cattle, this merely reflects the carrying out of the providential functions of different creatures, not the exploitation of an inferior species by a superior. The homilies of Ambrose do not neglect human sinfulness or consideration of sin's effects on the condition of man and nature, but the unmistakable impression left by his text is of a prelapsarian world, precisely balanced by the eternal laws built into the Creation from the beginning, elevating mankind to the highest place but balancing this elevation with a sense of the duties encumbent upon such a godlike creation. Ambrose describes a moral ecology in which the role of each creature within the natural order is defined by a set of spiritual obligations that create conditions of dependence rather than of exploitation.

Augustine's discussion of Genesis differs in substantial ways from those of Basil and Ambrose. For one thing, Augustine does not discuss the natural world—animals, plants, and the human anatomy—with the thoroughness or interest of either Basil or Ambrose. For another, his depiction of the human relation to the environment focuses more directly on the extent to which the created world satisfies human needs. In book three of *De Genesi,* Augustine discusses the significance of the creation of the animals with whom human beings shared the newly formed earth. After considering the terminology available for categorizing the various classes of fish and amphibians, Augustine turns to a gloss of Genesis 1:24–25. He makes a distinction between those animals called generically "cattle" (*pecora*) and other animals known as "reptiles and beasts of the earth."[80] "Cattle" is the name given to those animals who "serve man, either by aiding him in his work or by providing him with clothing." Augustine's discussion of what he calls "quadrupedia" indicates that, aside from considerations of morphology or taxonomy, one way to understand the distinctions between the types of animals named in Genesis is to consider their relations to human beings.[81] This anthropocentric conception of the organization and function of creation is also reflected in Augustine's assertion that harmful plants exist as a consequence of human sinfulness, not because of a perverse act of creation on God's part.[82] Indeed, the primary consequence of original sin was the loss of human sovereignty over the natural world. Augustine makes this loss the theme of much of *De Genesi,* and the influence of his discussion colors the whole history of hexaemeral commentary.[83]

As several long passages in *De Genesi* make explicit, the world was created to be receptive to human needs. Augustine contrasts mankind's upright posture with the bent and abject posture of beasts; human beings look heavenward while the "earthly" beasts look toward the ground. Because man was created in the image of God, he is the master of all other creatures. Animals have the distinction of being created by God, but to man alone belongs the excellence of having been made in God's image.[84] All of the qualities that once defined the unique and superior status of human beings were undone by the effects of original sin. Sin causes nature to become hostile and unreceptive; animals, once obedient, resist human domination; and even the rose grows thorns. That which assists human beings in reestablishing control over the environment—that which came to be called technology—had its origin in the sin of pride, in the aspiration to divinity that broke the natural bonds of domination linking human beings to nature.

Augustine's Platonism also shapes his attitude toward the relation between human beings and the natural world. Since all created things participate in the Divine Ideas seeded into the material creation, everything has an inherent spiritual value. But while every created thing is relatively perfect within its own sphere, all things are arranged hierarchically from the lowest (and most material) creature to the highest (and most spiritual). Human beings occupy a point somewhere in the middle of this scheme; they are lower than the angels or other pure "intelligences" but higher than any other creature with whom they share the earth. While members of a particular class of beings do not "evolve" toward a higher state of being, the whole of creation unfolds in linear time toward a greater completeness and perfection. The forms of things (their *ratio*) is realized with time, and the world as a whole grows toward a fuller articulation.[85] Unlike the other inhabitants of the earth, man was not created "according to kind" but solitary, as an "original seed" in which species and genus were one. Indeed, before the Fall, man was unique in many respects: reproduction occurred without desire or "coupling," nourishment without hunger, governance without exploitation, life without death.[86] The prelapsarian couple had two functions—to worship God and to rule the earth—though Eve also had the third duty of obeying her husband.[87]

In book 13 of *De civitate Dei*, Augustine writes that the story of the Creation and Fall can be read in a spiritual sense without doing any damage to the meaning of the literal text.[88] Although the account of *De Genesi* focuses on the specific interpretation of difficult passages and perplexing concepts—how, for example, can God "rest" on the seventh day?—Augustine does not neglect the spiritual sense of the text in his readings or lose sight of the larger context of salvation history of which the Creation is a part. Thus, while Adam ruled Eden and had the power of a god, his sin overthrew his rule and undermined his power. Where the prelapsarian Adam used nature and lived wholesomely within it, the fallen Adam exploited nature and lived off its bounty. In order to restore the original perfection of the prelapsarian world, Adam's successors must remake themselves morally and spiritually; merely making over the natural world and restoring physical domination over its creatures is not sufficient.

The question of the relationship of the literal and spiritual meanings of Adam's place in nature arises in the writings of Bede as well.[89] In his Hexaemeron, Bede notes that certain creatures of the earth are under the care of human beings while others remain untamed.[90] The earth has been prepared for man based on an idea in the mind of God, and man is created for a spiritual rather than a corporeal ideal. This fact makes mankind superior to the rest of creation, and this superiority is symbolized by Adam's upright stature.[91] For Bede, as for Augustine, this position of natural domination—a position based on moral superiority—was lost with the Fall. Likewise, nature loses its benevolence with the Fall. Where once all things were both useful and productive, nature now produces plants and animals that are harmful to man. Before the Fall, Adam and Eve were vegetarians, eating only herbs and the fruits of the various trees; the agriculture they practiced was not necessary for survival but a pleasant avocation, symbolic of the cooperative nature of the relations between sinless human beings and a benign nature.[92] Furthermore, Adam's moral superiority was demonstrated before the Fall through the naming of the creatures of the earth. Bede doubts that every species literally appeared before Adam for names, but he does think that God could have commanded all the creatures to appear and thereby demonstrated both his own power and his recognition of human superiority over nature.[93] The prelapsarian human race enjoyed moral domination over an earth that cooperated by producing sustenance without the intervention of productive labor. This domination did not involve any form of exploitation, but rather a recognition of relative status based on a divinely ordained hierarchy. It is only with the introduction of sin that this relationship becomes exploitative, and then not as a sign of human superiority but because of the loss of natural sovereignty. It is precisely when human beings demonstrate their unworthiness to rule the earth that they are forced—by its recalcitrance and sterility—to attempt to do so.

In the *Interrogationes et responsiones in Genesim*, Alcuin (730–804) also noted that God created a domicile for man that was fruitful and subservient to human needs. Like Bede and Augustine, whom he follows closely, Alcuin writes that even before the Fall Adam performed labor and that this labor was not an affliction but a pleasure: "For it was not the affliction of labor in paradise but the gladdening of the will when those things which God had created grew gladly and fruitfully with the help of human work."[94] The tradition of nonodious prelapsarian manual labor may be traced back at least to the *Book of Jubilees*, where it is reported that Adam and Eve, "in the first week of the first jubilee" (which lasted for seven years), tilled the soil, planted, and sowed crops. God instructed Adam in the techniques of farming, and the fruits of this labor were stored away for the maintenance of the first family.[95] With the introduction of sin, this cooperative relationship with nature was lost, as was the pleasure of work.

Eriugena treats the question of the human domination of nature indirectly during his discussion of the relation between rational and irrational life.[96] "Universal Life" is divided into rational and irrational components. Human beings and angels comprise the former category, while irrational life is divided into "what participates in sense and that which is without sense." Animals possess senses; plants and trees are examples of life "without sense." He next discusses these four species of life in general terms—the intellectual (angels), the rational (human beings), the sensitive (in beasts), and the insensitive (in plants). Only man participates in all four forms of life, and he is therefore called the "workshop" of all creatures "since in him the universal creature is contained." With this division of nature in hand, Eriugena discusses the origin of souls. It is not until the fifth day of the creation that any mention is made of "living souls," because before the creation of "creeping things" out of the primordial seas there was nothing created that possessed intellect or reason.[97] The life that generates trees and plants is not the same as the life possessed by the "living soul" because the life of shoots and plants and seeds can do nothing outside the body that it animates, it has no "perfect life independent of bodies." The rational life possessed by the human soul can, however, stand apart from the "germinal life" and contemplate it. The upshot of Eriugena's complex argument is that the life of plants and animals is of a different order than the life of human beings and angels, for the life of human beings is nutritive and sensitive as well as rational. Thus, he concludes, we should heed the advice of Augustine (in *De vera religione*) and "not make a religion of the cult of that life by which trees are said to live" since this lower form of life is really no different from the generative life that causes our hair or fingernails to grow. "We ought not to worship the life of beasts" is Augustine's lesson, and one that Eriugena underscores in his establishment of the divisions of nature.

The physiological basis of the distinction between human beings and animals is more fully developed by Eriugena in his exegesis of the fifth day of creation. The soul of an animal is contained within its blood, and since blood decays with the body, animal souls are "earthly things." However, he also acknowledges that the souls of animals, being "simple" (while bodies are "complex"), do not dissolve with the body but instead return to participation in the "one primordial life or soul."[98] The evidence that the souls of animals are more than merely "earthly" comes from the observation, first made by Basil, that certain animals possess physical powers greater than any possessed by human beings: Eriugena cites the vision of the eagle, the memory of the dog, and the chastity of the griffin as examples. He apologizes to the renowned Fathers for preserving the integrity of the irrational soul beyond death by noting that, unlike those "holy and philosophical men" who were so skilled in the observation of nature, he is not so constrained by the necessity of instructing men who are entirely given up to the flesh like brutes. While the Fathers had to draw a clear distinction between men and animals because, at the time they wrote, the actual difference was so small, he does not have to make the same concession to human weakness. This evocation of moral progress adds a new element to the hexaemeral literature, as does Eriugena's granting to animals some share in a primordial soul that animates all living things. This is not to suggest that he elevates the irrational animals to the same moral plane as rational human beings—he repeats Gregory of Nyssa's view that "true soul" is to be found only in men—but suggests that while animals are made from the elements most appropriate to their physiology (fish from the "gross waters," birds from the air), they nonetheless retain a link to the animating life of the world.[99] Adam is created in the image of God and according to the paradigm of the whole creation, but he has a "mixed" nature encompassing both an animal body and a divine soul. Thus, while humanity properly exercises mastery over the animals, it does so from a position within the creation rather than above it.

The "mixed" nature of human beings, their kinship with both the animals and the angels, is a theme of the hexaemera of a great number of later writers, including Bernardus Silvestris, Thierry of Chartres, Rupert of Deutz, and Peter Comestor.[100] Bernardus wrote in the *Cosmographia*—a work influenced by both the Platonism of Eriugena and the Aristotelianism of the twelfth century—that the first man was created to crown nature and to combine in unity the diverse elements of the heavens and the earth.[101] This composite creature is given sovereignty over creation, and while brute beasts shall walk with their "heads cast down," man will "lift up his head to the stars" so that he may use their patterns as

a guide in formulating the principles of his own life—yet another variation on the theme of man's upright posture.[102] Bernardus shows the
influence of the *Timaeus* in his description of the functions of various
body parts: the head, as the seat of reason and the dwelling place of the
soul, is compared to the firmament of the heavens, and, like the heavens,
it rules over those lesser parts of both the individual body and the natural
world as a whole.[103] Yet this portrait of man as the masterpiece of *Natura*
is tempered by Bernardus's closing remarks on the mutability of all created things, and the passing of the body and the merging of the soul with
the sum of all that exists immutably.

In the writings of Thierry of Chartres and Bernardus, the elevation of
humanity to a position above the rest of creation is a structural conceit;
human beings rule the microcosm as the heavenly bodies rule the macro-
cosm, but they do so only at God's pleasure, and only through their
temporary immersion in the divine love that orders the universe. Thierry
believed that the creation of the entire physical world took place simulta-
neously, in the first moment of time. Matter then interacted under the
direction of divine Providence to unfold the seminal causes imbedded in
nature. Thus the human position at the "head" of creation is by no means
a recognition of human superiority, but rather an acknowledgement of
the movement of Providence down the chain of being. There is nothing in
Thierry or Bernardus to suggest that human beings are enjoined to exploit their position in nature; rather the emphasis in their work is on the
moral obligations that bind humanity as a consequence of its position
between God and nature.[104] Likewise in the commentary of Arnold of
Bonneval (died about 1156), the subjection of nature to the human will is
seen as a manifestation of God's power given to man, and the exercise of
sovereignty should reflect on its origins as much as on its wielder.[105]

Robert Grosseteste's *Hexaemeron,* composed in the 1230s, shows the
influence of Augustine's *De Genesi* and Basil's *Hexaemeron* but otherwise reflects Grosseteste's interest in a body of texts outside the hexaemeral tradition.[106] Grosseteste notes in his comments on Genesis 1:28
that the earth is given over to man's dominion, and that before the Fall
human beings controlled all of the regions of the earth. Before the Fall,
the earth provided man with food; it was fruitful and there were no
harmful creatures for man to fear. Man lived by consuming the fruits of
the earth; neither he nor any of the animals ate meat, and there was

harmony among all creatures: "The authority of [Bede and Augustine] shows that man and all the earth's animals . . . would have lived commonly and peacefully had man not sinned."[107] Nature obeyed God's law before the Fall; each creature had a proper role to play, and man's role was to rule the earth. Grosseteste, in discussing the meaning of human domination, cites a key text from Augustine's *City of God* (bk. 19, chap. 15) which says that God wished that human beings dominate not other human beings but instead the beasts. The first just men were shepherds of flocks rather than kings of men, and the word slave (*servus*) is therefore not found in Scripture until Noah punished his son with it (Genesis 9:25). The point of Grosseteste's passage is to illustrate the change in the meaning of "domination" with the Fall of man. Servitude is a punishment for sin, and, as Augustine notes, the lust for domination is itself the source of slavery.[108] Natural domination does not employ coercion or punishment but grows spontaneously from a love of justice. Man rules the irrational creatures through the exercise of reason; when reason falls, man loses his natural sovereignty and resorts to irrationality. Like Basil, Grosseteste sees the control of irrational creatures as a measure of faith rather than an excuse for exercising power.

Thomas Aquinas considered the question of human domination in the *Summa theologiae,* and his analysis brings into focus the issues discussed by most of the writers within the hexaemeral tradition. He begins his reply to the question "Whether man dominated the animals in the state of innocence" by observing that "in the course of nature" the less perfect is subject to the more perfect. Man, created in the image of God, naturally holds power over the animals as well as the rest of the natural world.[109] He also agrees with the hexaemeral commentators in holding that before the Fall Adam did not require animal food or any clothing, so that the use to which animals were put was benign—for one thing, Adam wished to have experiential knowledge of their natures. In the state of nature before the Fall, all of the animals were obedient to man in much the way that domestic animals are now. Was this domination exploitative? Aquinas summarizes the views of the hexaemeral writers when he notes that the power of man over nature existed to the extent that men hold power over themselves.[110] Adam ruled by force of reason. He ruled the animals by command, his body by use, and plants by changing them "without any impediment." Yet this command was for the common good and followed from the natures given to plants, animals, and human beings. There was nothing unnatural or exploitative about the mutual relationships binding the various levels of creation together; only with the fall of reason was the providential order overthrown.

THE MEDIEVAL ETHIC OF COOPERATION

When Lynn White wrote that "no item in the physical creation had any purpose save to serve man's purposes," he was expressing the view that Christianity provided a rationale for the domination of nature by Western technology. As I have noted, other writers have countered White's argument by introducing biblical texts to support variant readings of the human relation to nature.[111] But the formative theological descriptions of the prelapsarian world strongly suggest that human beings are to be stewards rather than despoilers of nature. God puts Adam in a position of dominance, and he allows Adam to use nature for the fulfillment of his needs; but God intends Adam to learn moral lessons from the structure of nature and from the behavior of animals.

A careful reading of Basil and Ambrose, Augustine and Bede allows us to construct an ethic of cooperative partnership with nature. As Genesis makes plain, it is only with the corruption of the human will that the earth withdraws itself from the benign symbiosis that had characterized the prelapsarian world. Adam and his progeny must restore perfection both through the labor of the hands and through the reshaping of moral character.

However, the restoration of perfection need not have as its means or goal the exploitation of nature. Even if it were unambiguously true that Genesis supported an ethic of human domination, it is by no means clear that this ethic need sanction a destructive attitude toward nature. The control of nature may be accomplished through the use of tools that extend human capabilities and put to efficient use the powers inherent in nature, rather than through machines that pit the inventive powers of man against nature. Indeed, ethological studies of primate tool use suggest that *homo faber* might have been content to use nature's forces, including the body's own organic potential, in order to develop tools that enhance the ability of human beings to live within a particular ecology.[112] An ethic of domination, with or without biblical sanction, might just as easily encourage the construction of windmills as of nuclear power stations, and a stone hammer is as much a weapon in the "struggle with nature" as a pneumatic hammer.

In other words, even with the origins of the Western "ethic of domination" clarified, the question of why this ethic sanctioned particular kinds of technological choices remains. A Christian theology that supports human ascendancy over nature is not enough: to have created the world it did, this theology had to be receptive to other ideas—to the idea of a technological determinism that sees the stone hammer as merely a stage in the creation of the pneumatic hammer; to the idea that nature should yield more than sustenance, more even than a surplus; to the idea that nature is not merely a passive source of material that gives shape to human ambitions, but itself a tool that can be reshaped and reorganized in the interests of productivity; to the idea that it is not enough to control nature for the sake of personal or communal survival, but that it is necessary to develop exclusionary claims over nature and over what nature produces. In other words, the idea of domination explains only the attitude that nature exists to be used; it does not help us to understand the specific uses to which it has been put.

For an explanation of these specific uses we should perhaps take the lead of Lewis Mumford and look at the "overweening pride and indifference to the future" that caused Western peoples to give up small-scale "democratic polytechnics" in favor of "authoritarian megatechnics."[113] After all, the direct result of the medieval Christian ethic of domination was a long-lived tradition of craftsmanship and subsistence farming, and, in Mumford's view, it wasn't until Francis Bacon reintroduced a "power-hungry technical mentality" that the West took off on the self-destructive course it now follows.[114] Bacon himself supplies ample support for the Western idea of domination. He wrote, for instance, that the goal of human knowledge is "a restitution and reinvesting (in great part) of man to the sovereignty and *power* (for whatsoever he shall be able to call the creatures by their true names he shall again command them) which he had in his first state of creation."[115] But, as Paolo Rossi has shown, even this seemingly unambiguous call to exploitation is subject to interpretation and must be heeded with care. In fact, Bacon thought that the role of the scientist or mechanic was to assist nature in its natural operations.[116]

The search for the connection between the idea of dominating nature and the facts of Western technological hegemony needs to be revised in the light of three points. First of all, it seems just as likely that the Christian interpretation of the human relationship to nature could have created a nonexploitative form of technology. Second, it seems that the Christian attitude toward nature, whether expressed in a medieval hexaemeral commentary or in a nineteenth-century sermon, could just as likely have been a compromise with existing relationships—political, social, technical, ecological—as the cause of those relationships. Third, it seems obvious that the really significant question for the history of technology is not what Christianity taught about the domination of nature, but what Christianity taught about the domination of human beings by other human beings.[117] After all, the call to use nature for human ends presupposes the existence of a compliant labor force, an organizational structure capable of directing this labor toward the accomplishment of particular ends, and the distribution of the wealth created by human labor so as to maintain both productivity and the productive social system.

Social relationships are central to the development of Western technological hegemony. The natural world described by the hexaemeral commentators is benign and by no means intended solely for human exploitation. Readings of early Christian theology that attempt to find a rationale for exploitation are searching for a moral sanction supportive of economic, social, and technological changes that occurred for other reasons, reasons more accurately ascribed by Lewis Mumford to human rapaciousness than by Lynn White to divinely sanctioned homocentricity. If it is true that social relationships are more important to understanding the history of Western technology than either divine craftsmanship or biblical attitudes toward nature, then the next places to look for the sources of our technology are medieval social and educational systems. Therefore, following the lead of Weber and Mumford, I would like to examine Benedictine monasticism—a system of work and worship that these modern writers thought provided a paradigm for the rationalization of production—as a possible source for the Western ideology of labor and technology.

CHAPTER 3

Labor and the Foundations
of Monasticism

THE VIEW that monastic attitudes about manual labor have influenced the course of Western economic, social, and technological development may be found in a variety of studies, and this perception figures prominently in many accounts of the West's economic success. For example, Herbert Workman, in discussing the contributions of Benedictine monasticism to Western culture, had this to say:

> Benedict's success in linking Monasticism with labor was the first step in a long evolution upon whose details we cannot dwell, but whose main features demand attention . . . the change [from eremiticism to cenobitism] itself would have been of little value, at any rate viewed from the standpoint of social development, had it not been accompanied by the glorification and systematization of toil. With this addition the change lay at the root of all that was best and most progressive in Monasticism. Instead of the dervish of Eastern fancy, we have a colony of workers . . . we have the organized community . . . whose axes and spades cleared the densest jungles, drained pestilent swamps, and by the alchemy of industry turned the sands into waving gold, and planted centres of culture in the hearts of forests.[1]

Workman finds in the impulse to labor a mixed blessing: the working monk, busied with the exploitation of nature, loses sight of the ascetic ideal that first prompted him or her to retire from the world. Monasticism's contribution to economic progress came to "[prove] fatal to the principles of Monasticism."[2]

A few years before Workman, Max Weber made what proved to be an even more influential analysis of the role monastic labor and organization had played in Western society:

> The great historical significance of Western monasticism as contrasted with that of the Orient, is based on this fact [i.e., "a definitely

88

rational character"], not in all cases, but in its general type. In the rules [sic] of St. Benedict, still more with the monks of Cluny, again with the Jesuits, it [the *Lebensführung* or "plan of living"] has become emancipated from planless otherworldliness and irrational self-torture. It had developed a systematic method of rational conduct with the purpose of overcoming the *status naturae,* to free man from the power of irrational impulses and his dependence on the world and on nature. It attempted to subject man to the supremacy of a purposeful will, to bring his actions under constant self control with a careful consideration of their ethical consequences.[3]

Weber has conflated two separate activities in this analysis, namely the domination of nature and the domination of the self, and he has identified the institution of a "rational plan of living" as the medium through which these two activities merge into one. Weber's view was that the planned economy of the monastery, when coupled with the austerity of a devotional and otherworldly existence, created economic self-sufficiency and destroyed any illusions about the proper relations between humanity and nature.

In his discussion of "the Benedictine Blessing," Lewis Mumford wrote that "the first comprehensive effort to reconstitute the machine on a new basis . . . took place in the Christian Church. This was largely responsible for the fact that Western civilization caught up with, and then surpassed, the technical inventiveness of China, Korea, Persia, and India."[4] Mumford feels that Christianity added to its "reconstitution" of technology "a commitment to moral values and social purposes," and that the first example of technology combined with moral force was Benedictine monasticism. Monasteries abandoned "large-scale military and paramilitary" economic organization for small-scale labor "not as a slave's curse but as part of a free man's moral commitment." Monastic establishments organized "a new ritual of daily activity" that included both manual and spiritual labor. Mumford also notes that the "Benedictine monastery laid down a basis for order as strict as that which held together the early [e.g. Egyptian and Greco-Roman] megamachines: the difference lay in its modest size, its voluntary constitution and the fact that its sternest discipline was self-imposed."[5]

In many ways, the picture of the relations between monasticism and labor that emerges from Workman, Weber, and Mumford is persuasive.[6]

Also influential has been Lynn White, Jr.'s work on the "cultural climate" of technological change (see the introduction). Although his analysis is far more complex than Weber's or Mumford's and takes into account more factors, White also finds that "the monks insisted that *laborare est orare*, work is worship," and that "[the monks] worked in fields and shops not as a form of asceticism, but . . . because it was God's will."[7] Other scholars, interested in modern Western attitudes toward what Weber called the *status naturae*, toward the use and abuse of nature for human ends, have also traced these attitudes back to medieval Christianity and, in some cases, to medieval monasticism.[8]

What remains puzzling as one reviews these discussions of monasticism's effects on the history of Western attitudes toward labor, craftsmanship, and the use of nature is this paradox: how does one reconcile monastic asceticism with worldly attitudes and material achievements? In order to resolve this paradox, or, as may be the case, in order to discover if there really is any paradox at all, I will examine the traditions of thought regarding labor and "rational living" that preceded, and influenced, Benedict of Nursia's *Rule* for monks. Since this paradox lies in the tension between asceticism and worldly achievement, a close scrutiny of a few early texts from the fourth and fifth centuries seems especially appropriate: the *Historia monachorum in Aegypto*, Palladius's *Lausiac History*, the *Apophthegmata patrum* (Sayings of the Fathers), and texts by Augustine, Jerome, Basil, and Cassian, as well as some of the monastic Rules written prior to Benedict's—Rules collected in the ninth century by Benedict of Aniane in the *Codex regularum*. This investigation should make it possible to describe the nature of the early monastic commitment to manual labor, and to discover if this commitment was such that a program supportive of economic and technological progress could have been born in the monasteries of the West.

HERMITS AND CENOBITES

In describing the sect known as the *Therapeutae*, Philo Judaeus discusses how these contemplatives abandoned their property, families, and native lands for the solitude and spiritual freedom of the desert. Philo wrote during the first century of the Christian era, and he was the first to describe monastic life, indeed, the first to use the word *monasterion* to describe the holy place where an ascetic, solitary life was lived. By the

Labor and the Foundations of Monasticism

middle of the fourth century, the deserts of Egypt were heavily populated by men and women who practiced Christian asceticism and who lived the harsh life credited by Philo to the *Therapeutae*.⁹ Beginning in 357 with Athanasius's *Vita Antonii*, a procession of visitors journeyed to the Egyptian monastic communities, hermit cells, and wadis to witness a spiritual phenomenon that had already begun to penetrate the West. The lives and words of both eremitic and cenobitic monks have been well documented, and a picture clear in outline, if not in detail, emerges from these lively and fascinating accounts written by some of the visitors to the desert fathers. Among other things, we learn a good deal from these accounts concerning the role of manual labor in the heroic devotions of these men and women.

We know, for example, that St. Anthony, the "founder" of eremitism—if such an idiosyncratic movement can be said to have a founder—labored with his hands.¹⁰ The *Apophthegmata patrum* contains many anecdotes that demonstrate the importance of manual labor to those fourth-century hermits who followed Anthony's example, an importance created by the desire for material self-sufficiency and for the subjugation of the flesh. John the Dwarf, an influential figure who, despite his yearning for solitude, gathered many followers, was tempted when he was a young man to renounce labor for an idle, angelic existence. His devout brother, swayed more by practical considerations than John, reminded him that unless he really were to become an angel he must work in order to eat.¹¹ Such lessons, repeated frequently in early Christian literature, stem from certain key biblical texts, such as St. Paul's injunction in 2 Thessalonians 3:10, "If any man will not work, neither let him eat." This text serves to remind us, as Tertullian and others make clear, that Christianity was a religion for the humble, and that, unlike the pagan sects it displaced, it did not disdain manual labor or associate work with the shame of slavery.¹² Indeed, labor was a sign of humility and was practiced by the monks for precisely this reason. Therefore when John the Cenobite was greeted by visitors he did not interrupt his work, because as a sinner he had no time to distract himself from his weakness.¹³ When St. Jerome came to settle in the Syrian wilderness—he stayed only briefly, from about 374 to 376—he supported himself "by the daily labor of [his] hands and by [his] own sweat"—this despite the fact that he also spent a considerable amount of time in scholarly pursuits.¹⁴ For Jerome, John the Cenobite, and others this labor consisted in gardening, weaving mats from palm branches, rope making, water collection, and, as was the case with Dorotheus, the construction of stone cells for other monks.[15]

At times this menial labor, which often seems so tedious in the accounts, was invested with a miraculous association or occurred as a backdrop against which great spiritual changes took place. Thus, for example, Arsenius "had a hollow in his chest created by his tears," which grew deeper as he performed his labor. Palladius narrates the story of Piamoun, a virgin who spent her time spinning flax and prophesying. Valens, an arrogant hermit, lost his sewing needle while making a basket; his constant companion, a demon, retrieved the needle for him; only after being bound in chains for a year did the misguided Valens lose his pride and foresake the devil. For good or for evil, the laboring monk lived out the spiritual struggles of desert life against a backdrop of work that chastened the body but was inadequate to sustain it. As the monk Serinus put it, "I have spent my time in harvesting, sewing, and weaving, but if the hand of God had not sustained me, I would not have been fed."[16] This dependence on God for survival indicates that manual labor, whatever its benefits, was not enough to make the ascetic life viable; the spiritual commitment remained central and filled the spirit with the food often left unprovided by even the most difficult labor. When the monk Gelasios asserts that one should remain inside one's cell, "weeping for sin," if "you are not able to perform the [spiritual] works of the desert," he is merely saying that personal sanctification, through penance, is the primary mission of the hermit, and that other things, including labor, are of secondary importance.

In the literature of the desert, both spiritual and manual labor are personal and inward-directed. The amount, type, and mix of the *opus manuum* with the *opus Dei* are determined first of all by the soteriological mission of the individual hermit and not by any considerations of social utility. The product of this labor is a heightened spirituality, which is what saves and sustains: the monk Pambo, according to Jerome one of the "masters of the desert," instructs two visiting monks by telling them that the sale of labor for charitable purposes is good, but will not save their souls; however, if they guard their consciences toward their neighbor, then they will be saved.[17] Indeed, the life of the desert was antithetical to productivity, and subsistence living, the assumed economy of the monastic community, makes excessive labor problematical, especially since the monk eschews trade, the amassing of objects, and the acquisition of money. In the *Historia monachorum in Aegypto,* John of Lycopolis tells the story of a monk who obtained his bread through manual labor, but who was nonetheless tempted to sexual transgression by the devil. A page later, the *Historia* has John describe another monk who did not perform any labor at all, and who consequently grew indolent; before long this monk also ceased to pray and thereupon succumbed to the sin of concupiscence.[18] John uses this story to illustrate the dangers of spiritual indolence, not of physical idleness; but the two stories taken together indicate that neither activity nor quietude protect the weak from temptation. To rise above earthly concerns is the monk's ideal, and stillness, forgetfulness of self, and unworldliness are some of the means to that end: "Better and greater is the monk who is contemplative, who has risen above active works to the spiritual sphere." This Brahminlike denial of the world and its works—including even self-supportive manual labor—provides the counterpoint to the theme of virtuous manual labor, and it demonstrates the function such labor had as a tool designed to help shape the personal spiritual life of an individual hermit.

The tension between eremitism, with its self-contained, world-denying element, and cenobitism, with its communal labor and productivity, is captured nicely in the story of Paesius and Isais, narrated by Palladius in the *Lausiac History.* Upon the death of their father, the two sons of a wealthy Spanish merchant decided to enter monastic life. They disagreed, however, as to the proper disposition of their inheritance: "One divided everything among monasteries, churches, and prisons. He then learned a trade so that he could be self-supporting and spent his time in ascetic practice and prayer." The other brother chose not to distribute his share of the inheritance, but instead built a monastery for himself and a few brethren. This brother took in and cared for strangers, invalids, the old, and the poor. After both brothers had died, various opinions were offered as to the comparative sanctity of their two ways of life. Finally, blessed Pambo, a great and holy hermit, offered the opinion that "both were perfect—one showed the work of Abraham, the other of Elias."[19] Two further points should be made about this particular story and its lessons. First of all, the solitary life practiced by so many during the third and fourth centuries was clearly seen to be fraught with spiritual hazards. One finds in the *Historia monachorum* and the *Lausiac History* numerous anecdotes showing hermits in competition with themselves and with other hermits to achieve even greater heights of ascetic rigor. Palladius, for example, tells of the "self-conceit" of Abramius, who thought of himself as a priest ordained by Christ and who had to be brought to a less exacting way of life in order to be shown his own weakness. Among the champions of desert asceticism was surely Ammonius, who burned his cupidinous flesh with hot irons, ate only raw foods, and commited the entire Bible, plus sixty thousand verses of commentary, to memory.[20] The temptation of pride growing out of such superhuman exertions was truly felt, especially by those observers who came from the outside world to record the idiosyncratic styles of ascetic Christianity.

The second point about the story of Paesius and Isais is that we may reasonably doubt that Pambo's judgment of the equality of the eremitic and cenobitic lives was shared by all contemporary witnesses. For example, in the first *Vita S. Pachomii* the story is told of how Zachaeus, a Pachomian monk, questioned St. Anthony about the merits of the solitary and communal lives.[21] The author of the *Vita* has Anthony admit that the apostolic life is superior to the solitary life and that he and the other hermits came to the desert too early to benefit from the Pachomian innovation. Such an anecdote leaves little doubt that the cenobitic communities felt their form of life to be superior to the solitary life, and, one assumes, they thought so at least in part because communal labor extended the potential for self-effacing charity and helped to reduce the risks of self-aggrandizing feats of ascetic heroism.

The organization of religious life into a productive organic whole by Pachomius must surely stand as the most significant social innovation in early Christian history. St. Benedict's contribution to Western monasticism is incomprehensible without the Pachomian achievement. Palladius writes that the Pachomian rule was given to the founder in a dream and that the division of labor according to relative physical strength was one facet of this angelic legislation. At Panopolis, an offshoot of the original Pachomian settlement, Palladius saw three hundred monks, including "fifteen tailors, seven metalworkers, four carpenters, twelve camel-drivers, and fifteen fullers." Palladius also reports that the monks worked at every kind of craft and created enough of a surplus to provide for both nuns and prisoners.[22] The organization and efficiency of the Pachomian monasteries was astonishing: from the *Vita* we learn that supervisors were appointed by Pachomius to oversee the labor of individual groups of monks and that these supervisors would, in turn, report to Pachomius himself. An interesting story in the *Vita* reveals the Pachomian dedication to productivity: a young boy, seeing Pachomius threshing, instructs the founder in a more efficient technique.[23]

At the same time, spiritual exercises and spiritual discipline were by no means neglected. The monks who labored as husbandmen, gardeners, smiths, bakers, weavers, fullers, shoemakers, and copyists are all said to learn the holy Scripture by heart—a feat, as we have seen, associated with the most dedicated of holy men and women. The success of the Pachomian establishments may be judged by the numbers of monks who were supported by this rule—some seven thousand according to Palladius, or, as Jerome tells us, "a [monastic] house has about forty brothers . . . there are thirty or forty houses in one monastery, and three or four houses are joined in a tribe."[24] Although this organization suffered with the death of the founder, its influence was spread through the translation and dissemination of its Rule and of the *Life* of Pachomius himself.

The commitment to manual labor in both the eremitic and cenobitic communities was, therefore, substantial. The hermits whose lives and sayings were collected by curious travelers and devoted chroniclers found a compelling, if perhaps ambiguous, call to manual labor in the Bible, especially in the Pauline Epistles and in the apostolic life portrayed in the synoptic Gospels. The hermits worked alone to support themselves; the Pachomian monks worked cooperatively to support a broader constituency. In both cases there is little to suggest that this labor was purely penitential or deliberately nonproductive; and while there are some doubts expressed about the appropriateness of labor for those who have renounced the world, the judgment in the majority of cases suggests that productive labor is beneficial in both material and spiritual terms. Thus, in the *Apophthegmata* a brother tells the holy man Pistamon that he is worried about selling his labor. The holy man replies that "it is not dangerous to do so," though it is good to "lower the price a little if you can." Pistamon then says that "even if you can satisfy your needs by other means, do not give up manual labor."[25] The benefits of such labor were thought to be very great, for, as one modern writer has put it, "the chief sphere of monastic labor is self-control, the pursuit of inner peace, self-transcendence."[26]

Other testimony exists to support the evidence found in the lives and sayings of the desert fathers. Basil, for example, wrote a long work on asceticism when he was bishop of Caesarea which became known as the *Asceticon.* Rufinus translated a section of this work that came to be called "the short rule." The full version of the *Asceticon*—the so-called "long rule"—contains a discussion of the relative merits of eremitic and cenobitic monasticism as well as a discussion of manual labor in ascetic life. In this text, Basil explicitly judges the communal life to be superior to the solitary life in that the former presents opportunities for charity denied by the latter.[27] Further on in the "long rule," Basil considers the matter of manual labor directly. In answer to the question "whether prayer and psalmody should be a pretext for avoiding our work," Basil offered the opinion that manual labor allows us the opportunity to offer something to those who suffer need. The monk must toil diligently and not think that the search for piety allows him to escape from difficult labor; indeed, those who would be holy should endeavor to work even harder as a means of learning patience in tribulation. Basil goes on to cite 2 Thessalonians 3:10 in order to clinch his argument: why discuss the evil of idleness when the Apostle has made it clear that "for daily sustenance" everyone must work according to his or her ability and strength?[28] Similar themes are repeated in the writings of Gregory of Nazianzus and, in the West, in the writings of Jerome as well as in the monastic rules that preceded Benedict of Nursia's.[29] Labor considered from the perspective of the individual monk protects against the risks of idleness. When considered from the perspective of the Christian community as a whole, labor provides the means of sustaining those who cannot sustain themselves.

While the personal value of manual labor is increasingly stressed at the expense of its social value, in the earliest accounts of monastic organization it is the communal nature of work that explains the cooperative basis of daily life. Thus, in his preface to the Pachomian *Rule,* Jerome noted the centrality of organized labor to the Tabennesian monks: "Brothers of the same craft live in one house under one master. Those, for example, who weave linen are together, and those who weave mats are looked upon as being one family. Tailors, carriage makers, fullers, shoemakers—all are governed by their own masters, and each week they render an account of their work to the abbot of the monastery."[30] Yet Jerome's own career and writings attest to the personal, inner-directed value of manual labor as well. In Epistle 125, written in 412 to a young man named Rusticus,

Jerome used Proverbs 13:4 ("Everyone who is idle is prey to vain desires") to inform his correspondent of the value of work, as well as the
example of the Egyptian monks "who allow no one [into the monastery]
who is unwilling to work, for they think labor is necessary not only for
supporting the body but also for the salvation of the soul."[31] Jerome
recommends such labor as weaving, gardening, irrigation, apple growing,
beekeeping ("so you might learn from these tiny creatures how to structure a monastery and order a kingdom"), fishing, and book copying.
Since this list is so long, and since Jerome also cautions Rusticus "never to
take his eye off his book" and to memorize the Psalms, it seems likely that
what Jerome was actually advocating was a mixture of prayer, reading,
and labor—precisely the trio of monastic activities recommended by the
majority of monastic Rules. We know that when Jerome himself was
living in the desert near Chalcis in northern Syria, he labored with his
hands and supported himself by the sweat of his brow.[32] We also know
that he took a substantial library with him, that he periodically sent for
more volumes, and that, according to Epistle 5, he had assistants who
were busily engaged in copying while he pursued his biblical studies. This
workshop in the desert, while hardly in the tradition of the early hermits'
ascetic existences, nonetheless was in keeping with the communal life that
Jerome himself later described in his account of the Pachomian community.

Yet, while in the early monastic communities the impetus to labor
remains central to our understanding of the "plan of living" created in
the fourth and fifth centuries, we must not forget the purpose served by
this communal organization, and we must be careful not to project a
"work ethic" onto cenobites whose primary interests were spiritual. In
manual labor, as Jerome wrote in paraphrasing St. Paul, "you will forget
what is behind you and reach out for what is before you," toward, that is,
the perfection of the spiritual life. Even in the best-organized monastic
communities labor had primarily a spiritual purpose: Jerome notes that
in the Pachomian communities the brothers had their work assignments
shifted periodically so that they might learn to be "ready and obedient"
in everything and so that they might be more fully prepared to be employed in God's service.[33] If the purpose of labor was the creation of a
self-sufficient monastic economy, the primary byproduct of this economic purpose was the creation of an environment that fostered self-
effacement, obedience, and the "repose of the spirit" (*quies mentis* or
quies contemplationis). That these qualities were the primary goal of

monastic labor is clear from two influential texts—Augustine's *De opere monachorum* and Cassian's *Institutes*.

EARLY CENOBITIC RULES

Augustine wrote *De opere monachorum* about 400 at the request of the bishop of Carthage. Augustine was asked to mediate a dispute between a group of monks who, following St. Paul's injunction of 2 Thessalonians 3:10, labored with their hands, and another group of monks who, following Matthew 6:26, behaved as did the "birds of the air" and tried to live on alms. The focus of Augustine's argument against the latter group was precisely the point that had divided hermit from cenobite, namely the issue of how one can reject the world for God's sake and then demonstrate concern for its conventions, and the body's needs, by laboring for a living. Augustine writes that one must certainly labor, yet without feeling any anxiety for the fruits of labor. God will provide what is needed if a monk cannot provide for himself; but for the monk who is physically capable of labor, idleness is dangerous and contrary to the teaching of St. Paul.[34] Like Basil, Augustine partially deflects the purpose of productive labor outward, into charitable acts, and asserts that the able-bodied are required to supply the needs of those who, because of their duties (such as preaching or intellectual labor) or their physical infirmity, cannot be self-supporting.[35] Furthermore, Augustine wonders how idle monks might profitably fill their time; if the answer is that they will pray, then let them pray while they work, for "persons working with their hands can easily sing the Psalms and thereby ease their labor at the divine call."[36] Neither is reading an adequate substitute for manual labor "for [in] reading good books, one grows more quickly by putting into practice what one reads" and working for the sake of charity. Idle monks are a disgrace to the religious life as well as a danger to themselves, and arguments that deny the religious duty to "set aside for the morrow" neglect the fact that many biblical passages (for example, John 12:6 and Acts 11:28–30) encourage the monk to make provision for the future.[37] The point is that productive labor, if consecrated to God and balanced with the *opus Dei*, is both personally and communally desirable.

Augustine's arguments in the *De opere monachorum* were carried over into his own Rules, the *Obiuragtio*, the *Ordo monasterii*, and the *Praeceptum*.[38] In the first, Augustine directs the nuns to whom he is writing to "work for the common good" and to accept food and drink according to bodily strength and need. In the *Ordo monasterii,* Augustine provides a daily schedule of alternating prayer and work, and he warns of the dangers both of idleness and of labor that is performed outside the confines of the monastery. In the longest of his regulatory texts, the *Praeceptum,* Augustine cites the principle of Acts 4:32 and 35—"that all things be held in common and distributed according to the needs of each"—as well as the principle that labor allows the monk to practice charity and accrue spiritual benefits.[39] Labor also has a democratizing power because its universal pursuit eliminates any pretension to superiority among the monks.

Of equal stature, and of even greater influence in defining the conventions of Western monasticism, was John Cassian. Cassian's travels among the Egyptian monks, his personal commitment to the ascetic life, and his influential writings—the *Collationes* and *De institutis coenobiorum* were read by Ceasarius of Arles and Benedict, among others—all made him the key figure linking Eastern and Western forms of piety. His *Collationes* and *De institutis* say a great deal about the role played by manual labor in eremitic and cenobitic life. For example, in book 23 of the *Collationes,* Cassian writes of the "value of labor and the harm of idleness" and provides an argument against the acceptance of charity by those who are capable of sustaining themselves. Indeed, "the whole human race, except for monks—who live by the daily labor of their own hands and according to the precept of the Apostle—hopes for the charity of others."[40] Clearly, then, since everyone would like to be supported by others, and since, in fact, many already are so supported, those who can work should do so, in accordance both with St. Paul and with the social good.

In *De institutis,* Cassian devotes several sections to a discussion of labor's importance to the monastic community and to the individual monk. "Monks supplement their prayer with labor," Cassian writes, "so that [spiritual] sleep does not steal upon them."[41] The ideal spiritual life balances the virtues of body and soul, controlling the unsteady heart and capricious mind with the burden of work. Here Cassian is describing a form of labor whose intentions are primarily spiritual: "[it is difficult to say whether] they [the brothers] practice incessant manual labor for the sake of spiritual meditation or if it is for their labor that they require such a light of knowledge and spiritual skill."[42] Cassian relies on both St. Paul and the Book of Proverbs to bolster his arguments for the centrality of manual labor: from Paul, Cassian cites the perennial 2 Thessalonians 3:10 as well as Ephesians 4:28, and, to demonstrate that Paul practiced labor himself, Acts 18:1–3; from Proverbs, Cassian uses 23:21 and 28:19. Labor, as revealed in these passages, not only strengthens and protects the spirit, it makes charity possible as well.

Cassian not only argued for the personal spiritual efficacy of labor, he also argued that labor makes monastic life economically viable. After describing how the Egyptian fathers collected a surplus of provisions through their labor, Cassian describes the radically different situation in the West: "Thus it is in [the West] that we see no monasteries with such numbers of monks, for they are not supported by the products of labor in such a way that they can remain in the monastery continually; and if, through the generosity of another, there should be adequate provisions to support them, yet love of ease and restlessness of heart do not allow them to remain in the [monastery]."[43] The failure to perform manual labor poses a double threat—to the spirit of the individual monk and to the very concept of communal life. However, it is not the material risks of idleness that concern Cassian the most. Productivity is not an end in itself, but only a mechanism for the creation of conditions conducive to the individual monk's spiritual life. Indeed, we know that Martin of Tours, one of the exemplars of the monasticism that Cassian was so desirous of seeing created, was willing to forego the benefits of manual labor for the greater benefits of continual spiritual devotion. In the biography of St. Martin composed by Sulpicius Severus about 397, we learn that Martin and those who followed him into retreat at Marmoutier (outside Tours) practiced only the art of copying, "and [that] only the youthful were assigned to this work so that the elders had their time free for prayer."[44] Likewise, the surviving writings of Paulinus of Nola (died 431), which include a substantial correspondence with many of the most important churchmen of the early fifth century, contain not a line about any labor other than gardening. Likewise, Paulinus's *Rule* for monks has nothing to say on the subject of manual labor.[45] Thus while the testimonies of Augustine, Jerome, and Cassian are clearly supportive of monastic labor as a means of achieving both personal sanctity and communal viability, still, there is room for intellectual labor and for the devotions that occupy the full attention of older monks.

Four closely related monastic rules, composed during the fifth century and collected in the ninth-century by Benedict of Aniane in the *Codex regularum,* offer a view of the status of manual labor during the formative decades of Western monasticism. These rules, collectively known as the *Regulae patrum,* were put together by the secretaries of abbots who attended meetings for the purpose of formulating guidelines for monastic governance.[46] The earliest of these texts, the so-called "Rule of the Four Fathers" (*Regula sanctorum patrum*), prescribes devotion to God during the first through third hours of the day, "but," the text continues, "from the third hour to the ninth, whatever has been enjoined must be performed without murmuring."[47] This injunction, based on a text in Philippians 2:14 ("And do ye all things without murmurings and hesitations"), reminds the brothers about "the work that must be done." The *Regula sanctorum patrum* goes on to suggest that the "work of the hands" prescribed by the Apostle should not burden any monk overcome by weakness of the body, but that the monk who is weak in spirit—"*quod si infirmus est animo huiuscemodi frater*"—should work even harder to "restore the body to subjection." That this labor is penitential rather than productive is made explicit in the concluding sentences of chapter 11: "Therefore, this [practice of labor] ought to be observed so that in nothing will the brother do his own will."[48]

A fuller treatment of manual labor is found in the "Rule of Macarius" (*Regula Macharii abbatis*), written late in the fifth century. Chapter 8 of this Rule admonishes the monk not to hate difficult labor and, instead, to shun idleness.[49] Furthermore, the last chapter of the Rule says, "This also must be done: inside the monastery no [monk] may practice a craft, except for him whose faith is proved, who does what he is able to do for the utility and necessity of the monastery."[50] This regulation suggests that craftsmanship for its own sake is a distraction from the goals of worship, and a monk of unsure faith may find himself tempted by the self-indulgence of personal labor. The fact that this regulation occurs at the end of a series of proscriptions against monastic misconduct (such as fast breaking, improper dress) indicates that the primary function of labor was not the creation of objects but rather the subjugation of the will and the sustenance of the community.

In the *Regula magistri,* the long sixth-century rule that influenced St. Benedict, the situation is different.[51] First of all, St. Paul is quoted to prove that labor must be physical as well as spiritual, but "physical labor" is broadly defined and includes reading (during the winter months) and, for illiterate adults, the study of Latin. Also included are handicrafts, which must, however, be practiced under supervision, in silence, and while listening to a reader. During the summer months, light agricultural labor is also performed, but with this proviso:

> Field work and missions requiring travel should be considered the province of those brothers who are not skilled in the arts and have neither the ability nor the desire to learn them. The skilled craftsmen, however, are to stay at their respective crafts every day, having their daily quota of work assigned and checked. Delicate and weak brothers should be assigned such work as will nourish them for the service of God, not kill them. As for the hard of heart, or also the simple brothers and those who have neither the ability nor the desire to learn letters, let them be tied down by rough labor, but in a measure consonant with justice lest they be the only ones continually oppressed with various kinds of work.[52]

It would appear that in the *Regula Magistri* labor is organized toward optimum productivity. Labor quotas are assigned and work is checked by foremen, and the work itself is fitted to the physical and intellectual constitutions of individuals—indeed, a class system based on literacy and physical strength is instituted. But, reading further, one also notes that this organization is aimed primarily at the production of spiritual capital and that the "profits of the flesh" are explicitly denied precedence over those of the spirit. Thus, manual labor is suspended for those who would devote greater energies to spiritual labor, while harsh work like farming is not practiced. In chapter 86, the "Master" writes that "the lands of the monastery should be rented out so that a secular workman may be busy with secular matters . . . and, as is proper, we should not let our thoughts wander off to things that remain in the world after our death and which cannot follow our soul."[53] Labor may be prayer, but it is only one form of prayer, a form that can and should be given over to pure prayer whenever the mind threatens to dwell on earthly things. As the experience of later medieval monasticism shows, the *opus manuum* is easily superseded by the *opus Dei,* and work may be passed on to others—to the *conversi* and lay brothers, for example. The problem posed in the early monastic rules was to respect this priority while at the same time creating an economically viable communal structure. For the most part, this difficulty was not directly addressed. Instead—and this has direct bearing on the claims made for monasticism by Workman, Weber, Mumford, and

White—the tendency was to mandate labor for spiritual purposes and then to qualify its inclusiveness to insure that the spiritual life of the community was not compromised over economic interests. While the rationale for including manual labor in the structure of the monastic routine was firmly embedded in the tradition by the fifth century— Cassian had made the case for economically self-sufficient communities and Augustine had demonstrated that labor served God by serving communal interests—these early Rules express an ambivalence toward labor that stems from their authors' inability to integrate the spiritual and economic functions of the monastery. Like John the Dwarf, the inhabitants of Western monasteries wanted, I think, to "live freely as the angels" and could not quite fit productive physical labor into the heavenly microcosm of the world they had created. To put the same point in another way, the early monastic Rules seem more concerned with protecting personal spiritual autonomy than with creating a viable communal structure.

THE RULE OF ST. BENEDICT

The most effective reconciliation of personal spiritual needs—the eremitic tradition—and communal economic needs—the cenobitic tradition—is found in the rule composed by Benedict of Nursia in the early sixth century. On the personal level, Benedict, like Cassian, saw labor as a protection against idleness. "Idleness is the enemy of the soul. Therefore the brothers should have specified periods for manual labor as well as for prayerful reading" is the way Benedict puts it in the opening of chapter 48, a formulation that surely caught Max Weber's eye as he searched for the source of the "spirit" of capitalism. For the individual monk, physically demanding manual labor occupies a large part of each day—during Lent, for example, the brothers are to work from the third hour until the tenth hour—and "when they live by the labor of their hands, as our fathers and the apostles did, then they are really monks."[54] Yet, at the same time, this labor is not penitential in harshness but moderated on account of the weak: "Yet all things are to be done with moderation on account of the faint-hearted." This qualification stands in opposition both to the eremitic tradition of laboring beyond the limits of endurance and to the later tradition, exemplified in the writings of Columbanus, of laboring primarily as a means of chastening the flesh—"The greatest part of the rule of monks is mortification."[55] In the *Rule of St. Benedict*, the communal structure of monastic life necessarily entails manual labor, and, in fact, Benedict's discussion of labor occurs in the section of the *Rule* that outlines the basic structure of the monastic day. Labor and worship are inextricably bound together, complementary aspects of a total communal life. The monastery as a whole is pictured as a workshop of the soul, a workshop designed to be materially self-sufficient and appended to, but not dependent upon, the surrounding community: Benedict says, "the monastery ought, if possible, to be so constituted that all things necessary, such as water, a mill, a garden, and the various crafts might be contained within it."

Likewise, in comparing Benedict's *Rule* to that of the Master, we can see the extent to which economic and labor concerns affected the organization of everyday life. Adalbert de Vogüé has demonstrated, for example, that in Benedict supplements to the monks' diets were determined by the amount of labor performed and not, as in the Master's *Rule,* by the occurrence of holidays or the appearance of visitors.[56] This incidence of the principle "to each according to his need" is in keeping with the economic communalism that structures the *Rule:* chapter 33 reminds the monks that the private ownership is the "greatest evil" and cites the precedent of Acts 4:32 ("All things should be the common possession of all").

It is in the same spirit of communalism that the contributions of the monastic artisan are considered in Benedict's *Rule.* The craftsman practices his craft with all humility and only with the permission of the abbot.[57] Whatever is produced through the work of the artisans is sold at a price "a little below that which people outside the monastery are able to set," and this is done not, as one might think, to undercut the competition, but so that "in all things God will be glorified." Thus Benedict moralizes labor and demonstrates that no matter how important work is for the maintenance of the community, it is not assigned, performed, or sold at the expense of the monks' moral and spiritual health. The reason Benedict's *Rule* was so successful in merging economic and spiritual concerns was that it saw the two as interdependent, and it grounded the life of the community in the recognition that neither aspect of life, private or public, spiritual or material, can be neglected.

Benedict even uses the language of craftsmanship to describe the spiritual tools needed by the monk. In chapter 4, entitled "The Tools for Good Works," Benedict discusses the spiritual counterpart of the tools of manual labor. Renunciation, discipline, humility, patience, obedience, fear of judgment—these and other virtues constitute the background against which the *opus Dei* is practiced; they are, in Benedict's own felicitous phrase, the "instruments of the spiritual craft," and when they have been used they may be returned—as one returns daily the tools of one's manual craft—and the worker will be paid the just wage he has earned. The monastery, Benedict writes, is itself a workshop, a place where the monk labors physically and spiritually, alone and within the community, to achieve the reward prepared by God for those who love him (1 Corinthians 2:9). The last sentence of chapter 4 provides a clear sense of the way, in labor that is physical and spiritual, the monastery functions: "The workshop where we are to toil faithfully at all these tasks is the enclosure of the monastery and stability in the community."

MONASTIC LABOR AND THE *OPUS DEI*

Benedict's *Rule* created in theoretical form a world that trod the middle ground between the eremitism that was a dangerous source of pride and the communalism that threatened to reimmerse the ascetic in the world he or she sought to flee. Benedict's contribution to monastic world-building was the reconciliation of these two alternatives, and he succeeded in this reconciliation because he placed the practical life of the *opus manuum* within a spiritual context created by the needs of the *opus Dei*. The later history of Benedictine monasticism shows that this construction faced important problems in practice—not the least of which was the inability of individual monasteries to sustain the level of personal manual labor necessary for material self-sufficiency—but within the early history of monastic theory, Benedict's *Rule* stands as the most fully realized attempt to integrate the opposition between the spiritual impulses that drove men and women away from society and the economic needs that arose whenever the solitary hermit joined forces with others of his kind. Perhaps one should read the history of these experiments in spiritual living as a part of the tradition of utopian thought, for, like the utopians of the eighteenth and nineteenth centuries, the monks of the fourth and fifth centuries sought to integrate life as it could be lived with life as it must be lived.[58]

However, this is not to say that monasticism as it was envisioned in the early Rules or as it was practiced in the early communities supplied the

West with a model "plan of living" that supplied the impetus for the economic and technological success of the West. What Weber in particular saw in Benedictine monasticism was there—social planning, economic organization, dedication to manual labor, tolerance of craftsmanship and of technical innovation—but what he did not see correctly—the spirituality that created this rational structure—was far more important to the history of medieval monasticism. The Weberian capitalist, like the medieval monk, was inspired by a religious ethic to work indirectly on himself by working in the world; but while the "virtue of the English gentleman" was restraint and self-effacement in the interest of achievement, the virtue of the monk was restraint and self-effacement in spite of achievement. Capitalism finds the significance of labor in its products and uses technology and invention quantitatively, as a means of enhancing productivity. Monasticism, as shaped by the early history of asceticism and by the earliest monastic Rules, saw significance in the process of labor, not its products; it was centripetal and socialistic in its pursuit of communal self-sufficiency. The tradition of monastic labor does indicate the existence of economic organization, as is clearly the case in the *Regula Magistri;* but for that matter, the labor Pachomius performed with his mentor Palamon was organized as well. The existence of organized labor tells us far less about the spirit of monasticism than does the existence of the sustaining structure of the *opus Dei* in monastic practice. By the tenth century, manual labor could be justifiably abandoned by the monks of Cluny so that they would have enhanced opportunities to perform the true work that had called them to monastic life in the first place. Later medieval commentaries on the Benedictine and Augustinian *Rules* contain ample evidence in support of the contention that the founders' commitment to labor was provisional, being subject especially to devotional changes and, increasingly, to the even more "rational" capitalistic practice of hiring others to do what one does not wish to do oneself.

The legacy, then, of the first ascetics and the first monastic theorists favored manual labor, but always as a means to a spiritual end. Work was worship, but it was also a material precondition to prayer and a distraction easily surrendered. Perhaps the idea to hold in mind when considering Weber's analysis, or when thinking about the role played by the religious life in the economic history of the West, is this one, found in book 10 of Augustine's *Confessions:* "O Lord, I am working hard in this field, and the field of my labors is my own self."

CHAPTER 4

The Mechanical Arts in the
Order of Knowledge

ROM THE TIME of the first systematic classifications of learning by
the Greeks, the organization of knowledge has been in part determined by the perception of the cultural value or practical utility of
a particular branch of knowledge. In order to examine the status of
technical knowledge in the Middle Ages, it is essential to understand the
effects that cultural values have had on the classifications of knowledge.
Before addressing the specific role played by the mechanical arts in the
history of medieval classifications of learning, I would like to make a few
general remarks on the significance of the the classificatory tradition
itself.

First of all, any classification of disciplines, subject matters, methodologies, or educational goals has for one of its purposes the organization of
what is known so that a teacher or student can better understand the
relationships that exist between information in different subject areas. If
these relationships can be specified, then the location of information
within a particular discipline is possible, and, what is more important,
new kinds of information can be more easily assimilated. Second, classifications of knowledge specify programs for education because they help
students to identify what is not known as much as what is known. Thus
the accumulation of anomalous facts leads either to the expansion of
recognized disciplines or to the creation of wholly new branches of learning. Classifications are storage bins where facts may be collected and
from which they may be retrieved so as to be manipulated, related to
other facts, and eventually replaced or updated.

Less obvious is the evaluative function served by classifications of
knowledge. Classes or categories may be storage places for new information, but they themselves are also units of meaning whose location within
the classificatory scheme may be determined by considerations that have
nothing to do with their educative function. The organization of knowledge reflects the values of a culture as well as the intentions that culture
has for those who acquire and disseminate knowledge. Every classifica-

tion of learning is both inclusionary and exlusionary; the possibility of learning some kinds of things rather than others reveals something about what a particular society takes to be worth learning. Classifications of knowledge reveal something of the aspirations of those who formulate and control them.

A classificatory scheme allows a culture to fit information into a preexistent order of educational, social, political, and economic assumptions. Furthermore, when taken as a whole, a classificatory system allows both the system makers and its users to discover larger relationships among bodies of information. For example, when a system of classification is conceived vertically, it may show hierarchical relationships among its various categories or disciplines; when it is conceived in horizontal terms, it may show causal relationships. In either case, the ordering of disciplines suggests something about their relative value: in a vertical list, the higher discipline is greater than the lower and subsumes it; in the horizontal list, the prior discipline is necessary for those that follow it.

Throughout the Middle Ages, the classificatory systems devised by the theologians who were the primary arbiters of culture had as their purpose the demonstration of the relation of human knowledge to the knowledge of God. Theology was the highest science, and other sciences were related to theology in a descending hierarchical scheme of value. The subject matter of theology was, of course, God; the subject of the physical sciences was the world that God had made; the subjects of the logical and verbal sciences were the tools whereby the world was understood and expressed; and the mechanical sciences, if considered at all, consisted of knowledge that allowed an individual to manipulate the materials of the world. In this chapter, I will explore the history of medieval classifications of knowledge in order to show how, and why, technical knowledge—the "mechanical arts"—was undervalued in spite of its contributions to the material life of the period. Apart from what particular writers thought of the various disciplines classified as part of the mechanical arts, the form and ideological purposes of the classificatory scheme were responsible for the lowly status of technical knowledge.

GREEK CLASSIFICATIONS OF KNOWLEDGE

The Greeks distinguished between philosophy and scientific knowledge (*episteme*) on the one hand, and the productive arts (*techne*) on the other.

This basic distinction between theoretical and practical knowledge reflected the Greek view that speculation was "higher" than practice and that the natural course of an individual's education should carry him from lesser arts to greater wisdom—from techniques to philosophy. The clearest example of this hierarchical scheme of classifying knowledge may be found in Plato, though Plato's ideas on the organization of learning owe a great deal to earlier writers, especially to Pythagoras and Parmenides.[1] First of all, Plato assumes that the status of a branch of knowledge is determined not just by content but by the relation between the subject and the Being or Oneness that is the object of learning. In the allegory of the line (*Republic* 509d–511e), Plato shows that the lowest form of knowledge is opinion (*doxa*) and that its object is the physical world. Physics is therefore the lowest form of knowledge on a line that schematizes the relations between the objects of learning and the disciplines through which learning is pursued. The next highest form of learning is mathematics, which is subdivided into geometry, astronomy, arithmetic, and harmonics. Mathematical learning applies hypotheses framed with the help of physical models in order to understand mental objects, like triangles. Thus the movement away from opinion and into true science (*episteme*) corresponds to a movement away from the "shadows" of the physical world and toward the abstractions of thought; and *episteme* is opposed to *praktike* and *poietike,* the forms of practical knowledge.

Plato notes the contribution made by physics, a lower form of knowledge, to mathematics, a higher. Uniting the world of appearances and the higher realm of mathematical knowledge are the *eide* or "forms" (also "appearances" and "species"). As Plato explains in *Phaedo* 100b–101c, earthly appearances are derived from eternal, absolute forms. In the organization of knowledge, an interrelationship exists between what is perceived in a lower discipline and what is known in a higher. Mathematics was for Plato—as Aristotle reports in *Metaphysics* (987b14)—an intermediate form of learning because its objects are entities that exist somewhere between forms and physical things.

For Plato, the third and highest form of learning is dialectics or metaphysics, and this discipline has as its object pure Ideas. These Ideas are apprehended directly, without the mediation of material forms or mental images (the eternal *eide* as opposed to their transient, sensory models). The pure forms apprehended through metaphysics have both an ontological and an epistemological status; that is, they are not only objects of knowledge but also the sources of knowledge. With dialectic or metaphysics, as with mathematics, Plato posits a progression of abstraction and complexity, a progression that builds on certain features of the "lower" forms of knowledge in order to move toward the "higher." Plato equates the status of a particular form of knowledge with the ontological status of its object: "assume these four affections occurring in the soul: intellection or reason for the highest [dialectics or metaphysics], understanding for the second [mathematics], belief for the third [physics], and for the last, picture thinking or conjecture [perception]—and arrange them in a proportion, considering that they participate in clearness and precision in the same degree as their objects partake of truth and reality." (*Republic*, 511d–e).

Aristotle's division of knowledge is more complex than Plato's and relies on analyzing the content and methods of the various branches of learning rather than on evaluating their relation to Being. His general division of sciences into the speculative and the practical was the first recognition of this distinction and effectively undercut the Platonic hierarchical and progressive division described in the allegory of the line. Aristotle's classification of learning supplied the student of the sciences with a practical program of self-edification, and at the end of the lifelong process of systematically mastering discrete disciplines, the student arrived at a moral and political wisdom useful in the conduct of everyday life. Thus, in reconstructing Aristotle's division of the sciences on the basis of the *Metaphysics* and *Nicomachean Ethics*, one derives a scheme that turns, first of all, on a tripartite distinction among the productive arts (medicine, gymnastics, music, logic, grammar, statuary, rhetoric, and poetics), the practical sciences (politics, economics, and ethics), and the speculative sciences (metaphysics, including theology; mathematics, including arithmetic, geometry, astronomy, optics, harmonics, and mechanics; and physics or natural science).[2]

Although Aristotle did consider the objects of a science in his classificatory scheme ("And the highest science must deal with the highest genus, so that the theoretical sciences are superior to the other sciences," *Metaphysics* 1026a21), he focused more fully than Plato had on the methods of proof whereby knowledge is obtained. He wrote: "Knowledge, then, is a state of capacity to demonstrate" (*Ethics* 1139b31), and he maintained a strict distinction between what can be the object of knowledge and what cannot (*Ethics* 1140b31ff.). Furthermore, Aristotle described (in the *Posterior Analytics*) a universal methodology whereby certain knowledge may be had in any science, so that what the Aristotelian carries to the various divisions of learning is not a model obtained from a "lower" form of science but a method applicable to all science. Aristotle's division of knowledge was based both on degrees of certitude and on "family relationships" among branches of learning that were established by the supplication of an a priori set of assumptions about the nature of logical certainty. Therefore, Aristotle's classification of learning is epistemological rather than ontological. By the twelfth century, when the works of Aristotle were available to Western scholars, Aristotle's emphasis on the logical principles whereby certainty in the sciences is derived had been joined to the Platonic concept of certainty based on the nature of the object of knowledge to give the West a taxonomy of the sciences that was intended to unify human and divine learning.

Neither Plato nor Aristotle, however, developed a sufficient theory of the place of the mechanical arts in the divisions of learning. Plato's scattered remarks, such as in *Sophist* 266a–d, make it clear that human craftsmanship is the lowest form of imitation—the "production of images"—and that it corresponds to the kind of knowledge found lowest on the allegorized line of the *Republic*. Aristotle's discussion of *techne* in *Ethics* (1140a) focuses on the fact that the human arts or crafts are intended to be productive, and that while they can be taught, they must be distinguished from theoretical knowledge because their object is experience rather than causation. To say that a person "knows" how to make a chair means only that he can perform certain actions: "We think that the manual workers are like certain lifeless things, which act, indeed, but act without knowing what they do, as fire burns" (*Metaphysics* 981b1ff.). Indeed, a fully developed classification and analysis of the mechanical arts was not contributed to the tradition of classification until the twelfth century.[3]

EARLY LATIN CLASSIFICATIONS OF KNOWLEDGE

The first influential Latin classification of knowledge was the *Disciplinarum* of Varro (116–27 B.C.). Varro's canon of the liberal arts, written in the encyclopedic tradition of Posidonius (whose commentary on Plato's *Timaeus* influenced Chalcidius and therefore the whole Middle Ages), apparently treated each of nine disciplines systematically. Varro's lost work categorized learning into the disciplines of grammar, logic (dialectics), rhetoric, geometry, arithmetic, astronomy, music, medicine, and architecture. Once medicine and architecture had been dropped (as they were by the time of Martianus Capella, in the early fifth century), there remained the canonical seven liberal arts of the trivium (grammar, logic, rhetoric) and the quadrivium (geometry, arithmetic, music, and astronomy).[4] It was Boethius (ca. 475–524) who took over Varro's classification, grouped the quadrivial disciplines together, and added to the surviving works of grammar and rhetoric (by Donatus, Priscian, and Cicero) translations of Greek works dealing with the quadrivial sciences.

Martianus Capella's *De nuptiis Philologiae et Mercurii* was influenced by Varro as well as by Apuleius, Pliny, and others.[5] This cumbersome allegory, which describes the seven liberal arts in an encyclopedic fashion typical of the age, retains the division of learning found in Varro and collects a great deal of scattered information on each of the seven branches of knowledge. Martianus's poem, despite its limitations, nonetheless had a profound influence on writers from Fulgentius to John of Salisbury and beyond; indeed, Gregory of Tours assumes that his readers had probably learned of the seven liberal arts from "our own Martianus."[6] Yet no reader would have learned anything about the mechanical arts from Martianus; nor would any reader have learned respect for the two mechanical disciplines—medicine and architecture—included in his division of learning. "But since these ladies [Medicine and Architecture] are interested in mortal subjects, and since they have skill in mundane matters," Martianus wrote, "they have nothing in common with celestial deities, and it will not, therefore, be inappropriate to spurn and reject them."[7] Thus the two "lesser arts" were dropped from consideration in treatises dealing with the trivium and quadrivium, and the theme of the "baseness" or "unworthiness" of these manual disciplines was introduced. An interest in "mortal subjects" is distinguished from an interest in "higher" science, and the split between the theoretical and the practical found in Aristotle was institutionalized as a judgment of relative worth. Although medicine was later reinstated, the distinction between the mechanical and the liberal arts remained until the twelfth century.[8]

Boethius's contribution to the classifications of learning extended beyond his codification of the quadrivium to his comprehensive discussion of the principles whereby a system of classification could be constructed. First of all, in his commentary on Porphyry's *Isagoge,* Boethius preserved the so-called "tree" of the sciences that Porphyry (A.D. 233–302) had constructed by using hierarchical principles traceable to Plato. The "tree" of learning begins at its uppermost point with pure Being and descends downward, through a series of bifurcations, through particularized objects of knowledge (for example, body: animate and inanimate; animate body: sensitive and insensitive, and so on).[9] Illustrations of the *Arbor Porphyrii* may be found throughout the Middle Ages.

Boethius also preserved and extended the hierarchical ordering of the various branches of learning in his text *De trinitate*. Here he divided philosophy into speculative and practical parts. The speculative branch of philosophy consisted of physics, mathematics, and theology (*naturalis, mathematica, theologica*), and, as in Plato, the status of these three divisions was determined both by their subjects and by their relations to these subjects. Thus, physics or natural philosophy dealt with material bodies and the forms of material bodies in motion ("forms cannot be separated from their bodies"); mathematics with form alone (form set apart from both matter and motion); and theology with pure form (motionless and abstracted substance). The object of each branch of learning was form, considered either in conjunction with matter, apart from matter, or in an absolute sense. It is clear from the way Boethius uses this description of the division of learning that this tripartite scheme represents an ascent toward higher knowledge. Boethius did not include any discussion of the mechanical arts in his division of learning.[10]

Cassiodorus's account of the ordering of knowledge and his description of the life led by the monks at Vivarium provided the Middle Ages with both an important textbook for the study of the arts and an influential model of monastic life. When Cassiodorus founded his monastery at Scyllacium he gave explicit form to both the anchoritic and the cenobitic lives. His monks, living under a rule derived from the writings of Cassian, labored to produce copies of Scripture, the Fathers, and certain secular writers. Cassiodorus wrote the *Institutes* as a way to preserve classical learning and to extend this learning to the structure of monastic life.

Book 2 of the *Institutes* (written circa 544–545) describes the seven liberal arts of Varro—grammar, rhetoric, dialectic, arithmetic, music, geometry, and astronomy—and shows these and other disciplines as coming into existence because of their usefulness.[11] An "art" was also understood as a discipline that operated according to a fixed set of rules. This association of rulelike structure with the true arts anticipated a key element in the eventual legitimation of the mechanical arts in the twelfth century: traditional and informal practice had to be regularized before craftsmanship could attain the status of an intellectual discipline. What most clearly distinguishes "mere" craftsmanship from technology even today is the regularization of the rules whereby a craft skill is mastered and professionalized.[12]

Cassiodorus's own casual recitation of the skills and inventions necessary for the important enterprise of manuscript copying provided an indirect commentary on the way useful objects and processes were subordinated to the study of texts. In book 1, chapter 30, Cassiodorus describes bookbinders; "cleverly built lamps" that generate sufficient light for copying and that feed their own flames; sundials and waterclocks for measuring out the hours of divine labor. Cassiodorus continues this discussion of the tools of labor by writing that the "art of man has brought into harmony things that are naturally divided . . . these [clocks] have been provided so that the soldiers of Christ may be called to their godly work as if by sounding trumpets."[13] We also know from the *Institutes* that the monks of Vivarium used the flow of the Pellena River to power mills, irrigate gardens, and provide fish for the monastic table. The image of an environment carefully controlled in the interest of religious labor is underscored by Cassiodorus's description of the way the Pellena is present "when needed, and when it has fulfilled [the monks'] wishes, it goes far away."[14] The natural world and the tools of labor were subordinated to the intellectual task of Vivarium, as was the service of the peasants who contributed their work to the support of the monastic community.[15] All things—the seven liberal arts, the inventions of man, the labor of peasants, and even the forces of the natural world—come together within the context of this harmonious community, the purpose of which was intellectual and exegetical; one is reminded of Augustine's remarks, in *De doctrina christiana,* describing the usefulness of the earthly knowledge that creates a context for the acquisition of divine wisdom. The mechanical arts were an indirect part of the monastic life at Vivarium, but they stood outside the sphere of the intellectual arts that constituted a preparation for the study of Scripture. The mechanical arts were the province of the peasants whose labor supported the higher labor of the monks; Cassiodorus, like Augustine, could marvel over the contribution that these God-given mechanical arts offered to the scholarly monastic laborer, but the arts themselves remained unexplored and unsystematized.[16]

Cassiodorus's discussion of the division of learning was derived from Boethius and included the Boethian dichotomy between theoretical and practical knowledge.[17] In turn, Cassiodorus's second book, with its description of the seven liberal arts, influenced Isidore of Seville's discussion of the classification of knowledge in the *Etymologies* (circa 620). In books 1 and 2, Isidore describes grammar, rhetoric, and dialectic; the quadrivial arts are described in book 3. Isidore's definition of philosophy ("the study of divine and human things which help us to live well") prefaced a twofold division of the arts that constitute the study of "divine and human things." Isidore offers a tripartite division of physics (*naturalis*), ethics (*moralis*), and logic (*rationalis*)—a division derived ultimately from Augustine. He also includes a second division of philosophy based directly on Cassiodorus.[18] Summarizing the first of these taxonomies, Isidore asigns to physics the subordinated disciplines of arithmetic, geometry, music, and astronomy; to ethics (whose origin he attributes to Socrates) he assigns the study of four virtues of the soul—prudence, justice, fortitude, and temperance; under logic, citing Plato, he groups rhetoric and dialectic. He next indicates which books of the Bible may be most effectively used in the study of each of these subdivisions of philosophy. *Natura,* for example, is the subject of Genesis and Ecclesiastes; Proverbs discusses ethics. This establishment of direct correlations between divine and human learning represented a shift in emphasis from Cassiodorus's classifications of the arts. There, the arts are studied as a form of preparation for an immersion in Scripture. In Isidore, divine and human sciences are united in the study of Scripture. Furthermore, though he does not include any mechanical arts in his two classificatory schemes, Isidore does discuss medicine (book 4), building (book 15), farming (book 17), warfare (including "instrumentis bellicis," book 18), cloth-making (book 19), and other subjects that later came to be considered more fully as parts of the mechanical arts. Although Isidore was comprehensive, he was by no means thorough, and while this list of topics suggests that he gives useful accounts of the mechanical arts, the case is quite otherwise. As the title of his work suggests, Isidore's concern is not with the processes of a particular discipline but with the vocabulary through which these processes are described.[19] His inclusive and unsystematic discussions of the mechanical arts provide a link between the encyclopedic writings of the early Middle Ages and the more fully developed accounts of the twelfth and thirteenth centuries.

Between the time of Isidore and that of Hugh of Saint Victor there were few discussions of the classifications of the sciences and of the place of the mechanical arts in the organization of human knowledge. Those writers who provided an account of the arts generally repeated the Boethian or Stoic classifications.[20] For example, Rabanus Maurus's *De universo*, an encyclopedia of the ninth century, divides philosophy into physics, ethics, and logic. Rabanus asserts that the Greeks divided physics into seven parts—arithmetic, geometry, astronomy, astrology, mechanics, medicine, and music. This expanded version of the quadrivium may owe something to Isidore of Seville; in any case, Rabanus defines mechanics as the art of working in metal, stone, or precious stone.[21] He also maintains that the tripartite division of philosophy is a hierarchical one, reflecting an increasing certainty and increasing seriousness of subject matter, and he repeats verbatim Isidore's view that books of Scripture teach each of these disciplines.[22] Rabanus cites everyone—Stoics, Epicureans, Pythagoreans, Platonists, Atomists, and Varro—as a demonstration of the way philosophy, science, and opinion provide evidence in support of the truths of the Catholic faith. Although he provides accounts of the individual arts, including at least some of the mechanical arts, he does so in much the same way as Isidore—that is, apart from his discussion of the ordering and efficacy of the liberal arts.

An unusual division of learning is found in the *Periphyseon* of John the Scot (Johannes Scottus Eriugena). Eriugena's discussion of the four types of wisdom was included at the end of his brief hexaemeral treatise, which is itself only a portion of book 3 of the *Periphyseon*—a work concerned with "the primordial causes" of all things.[23] "Sophia" is divided by Eriugena into the practical, the natural, the theological, and the rational ("which shows by what laws each of the other three parts of wisdom should be discussed").[24] Practical wisdom is concerned with ethical behavior; natural wisdom with the causes and effects of "natures"; theology with the causes of all things; and rational wisdom with the methodology through which such investigations are pursued.

Eriugena agrees with Basil of Caesarea that the purpose of such divisions of thought was pedagogical. That is, every human science can be better communicated to the faithful by being divided into parts and ordered in sentences, words, and syllables.[25] Indeed, Eriugena uses the rhetorical method of division throughout book 3 of the *Periphyseon* in order to distinguish what is substantive in the "primordial causes" from what is accidental. Just as the creation is hierarchical, with earth and water seen as lower and inferior to air and fire, so too must the method of describing and understanding the Creation preserve the natural hierarchy. Eriugena's fourfold division of wisdom provides three ascending disciplines (practical, natural, theological) and one metascience used to study the other three. This recognition of the existence of a metascience of rational wisdom was Eriugena's contribution to the early tradition of classifications of knowledge. Rational wisdom could exist apart from the ascending hierarchy of knowledge and yet still be a valid intellectual tool; that is, rational wisdom could claim a place in the organization of learning on the basis of its usefulness rather than because of its subject matter. Such a possibility was an important move in the continuing history of taxonomies of knowledge. If a place was ever to be made for those forms of learning valued for their use rather than their subject matter, then this was a necessary first step.

TWELFTH-CENTURY CLASSIFICATIONS OF KNOWLEDGE

The tradition of the classification of the sciences reached its point of greatest development in the *didascalia* of the early twelfth century. The best known and most influential of these is the *Didascalicon* of Hugh of Saint Victor. Before the assimilation of Aristotle's *Posterior Analytics,* Hugh provided the most comprehensive solution to the problems of the ordering and goals of the various arts. The *Didascalicon* incorporates elements derived from the long tradition of classification outlined here; what it added to this tradition was a detailed consideration of the mechanical arts and a clearly articulated rationale for discovering in all human learning the means of enhancing the spiritual life of the individual student.

The text of the *Didascalicon,* written in Paris in the late 1120s, constructs a framework for the student's reading and meditation based on the fourfold Aristotelian division of the sciences.[26] The four branches of knowledge described by Hugh of Saint Victor are the theoretical, which has as its goal the contemplation of truth; the practical, which considers the cultivation of morals; the mechanical, which orders the actions of this life ("quae hujus vitae actiones dispensat"); and the logical, which provides the knowledge we need for correct thinking and effective argument.[27] The mechanical arts are further divided by Hugh into seven subordinate arts: fabric making, armament, commerce, agriculture, hunting, medicine, and theatrics.[28] Hugh asserts that these seven mechanical arts are like the trivium and the quadrivium in that three are concerned with external things and four are concerned with internal things, just as the trivium is concerned with words (the external) and the quadrivium is concerned with concepts (the internal).[29] This analogy was necessary as a means of legitimating the inclusion of the mechanical arts in the classification of learning. Hugh still stresses, however, the "adulterated" nature of technical knowledge:

> These sciences are called mechanical, that is, adulterate, because their concern is with the artificer's product, which borrows its form from nature. Similarly, the other seven are called liberal either because they require minds which are liberal, that is, liberated and practiced (for these sciences pursue subtle inquiries into the causes of things), or because in antiquity only free and noble men were accustomed to study them, while the populace and the sons of men not free sought operative skill in things mechanical.[30]

While Hugh of Saint Victor includes the mechanical arts in his classificatory scheme, he does so with the recognition of the unusual status of these "adulterate" arts. He asserts that one must continue to recognize that the mechanical arts are tainted both in their concern for products ("their concern is with the artificer's product, which borrows its form from nature"), a concern that is twice removed from the divine paradigm of true creation epitomized by Genesis 1:1, and in the "illiberal" nature of those who practice them.[31]

This last point is of particular importance because it introduces the important issue of the class bias built into classifications of learning. Historically, there has been a clear relation between the status of a particular form of labor (or learning) and the status of those who engaged in its practice. M. I. Finley has argued, for example, that the relative stagnation of technological development during the Greco-Roman period was due in part to the association of manual labor with the social status of the slaves or *plebi* who performed this labor.[32] According to Marc Bloch, in antiquity, mechanical inventions that eased the burdens of labor were greeted as a means of providing relief to workers.[33] In the early Middle Ages, manual labor was considered onerous enough to serve as a means of purifying the flesh and as a duty to assign to those individuals whose physical strength exceeded their intellectual acuity.[34] Jacques Le Goff has argued that labor continued to be regarded as burdensome throughout the early Middle Ages, and, as I shall argue in the next chapter, this attitude persisted throughout the twelfth century.[35] All of which is merely to state the obvious: certain types of manual labor, especially agricultural labor, were considered to be burdensome and the proper sphere of a particular, and lowly, social class. Nonetheless, whatever distaste for manual labor there was in the Middle Ages does not explain the status of the mechanical arts in the classificatory tradition. For one thing, there is the very great difficulty of ascertaining the exact effect of the ordering of the various arts on public perceptions of either the arts themselves or their practioners. While classificatory schemes provide us with a valuable insight into the view of labor and technology held by intellectuals, there is a legitimate question as to whether these views were widespread social attitudes or were merely held by a particular social class or profession. When, for example, Roger Bacon comments on what he has learned from practical men, he is paying an ambiguous compliment to those who work with their hands: "More secrets of knowledge have always been discovered by plain and neglected men than men of popular fame, because the latter are busied in popular matters . . . and I have learned more useful and excellent things without comparison from very plain people [ab hominibus detentis magna simplicitate] unknown to fame in letters than from all my famous teachers."[36] That the practitioners of the mechanical arts were "unknown to fame in letters" is precisely the reason it is so difficult to describe the reasons for the denigration of the mechanical arts: most of the evidence we have for evaluating the status of the mechanical arts is biased because the accounts are written by men who, like Hugh of Saint Victor, are far more interested in the metaphysical effects of the mechanical arts than in their methods or products.

It is in this metaphysical orientation of classificatory schemes that the key to understanding the status of the mechanical arts resides. In this context, Hugh of Saint Victor holds a crucial place. Although he broadened the categories of learning to include disciplines not directly related to the interpretation of Scripture, his interest in organizing knowledge was Augustinian in its insistence on the salvationary function of learning:

For the mind, stupefied by bodily sensations and enticed out of itself by sensuous forms [et per sensibiles formas extra semetipsum abduc-

tus], has forgotten what it was, and, because it does not remember that it was anything different, believes that it is nothing except what is seen. But we are restored through instruction [*Reparatur autem per doctrinam*], so that we may recognize our nature and learn not to seek outside ourselves what we can find within.[37]

Although Hugh followed Aristotle in dividing the sciences, he followed Augustine (and Plato) in arranging these parts according to their effects on the student. Hugh's division of knowledge was predicated not only on the subject matter of a discipline, but on its efficacy for salvation.[38] "There are those who say that what the arts are concerned with remains forever the same. This, then, is what the arts are concerned with, this is what they intend, namely, to restore within us the divine likeness, a likeness which to us is a form but to God is his nature."[39] Although Augustine had explicitly denied the value of the mechanical arts for the student of Scripture, writing that "among other teachings to be found among the pagans . . . teachings that concern the bodily senses, including the use and theory of the mechanical arts . . . I consider nothing to be useful."[40] Hugh sees that these arts, just as much as those called "liberal," have for their purpose the preparation of the student for wisdom and blessedness. In Hugh's view, the status of the mechanical arts was determined by the fact that their concerns are the most intimately worldly— that is to say, the needs of the body must be met before abstract reflection can take place. Thus, within the Victorine hierarchy of learning, the mechanical arts come first and are the lowliest, because they are concerned with the condition of the body in the world and can only serve as a preliminary step in the journey toward salvation.

Hugh's hierarchical classificatory scheme, and its synthesis of an Aristotelian organization of learning with an Augustinian rationale and intention, exerted an enormous influence on all succeeding classifications. Likewise, Hugh's essentially metaphysical view of the mechanical arts was incorporated into later commentaries on the organization of knowledge. His near-contemporary Godefroy of Saint Victor, for example, wrote a work entitled *Microcosmus* that included a division of the sciences and a detailed consideration of the mechanical arts. Godefroy included in his "mechanical subdivisions" a minimal list that includes armaments, fabric-making, agriculture, medicine, hunting, commerce, and building. He goes on to define each of these mechanical arts in terms of the "ends" or goals that they pursue. Thus, the goal of the merchant is to transport his wares across the land; the goal of the fabric-maker is to protect human beings from the discomfort of the cold; the goal of builders is to produce human dwellings using the natural materials of wood, stone, and metal. All of the various classes of workers who use these arts are engaged in the similar function of adapting the earth to the needs of human beings.[41] Godefroy did not dwell, as Hugh had, on the spiritual effects that such labor had on the laborer, but he did show that the microcosmic world of human skills and mechanical arts was both necessary and natural, as much a part of human life as intellectual or spiritual concerns.

In the next century, Bonaventure, writing his *De reductione artium ad theologiam* (circa 1250), returned to Hugh's basic system of classification as well as to Hugh's view that the arts move the student, through successive stages, toward union with God.[42] Bonaventure uses the metaphor of the diffused light of God—the *lumen* that is the manifestation of God's *lux*—in order to show the relation of the six lights of learning to the original creative act.[43]

The first light illuminates the mind regarding the created forms of things (*figuras artificiales*); this light is called the light of the mechanical arts, and it is lower than philosophical knowledge because it deals with physical things.[44] Bonaventure retains Hugh's sevenfold division of the mechanical arts as well as the explanation that these arts serve to console and comfort us in this world. Yet the servility of the mechanical arts in no way detracts from their significance in the scheme of learning: "Divine Wisdom is to be found in the mechanical arts, whose sole purpose is the production of objects. In this light we are able to understand the generation of the Word, the Incarnation, the ordering of life, and the union of the soul with God. And this is so if we consider the production, effect, or fruit of an artifact; it is also true if we consider the art of the maker, the quality of the effect of the object, or the usefulness of the thing produced."[45] Bonaventure, like Hugh of Saint Victor, sanctified the mechanical arts and placed them within the context of knowledge whose source and goal is the light of God.

Another important tradition in the history of medieval classifications of learning stretches back in time and outward in space to include the contributions of Islamic scholars. This tradition added different arrangements of the liberal and mechanical arts to the classificatory tradition as well as different rationales for the structure of these arrangements. Arabic-speaking scholars had access to the writings of Aristotle long before Western scholars, and their classifications of the sciences reflected their acquaintance with a range of texts that was only beginning to become available to Latin scholars in the twelfth century.

For example, al-Farabi (died 950) had written two works on the classification of the sciences in the tenth century; about 1150, Domingo Gundisalvo translated these two texts as *De scientiis* and *De ortu scientiarum*.[46] At about the same time, Gundisalvo also composed his own classificatory treatise, *De divisione philosophiae*.[47] In al-Farabi, Gundisalvo found that the sciences are arranged in an ascending hierarchy and that the relative position of a science in this scheme is determined by the relationship of that science to pure substance.[48] Al-Farabi leads his students of *falsafah* through arithmetic, geometry, mechanics, and "terrestial physics"—which is, in turn, divided into eight parts—before arriving at the study of the highest substance, namely God.[49] In *De scientiis*, a text that deals with the specific sciences in detail, al-Farabi writes that "the science of devices" is the branch of learning that considers the principles of things as things and not as theories about things. This science of machines teaches modes of invention (*docet modos excogitandi et ad inveniendi*) and the manipulation of natural objects "through artifice."[50] Using Euclidean geometry as a model, al-Farabi stresses the significant fact that this mechanical science of artifice employs measurement in devising the instruments used in the other sciences. The mechanical science described in *De scientiis* is, therefore, subordinated both to those sciences whose object is a higher substance (such as geometry, which considers pure figure), and to those specific practical arts for which it provides the devices of measurement and analysis.[51]

Gundisalvo, adapting al-Farabi's ideas in *De divisione philosophiae*, posits a tripartite division of natural philosophy derived from Aristotle, which is composed of physics, mathematics, and metaphysics.[52] Like al-Farabi, Gundisalvo divides physics into eight parts, making the point that the true subject considered by natural science is matter in motion, that is, matter considered apart from being or substance.[53] Yet Gundisalvo's version of the "science of devices" is not considered with the natural sciences but as a part of mathematics. His rationale for this switch is taken from Avicenna's *De anima* and from Boethius's *De arithmetica* and is an acknowledgment that, properly speaking, mathematics considers the pure forms of things according to syllogistic demonstration; the science of "devices" serves this study by providing the mechanical means whereby "pure forms" can be apprehended.[54] Thus constructed, the seven parts of mathematics are arithmetic, geometry, music, astrology, perspective (*scientia de aspectibus*), statics (*scientia de ponderibus*), and, subordinated to all the rest, the science of devices (*scientia de ingeniis*).

In his remarks on the final science on this list, Gundisalvo borrows from al-Farabi: "The science of devices is the science of inventing the methods for accomplishing all of those things whose modes were declared and demonstrated in the theoretical sciences."[55] Apart from its recognition of the role of the mechanical arts in providing the material means for the investigation of "pure form," what is striking about Gundisalvo's description is its lack of precision or concrete examples. He mentions, for example, the case of "a geometrical device for measuring bodies" used by stonemasons in their craft, but the name or exact function of this device remains unstated.[56] Likewise, his instances of "devices" in optics and statics remain unnamed formulas taken from al-Farabi's *De scientiis* without any elaboration or connection to the current state of medieval technology. Thus while the principle whereby Gundisalvo placed the *artes mechanicae* in the order of the sciences appears more in accord with actual practice—technology supplementing and sustaining theoretical science—the statement of this principle leads one to suspect that Gundisalvo had not worked out its implications by examining specific cases. He restated the views of his sources but did not modify in any essential way the pervasive tradition of viewing the mechanical arts within the context of their metaphysical value.

In order to understand this limitation of Gundisalvo's *De divisione*, we must return to his original tripartite division of learning and to the discussion of the position of metaphysics in the classification of learning. From Avicenna, Gundisalvo took a definition of metaphysics that says "Divine science is the science of things separated from material substance"; it is the "first and surest science," and it is the science to which all others are subordinated.[57] For Gundisalvo, as for Hugh of Saint Victor and Bonaventure, the ordering of the human sciences, and the status of the mechanical arts, were determined by the conviction that all learning is hierarchically arranged, descending from God to abstract entities (numbers, lines, planes) to the study and manipulation of material things. The "virtue" of the mechanical sciences is not questioned; it is because of the rationale demanded by a God-centered classification of human learning that technical knowledge remains subordinate to the other sciences. His interest was not in the ordering of knowledge per se, but in the ordering of knowledge in relation to the science of being.

Despite the metaphysical intentions of Gundisalvo's classification, there is a subtle difference between what he saw as the role of the mechanical sciences and what Hugh of Saint Victor saw as their role. The key point is that a clear distinction must be made between the theoretical and the practical intentions of the various sciences. This idea is also expressed in the *Didascalicon*.[58] In Hugh's view, the mechanical sciences have as their goal the creation of artifacts patterned after the manifold works of nature. These artifacts imitate nature's own imitation of divine exemplars.

Gundisalvo's view is rather different. For him, the mechanical sciences manifest the theories of the other sciences and provide the means of rendering the production of artifacts more accurate and efficient.[59] For Gundisalvo, the techniques of the mechanical arts are not directed primarily toward comprehending nature but toward the methods whereby other sciences facilitate this comprehension. The result of this shift in emphasis was to set the mechanical arts apart in a way that had not been possible until, with Aristotle's assistance, the distinction between theoretical and practical knowledge was incorporated into the classifications of learning.[60] To put the matter in another way, the mechanical arts could only be properly evaluated when seen in a context created by physical rather than metaphysical concerns. As a means to God, these human-centered arts were bound to remain the poorest of handmaidens; but as a means of enhancing the work of the other sciences and as the means of embodying theoretical principles, they could be more properly valued.

Yet another contribution to reevaluating the status of the mechanical arts was made in the middle of the twelfth century. John of Salisbury's *Metalogicon* (1156–1159) represents one side of an intellectual and pedagogical conflict that was to continue throughout the twelfth century, a conflict between the proponents of the trivium (like John himself) and the proponents of the quadrivium. What Mère Chenu has called the "professionalization of theology" in the twelfth century created a broad and sometimes bitter division between those "masters" who used new methods of scriptural analysis based on Aristotle's *Analytics* and *Topics,* and those upholders of the old theology, like Rupert of Deutz, who found the introduction of the *quaestio disputata*, of new analytic terminologies, and of complex logical demonstrations to be impediments rather than aids to the understanding of Scripture.[61] John of Salisbury's arguments against "Cornificius"—the enemy of grammar, rhetoric, and logic—provide a detailed view of one part of a complex set of disputes that involved many aspects of pedagogical practice, interpretive authority, and the acceptability of intellectual innovation.[62]

One of the first points John makes in the *Metalogicon* is that Nature has elevated human beings above "the burden of their earthly nature and physical body," providing them with the gifts of reason and speech.[63] Since speech unites human beings, its arts should be studied as a means of overcoming the terrible and unnatural loneliness that would otherwise oppress men; furthermore, speech helps to guard against the divisions that would be the consequence of an inability to exchange ideas and information.[64] John's bitter attack on Cornificius reveals the extent to which "false philosophers" had "renovated" grammar, rhetoric, and logic. In John's opinion, learning had become mere wordplay because a grounding in the basic arts had been lost, as had all respect for the earlier masters like Hugh of Saint Victor. Cornificius, like a modern-day sociobiologist, has argued (writes John) that one is either born with a gift for the trivium or one is not—no amount of study can rectify what nature has left out.[65] John's response to this argument is important, for he provides a rationale for supplementing the power of nature through human aids. Nature should be cultivated so as to yield its maximum benefits to the individual.[66]

John added to the discussion of the division of the arts an argument for the role they play in the development of the individual and for their value in enhancing a body burdened by the material nature of the flesh. "It is imprudent to expect from nature that which is the result of human activity." This affirmation of the appropriateness of human intervention in nature was intended to be a way to defend the trivium by supporting a philosophy of educational interventionism that sees nature as amenable to change at the hands of human beings. After all, as John wrote in chapter 11 of the *Metalogicon,* the arts are merely systems whereby human potential is realized. The arts atone for nature's wastefulness and inefficiency by using nature's tools (reason, memory, and innate talent) to actualize a person's natural potential.[67] The liberal arts, defined as aids to reason, have as their higher goal the liberation of consciousness from material concerns so that human beings may better apply themselves to the cultivation of wisdom.[68] The arts also make life easier and relieve human beings from excessive toil, which can dull innate ability. The mechanical arts have the same function as the other "helps" to human nature, and they are a means of extending the powers of innate capacity and of freeing the mind from material concerns so that wisdom can be pursued.

THIRTEENTH-CENTURY CLASSIFICATIONS OF KNOWLEDGE

The increased concern with the mechanical arts in classifications of learning continued during thirteenth century. In the twelfth century, classifications like Hugh of Saint Victor's had little practical effect on teaching; the monastic and cathedral schools continued to teach the traditional seven liberal arts, with more or less emphasis on the trivium or quadrivium depending whether "grammarians" or "dialecticians" dominated the school.[69] During the thirteenth century, with the appearance of the universities and the dissemination of a broader range of Aristotelian texts, new educational structures and new curricula changed the status of the traditional seven disciplines. Scholars like Robert Grosseteste developed new criteria for certainty in the human sciences and applied logical methods of proof to a broader range of subjects than had previously been considered. The rigorous analysis of propositions in the natural sciences helped foster a more rigid distinction between rhetorical, logical, and mathematical disciplines and undermine the simple dichotomy between the trivium and the quadrivium that had dominated educational theory for so long.[70]

The mechanical arts also underwent a reconsideration and a redefinition in the thirteenth century, one that altered their order and description but did not enhance their status. For example, the *De divisione philosophiae* of Michael Scot (circa 1175–circa 1253), which survives only in six fragments preserved by Vincent de Beauvais (died 1264) in the *Speculum doctrinale*, divides philosophy into two basic parts, the theoretical and the practical.[71] Michael then divides *theorica* into the natural, mathematical, and divine sciences, noting that the common relation among these three is their varied relation to movement and change.[72] Practical science is divided into two parts, the civil and the common (*in civilem et vulgarem*). Michael insists on distinctions of social classes in analyzing the various arts. Thus the "citizens' " practical sciences include speech or language, morals, and the contemplation of that knowledge which pertains to civil and honest men. The "vulgar" practical sciences include shoemaking and other such common occupations, all of which have to do with the use of tools or the production of artifice. However, the practical sciences are further classified according to their relations to the natural sciences. In this division, Michael followed Gundisalvo and al-Farabi by including medicine, agriculture, alchemy, necromancy (*scientia quoque de proprietatibus rerum, quae dicitur nigromantia*), augury, navigation, and others.[73] The fragmentary treatise breaks off here, but Vincent of Beauvais's *Speculum doctrinale*, if it has reflected as well as preserved Michael's views, does so squarely in the Victorine tradition established by the *Didascalicon*.[74] Vincent not only used the divisions of knowledge derived from Hugh, he also retained the ordering idea that the primary purpose of the human sciences is to restore fallen man to his prelapsarian condition.

Robert Kilwardby's *De ortu scientiarum,* written about 1250, provides the most comprehensive thirteenth-century analysis of the status of the mechanical arts and represents the culmination of the Victorine tradition.[75] It is useful to contrast Kilwardby's analysis of the mechanical arts with the scattered remarks made by Thomas Aquinas on the same subject. In comparing the two, one sees the influence of those Aristotelian texts that by midcentury exerted a profound influence on the content and methodology of university teaching. The accounts of Kilwardby and Aquinas represent the definitive late-medieval views of the place of the practical sciences in the organization of knowledge and confirm that the mechanical arts continued to possess a diminished status because of their methods, their goals, and the social status of their practitioners.

Kilwardby's *De ortu scientiarum* begins with a discussion of the nature of human knowledge, a discussion that displays the influence of both Aristotle and al-Farabi.[76] Particularly significant for an understanding of Kilwardby's discussion of the mechanical arts is his conviction that the sciences have a threefold origin. First of all, there are human needs whose satisfaction is necessary for salvation.[77] Next, there are the "useful" purposes served by the sciences, including their ability to teach us how to live well (*partim modum honesti vivendi*) but not how to be saved. Finally, there is science that takes the form of superstition—a vain and harmful misuse of reason. It is the second of these forms of *scientia* that we call philosophy, and it is with this form that Kilwardby is primarily concerned.

Kilwardby takes his definition of philosophy as the knowledge of divine and human things that teaches us how to live well from Isidore of Seville's *Etymologies*.[78] Human beings naturally desire to know, and they must use their senses to do so. Accepting this cornerstone of the Aristotelian view of science leads Kilwardby to affirm the importance of experience as a source of knowledge in terms far stronger than those employed by either Hugh of Saint Victor or Gundisalvo.[79]

After discussing the nature of speculative philosophy (physics, mathematics, and "divine science" or metaphysics), Kilwardby turns his attention to the practical or human sciences. These he divides into more complex parts than any previous commentator. His basic division splits the human sciences into the verbal and practical arts. The verbal arts are divided into grammar, logic, and rhetoric, while the practical arts are divided into ethics (including monastic rule), economics, civil rule, and mechanics, which includes farming, cooking, medicine, tailoring, armament, architecture, and commerce.[80] Like Hugh of Saint Victor, Kilwardby treats the mechanical arts as both imitative of nature and necessary for the provision of humanity's material needs. Also from the *Didascalicon* comes Kilwardby's familiar recitation of the "plebeian" practice of these arts.[81] Thus far there is little to distinguish *De ortu scientiarum* from the *Didascalicon*; however, beginning with Kilwardby's discussion of the specific nature of the seven mechanical arts the originality of his treatment becomes more apparent.

First of all, Kilwardby refines Hugh's sevenfold division of the mechanical arts by eliminating "theatrics" as inappropriate; in its place he substitutes "architecture," by which he means construction rather than design. Further, he revises Hugh's terminology, substituting "commerce" for "navigation" and then, adapting Hugh's scheme to suit his own ends, he divides the seven mechanical arts into those that are "intrinsic" to the body (farming, cooking, and medicine) and those that are "extrinsic" (tailoring, armoring, architecture, and commerce). That Kilwardby's ordering of the mechanical arts is predicated on the relation of each art to the body is in keeping with his conviction that it is the function of these arts to attend to material needs.

Kilwardby next considers the relationship of the mechanical arts to philosophy. How, he asks, considering Aristotle's conviction that the sciences are universal, can ethics and mechanics, which are immersed in the singular and contingent, be a part of science?[82] In answering this question, Kilwardby cites Eustratius of Nicaea (flourished about 1100) on Aristotle's *Ethics,* a text that quite clearly distinguishes between a demonstrative science and practical wisdom.[83] Aristotle's intention in the *Ethics* is to indicate the difference between the "judgments about things that are universal and necessary" that constitute scientific knowledge strictly speaking, and the "reasoned and true state of capacity to act with regard to human goods" that constitutes practical wisdom and which cannot be either the object of demonstration or the subject of a science.[84] Using Aristotle's criteria for a true science but subverting Aristotle's intentions, Kilwardby shows that there is a hierarchy of sciences proceeding from the more abstract and universal—from metaphysics and mathematics—to the more particular—like ethics and mechanics.[85] In other words, though Aristotle clearly denies that practical wisdom of the sort that constitutes ethics or mechanics could be a science "since it is concerned with the ultimate particular fact," Kilwardby, following Hugh of Saint Victor, allows these disciplines the status of true sciences:

> ethics and mechanics do not provide certain knowledge of those things that they show but neither does physics in all things . . . thus, first and greater knowledge was discovered in metaphysics and mathematics; however, metaphysics is the greater of the two because of the dignity of its subject matter while mathematics is the greater because of the certainty of its demonstrations. Physics originated later and is of less importance than metaphysics or mathematics; later still, and of less importance, is ethics. The last found, and least important knowledge of all belongs to mechanics.[86]

Kilwardby next considers the nature of the distinction between practical and theoretical science. In a most unusual move, he denies that such a distinction exists and asks if the carpenter or the stonecutter could work without the theoretical guidance of geometry. Does the navigator not use the findings of the astronomer in practicing his mechanical science? "We see, therefore, that the speculative sciences are practical and the practical sciences are speculative." This is an important point for Kilwardby and for the history of the classification of the sciences. Classifications like Hugh of Saint Victor's that relied on a strict separation between speculation and the production of some tangible result could not admit the importance of the mechanical arts as a means of applying theory to the solution of specific problems such as those faced by a craftsman or artist.

This is not to say that Kilwardby elevated the mechanical sciences above the speculative—"all of mechanics are subalternated to speculative science" is a clear principle for Kilwardby—but that the grounds for the subalternation were shifted toward considering whether the operation of a particular science produced knowledge quia or propter quid.[87]

The mechanical arts can only achieve ends and demonstrate quia; the speculative sciences can also determine why something is propter quid. Thus medicine cannot properly exist without astrology, nor astrology without astronomy; there is a hierarchy of methods, a hierarchy of proof, and a hierarchy of certitude that determines the place of a science in the order of knowledge. Like Hugh and Gundisalvo, Kilwardby saw the more abstract science as superior to the less abstract, but he saw this through the application of principles derived from Aristotle. Thus the status of the mechanical arts is determined by their methods and intentions rather than by their efficacy for salvation. Like any good theoretician, Kilwardby failed to consider the possibility that the abstractions of mathematics or the grand generalities of metaphysics could have been derived from particular experiences, or that, at least, the interchange between the craftsman's pragmatism and the mathematician's idealism might be a two-way passage, with theory and practice mutually correcting and sustaining each other. Kilwardby continued to have his eye on the *objects* of different kinds of knowledge rather than on the realities of the use of knowledge: the mathematician, forever a Platonist, works on numbers; the carpenter or stonemason works on wood or stone with various tools, including, in the form of measurement, concretized numbers. Kilwardby could see that there was a basic similarity between these two enterprises—indeed, it was this perception that led him to deny the distinction between theory and practice—but that the two enterprises had a value derived from their dependence, or that the carpenter could teach the mathematician a thing or two about the use of numbers, Kilwardby did not acknowledge.

In bringing the full weight of Aristotelian natural philosophy to bear on the question of the meaning and organization of *scientia,* Albertus Magnus and Thomas Aquinas significantly shifted the relations among the sciences and redefined the spheres within which each science was authoritative. Albertus's *Commentary* on Aristotle's *Metaphysics,* written in the late 1260s, presents an argument for the separation of natural science from mathematics and declares that natural science, as the investigation of matter in motion, has its own principles of research and its own inherent certitude. This argument for the validation of the natural sciences as having their own methodologies and concerns was applied by Albertus to the *scientiae mediae* as well. These "middle sciences" of optics, astronomy, and mechanics apply mathematics to the study of physical phenomena. Where Robert Grosseteste had insisted on the dependence of natural philosophy on mathematics, Albertus argued that the various disciplines of the *scientiae mediae,* while clearly subordinated to mathematics, could provide an authoritative account of their subject matters without depending on the principles of mathematics. Father Weisheipl has summarized the significance of Albertus's contribution to the classification of the sciences in these words:

> although Albertus Magnus utilized the traditional tripartite classification of the speculative sciences, his own understanding of the division was vastly different from that of Alfarabi, Gundissalinus, Grosseteste, Kilwardby, [and others]. For Albert the traditional division preserved by Boethius does not represent an ascending hierarchy of forms; nor does it represent an ascending hierarchy of scientific knowledge. Albert clearly conceives the mathematical sciences to be speculatively inferior to natural science and a preparation for the science of nature, physics. For him, applied mathematics (*scientiae mediae*) can be useful in the study of physical reality, but not a substitute for it. Finally, Albert insists on the autonomy of natural science, which needs neither mathematics nor metaphysics in order to solve its problems.[88]

Thomas Aquinas used the tools provided by his teacher—especially the texts of Aristotle—to create his own version of the relations between the sciences. In his early commentary on Boethius's *De trinitate,* Aquinas cites with approval Aristotle's division of the sciences into mathematics, physics, and theology (metaphysics) in the *Metaphysics* (6, 1, 1026a18). Aquinas argues that the seven liberal arts do not adequately divide theoretical philosophy but that instead they provide an introduction to the study of philosophy. Like Albertus, Aquinas accepts the autonomy of natural science and rejects the idea that the objects of mathematics exist apart from sensible things.[89] He does, however, maintain the idea that "one science is contained within another," and he argues that practical disciplines like medicine, alchemy, and agriculture are subalternate to physics. What Aquinas meant by "subalternate" was that a "higher" science, like physics or mathematics, has for its operating principles certain kinds of knowledge that are demonstrable within physics or mathematics itself; a "lower" science, like medicine, must borrow at least some of its operating principles from a "higher" science and, more to the point, the "lower" science must accept as true those principles it borrows, for it cannot demonstrate their truth on its own. Therefore, the practical sciences, like medicine, agriculture, and alchemy are subalternate to physics both because physics supplies principles to these practical disciplines and because physics has for its object the properties of natural things—a more abstract concern than that of any practical discipline.[90] In the commentary on *De trinitate,* Aquinas draws a sharp distinction between the object of a particular science—like astronomy or music—and the methods through which this object is achieved. Thus mathematics, which was for Hugh of Saint Victor the study of pure form abstracted from physical objects, became for Aquinas a means of demonstrating conclusions concerning natural things. The ordering of the various sciences was, therefore, dependent on both their objects and their methods; theology, being concerned with pure being, was the highest science of all, and in its two forms, as metaphysics and the study of Scripture, theology existed beyond matter and motion, mathematics and physics. Theology was the study of "substance, potency, and act."[91]

In his commentary on Aristotle's *Ethics,* Aquinas distinguishes between two different kinds of order: that which exists among the parts of a whole and that which exists between the parts and an end or purpose. Intellectual order, in turn, has a fourfold relation to the faculty of reason: there is an order of reason that simply examines what is; an order produced when reason organizes its own activities, as in the creation of a set of meaningful and internally coherent symbols; an order produced when the intellect spurs the will to action; and an order in which reason, through thought, operates in the production of external material things "as in the case of a box or a house."[92] For each of these orders of reason there is a corresponding science, not because the systematic study of rational order is more efficient, but because the reason and its powers can only be brought to perfection through the systematic habit of thinking. Thus, corresponding to the order of reason that examines what is but produces nothing, there is natural philosophy; corresponding to the order of reason that produces order within the processes of thought and expression there is rational philosophy or logic; corresponding to the order of the rational will there is moral philosophy; and, finally, corresponding to that use of reason which acts upon the material of the external world in the creation of objects there are the mechanical arts. What is most striking about this discussion in the *Commentary on the Ethics* is the recognition of a common source for each of the sciences. The four main divisions of thought are manifestations of natural differences in the application of reason to the self, the world, and those systems of discourse (symbolic systems) and action (ethical systems) through which interaction between the self and the world is regulated. Aquinas deepened the traditional classification of the sciences by looking for their common element in the habit of constructing rational systems that allow thought to govern human actions effectively. In the commentary on Aristotle's *Metaphysics,* Aquinas writes that "all of the sciences and arts are directed toward one end, namely, the perfection of man," and he argues that wisdom, the goal of metaphysics, is the object of the highest science.[93] Thus Aquinas retains the concept of a higher science that subordinates a lower, and, in particular, he maintains the distinction between the highest science— theology—and those lesser sciences that serve to advance the principles of what he calls "divine science or first philosophy." Nonetheless, within their respective spheres, each of the subordinated sciences, including mechanical science, has a legitimate contribution to make to the overall goal of human happiness and perfectibility. Aquinas did make occasional dismissive comments about the mechanical sciences—in his *Commentary on the Physics* for example—but in general his division and description of the human sciences offers a fully developed conception of how a variety of disciplines, with a variety of goals, materials, and methods, can be subsumed by the common goal of understanding first causes.[94]

Raymond Lull, who was Aquinas's contemporary (circa 1232–1316), offers an instructive contrast to the view of the sciences presented by Aquinas and, indeed, by the majority of late-medieval writers. In one of its versions, his classification of the sciences departs from the tradition surveyed thus far, and it suggests the means whereby the mechanical arts finally came to be reevaluated. Lull, whose idiosyncratic education included the the study of the Cabala, Arabic science, and Augustinian Neoplatonism rather than the more traditional liberal arts, composed some 292 works in three languages (Latin, Arabic, and Catalan) during an active lifetime of study, teaching, and missionary work.[95] The announced intention of Lull's life work was the conversion of the "infidel" Muslims, and he set out very deliberately to create an Art that would demonstrate in a compelling and rational fashion the essential truths of the Christian faith. Lull's Art stands as an alternative to the Scholastic summas: professing direct illumination through visionary experiences, Lull constructed a calculus of symbols and diagrams that provided the key to understanding the mysteries not only of theology but of philosophy, law, medicine, logic, mathematics, and astrology. At the center of this complex scheme lay the nine Lullian Dignities, assigned the letters BCDEFGHIK—Bonitas, Magnitudo, Duratio, Potestas, Sapientia, Voluntas, Virtus, Veritas, Gloria. In the *Ars brevis* (1303), Lull showed how, by combining these qualities into various geometrical relations, the master of the Art could deduce answers to questions in the physical and metaphysical sciences alike. Like Aquinas, Lull sought to provide his reader with a means of apprehending the Deity; unlike Aquinas, he also purported to offer a system that would unify all knowledge by reducing it to a set of logical relations. In this ambition, Lull anticipated—as others have noted—both the "universal algebra" of Leibniz and the analytic character of modern symbolic logic.[96] In the *Arbor scientiae* (composed 1295–1296), Lull creates a "forest" of categorized sciences in order to show the relations among the various branches of the Art. The unifying and reductive intentions of this work allow Lull to consider a broader range of relations among scientific disciplines than had previously been considered and to move away from the linear and hierarchical form of classification that had dominated the tradition since the twelfth century.

Lull's *Arbor scientiae* is a simplified version of the whole of the Lullian Art presented in other works (with Lull, the word "simplified" is used in a relative sense). The entire Forest of Lullian learning contains sixteen trees, including an *arbor elementalis,* an *arbor vegetalis,* an *arbor sensualis,* and so forth.[97] The forest as a whole thus includes classifications of virtually everything in the physical and spiritual worlds and demonstrates the common basis of all things in the mystic calculus of BCDEFGHIK. The tree of the sciences—the *arbor humanalis*—has eighteen roots, seven branches, seven fruits, and many flowers. The roots of this tree are primarily the virtues of God and, as such, are variations of the main scheme of the nine Dignities. Its roots and branches are further divided into the corporeal and the spiritual. The corporeal branches include the elementative, vegetative, sensitive, and imaginative powers of man, while the spiritual branches include the powers of the soul—memory, intellect, and will. There are two species of art in the *arbor humanalis*, the liberal and the mechanical. Lull defines the liberal arts as modes of knowing through reason; the subjects are the seven liberal arts. The purpose of the mechanical arts is to serve the needs of the body. None of this is particularly original, and the division of the parts of philosophy into natural, moral, and logical is nothing more than an adaptation of Hugh of Saint Victor's classification. Where Lull was original was in using the tree of learning, with its potential for describing a complex series of overlapping relationships, as a means of describing knowledge in a variety of subject areas. In *De ascensu et descensu intellectus* (1305), Lull used the linear, ascending "ladder of being" in order to show how the soul climbs from physical to spiritual knowledge. In the *Arbor scientiae*, however, Lull's "forest" with its trees rooted in Divine virtues and branching into complex relations of human knowledge suggests that the human sciences are ends in themselves, rooted in, rather than directed toward, the perception of spiritual truth, and that evaluations of relative worth among these sciences is less important because each science belongs to a taxonomic landscape where hierarchy is absent and where relationships are more important than subordination.[98] The idea that various disciplines were generative of "fruits" also made it possible for Lull to consider the various arts in terms of what they produced rather than merely in terms of their methods or practitioners' social status.[99]

MECHANICAL ARTS IN THEIR SOCIAL CONTEXT

The history of the classification of the sciences does not end with Aquinas and Lull. In particular, discussion of the status of theology as a science was a central concern of all theologians, and the question "whether theology is a science" (*utrum theologia sit scientia*), which appears in scores of commentaries on Peter Lombard's *Sentences*, involved broad discussions of the principles governing the definition and ordering of the sciences as a whole. In both of these contexts—in discussions of the status of theology and in treatises devoted to the classification of knowledge—the mechanical arts continued to be subordinated to all of the other sciences and to hold this lowly place on the basis of their preoccupation with the body or with the physical world. One reason for the lowly status of the mechanical arts was the fact that the authors of these texts were not themselves practitioners of any particular craft and therefore had little interest in, or sympathy for, either the craftsmen or the crafts themselves. Systematization alone could do little to raise the value of the mechanical arts in the hierarchy of learning because of the assumptions built into the classificatory schemes themselves. Medieval classifications of knowledge were established to demonstrate the value of a particular science in relation to the object of all sciences, namely, God. Graphic depictions of learning as well as written classifications call attention to this fact and demonstrate the extent to which the place of a particular form of knowledge was determined by its object rather than by the rigor of its methods or the social significance of its products.[100]

The mechanical arts were mired in the fallen world of matter and could not supply the practitioner with any knowledge of God. They were practiced by "the sons of ignoble men"—as Hugh of Saint Victor put it—and their products were useful objects whose value was suspect to those whose concern was the protection of cultural norms. It would take more than an intellectual decision to reevaluate technical knowledge in order to free the mechanical arts from their lowly place in the taxonomy of learning. It would take two related changes in social thinking to create the conditions for a new evaluation of technical knowledge: first, the separation of labor, and labor's tools, from the realm of the sacred and the control of the theologians; and second, a willingness to evaluate labor and the mechanical arts in terms of the products they produced rather than in terms of their effects on their practitioners' spiritual lives. In short, labor and the mechanical arts would have to be secularized before their function as social tools could be assessed. This secularization of labor began in the twelfth century as part of a broader effort to redefine the relations between the powers of church and state. As both Weber and Mumford suspected, manual labor and technology as we know them were shaped in part by the ideology of the medieval church. It will be helpful to turn now to the details of this shaping influence of late-medieval theology.

CHAPTER 5

The Secularization of Labor

THE TWELFTH century was a period of transformation in the history of the West. Fundamental alterations of perception and practice in theology, science, technology, law, and politics make the twelfth century central to any formulation of the medieval contribution to European culture. The "renaissance" of the twelfth century left its mark on the landscape, on value systems, and on ideology. There were "revolutions" in the natural sciences, law, theology, and economics; in technology there were developments of techniques central to the mechanization of European life; in theology there was even a counterrevolution, while in monastic theory and practice there were both revolutions and reactions—revolutionary new orders of monks with backward-looking programs of monastic reform. There was, in short, a mixture of chaotic change and tenacious traditionalism in the twelfth century, all of which makes it a period of special significance and daunting complexity.[1] Out of this mixture came wholly new and substantially revitalized social and intellectual views central to the formation of Western systems of thought and action. One product of this period is of particular interest to this study, for it was in the twelfth century that the relation between labor, technology, and the structure of society was most clearly and influentially defined. This act of definition profoundly affected both those who labored and the tools with which they worked.

While it is difficult to characterize the attitudes of medieval theoreticians of culture toward labor prior to the twelfth century, a few general remarks will help to place this discussion of the twelfth century in its proper context. The most important observation to be derived from a reading of early monastic documents, the hexaemeral literature, and treatises on the classifications of learning is that manual labor and technical knowledge were seen as having, at best, a subsidiary role in the spiritual life of the church. Monks worked to subdue the flesh, to provide substance for their brothers, and to open up possibilities for charity. The need to work reflected the sinful state of postlapsarian man, and the menial nature of most labor was a constant reminder of how far the human race had moved from the perfection of Eden. For scholars, the mechanical arts represented a debased form of learning intended to facilitate the higher labors of divine reading and contemplation. The common element in each of these views was the subordination of labor and mechanical knowledge to the spiritual life of the individual Christian and to the corporate life of the church as a whole. That work should be seen primarily as a means of creating wealth, or of altering the material world to serve human needs, or as an outlet for human creativity (in Mumford's sense) simply was not considered. At least in official expressions of Christian culture, labor remained the subordinate of spiritual purposes, and, as I have suggested, labor's products and the innovations of technology could receive no official sanction until this subordinate status was altered. This alteration took place in the twelfth century not by giving labor and technology a higher status, but by detaching them from the spiritual world, secularizing them, and creating for their practitioners a separate identity within Christian culture.

THE PRODUCTS OF TWELFTH-CENTURY LABOR AND TECHNOLOGY

In evaluating the role of labor and laborers in the twelfth century, the first thing to consider is the nature of the changes that occurred in European economic and social life during that century. The transformation of agriculture through modified techniques of sowing and planting altered the structure of society by requiring a revision of the relations between lord and peasant. A significant body of twelfth-century legal texts was created to redefine the triad of obligations binding the nobility and the peasants to the land and to each other.[2] More efficient plowing and land use— whose origins can be traced to the ninth century—gradually eliminated the cultivation of small plots of land and encouraged the cooperative development of open fields.[3] Three-field rotation (for example wheat, oats, fallow) together with the use of heavy plows equipped with colters, shares, and moldboards provided the tools necessary for increased productivity. Moderate weather and freedom from incursions by external enemies helped make twelfth-century agriculture productive. The use of the horse as the primary draft animal was also an enhancement of agricultural technology. When properly harnessed, horses work more quickly than oxen, though they are more expensive to maintain.[4] Apparently what was neglected was the proper manuring of fallow fields, and this neglect helps to explain the enormous expansion of land clearing as well as the abandonment of clear fields after only a few planting seasons.[5]

In fact, the deforestation of Europe during the twelfth century—especially during the 1170s and 1180s—may be seen as the first great ecological disaster, but it was also a catalyst for structured and cooperative labor. The technical resources that made the clearing of the wilderness and the cultivation of new land possible also had the social effect of encouraging both economic and and religious individualism. Peasants expanded their lord's holdings as well as their own, while religious houses reached out into the wilderness in order to establish new, isolated, and poorer daughter houses.

At the same time, harnessing wind and water power enhanced the efficiency of a variety of forms of production. Power technologies were used in grinding grain, powering saws, irrigating newly cultivated land, powering metalworking tools, and cloth production. Although water mills date from the Carolingian period, they became abundant in the eleventh and twelfth centuries. In the *Domesday Book* (1086), some six thousand mills are recorded in England; a lesser but still large number are noted in documents from central France.[6] In tenth-century Rouen there were two mills along the Seine; there were five in the twelfth century and a dozen by the end of the thirteenth century. In the county of Aube, there were fourteen mills in the eleventh century, sixty in the twelfth, two hundred in the thirteenth.[7] These mills performed a wide variety of functions: from their original function of milling grain, the water-driven mills of England and France came to be used to power water-lifting and irrigation machinery, oil presses, tanning and hemp mills, paper mills (in the thirteenth century), and, as illustrated by Villard de Honnecourt, sawmills.[8] Floating mills became common enough on the Seine to present an obstacle to river traffic and a hazard to bridges.[9] By the twelfth century, water power was used in the mining industry of central Europe to drive hammer forges and to produce drawn wire.[10]

This widespread use of water power by the twelfth century had both technological and social repercussions. In technological terms, the efficient use of water power demanded experimentation with a variety of gearing and cam arrangements in order to optimize the use of the water's motive force. Illustrations from later periods remain our best source of evidence for some of the experimental lines pursued by medieval engineers.[11] On the social level, efficient water power created a new class of intermediaries between lords and peasants, and displaced other types of laborers (like hand fullers), driving those displaced back to the land or into other crafts.[12] While the mechanization of tedious work like fulling or the grinding of grain might be counted as examples of technological progress, there is reason to believe that then, as now, those workers displaced from their occupations by mechanical power were less than grateful. Indeed, it was likely that water power and its practical adaptations were supported by the nobility as a means of further controlling the peasantry.[13]

With changes in agricultural productivity and technological capability came broadly based economic alterations in twelfth-century life. Between the tenth and the thirteenth centuries Europe moved from a fragmented to an interdependent economy. Regular trade routes were established between Mediterranean ports and the Middle East. In the north, trading patterns emerged that brought grain and foodstuffs to the Low Countries in exchange for cloth; fish came to Europe from as far west as Iceland, and timber was moved south from Scandanavia.[14] Again, as with the development of technology, it is important to note that trading did not begin in the eleventh and twelfth centuries; rather patterns of economic relationships that had been in place since the tenth century underwent expansion, with a greater variety and larger volume of goods moving between northern and southern Europe and among Europe, the Far East, and North Africa.[15] The rise of Flemish cloth manufacturing in the twelfth century exerted a particularly strong influence on England, and the two countries entered into a fruitful and mutually profitable trading partnership with the English exporting some thirty to fifty thousand sacks of wool (the fleeces of some five million sheep) to Flanders by the early thirteenth century.[16]

A related development was the growth of trade fairs in northern Europe and Italy. The existence of these fairs indicates the maturation of what one scholar has characterized as "intricate and sophisticated techniques of finance and business" among the rising merchant class.[17] In turn, the production of an agricultural surplus, the expansion of domestic and international trade routes, and the establishment of sophisticated business practices created the need for dependable currencies and for organized regulation of capital exchange. Governments began to mint gold coins, thereby giving the European economy a vitality and flexibility it had not previously possessed. By the end of the twelfth century, banks and moneylenders had become an important part of the European economy.[18] The money supply of Europe was increased during the twelfth century as a result of several factors, for example: the success of Christian military campaigns against Islam produced tribute payments, and the successes of the manorial economies of Western monasteries produced profits that were invested in building projects and other ventures.[19] Letters of credit were introduced by merchant-bankers so that the movement of goods across Europe could proceed with greater ease; indeed, the bankers and merchants added a transnational element to the expanding European economy by exchanging currencies and by establishing fiduciary money for the use of their customers. All of this economic activity took place in an environment that was increasingly urbanized but still dominated by agrarian villages; the period from 1000 to 1300 also witnessed an overall increase in population of between 100 and 200 percent.[20]

The "commercial revolution" involved not only the expansion of agriculture, trade, and population, but also the redefinition of social relations and obligations. Marc Bloch has warned historians of the "pseudo-dilemma" posed by a rigid distinction between natural economies and money economies, and he has argued that both forms of exchange existed side by side during the Middle Ages.[21] Nonetheless, it is important to note those well-documented cases in which the exchange of money or goods became a substitute for the forms of personal obligation that were the norm until the twelfth century. For example, beginning in the twelfth century, a knight could pay scutage to fulfill his military obligations; the recipient of this tax would hire a mercenary to take the knight's place.[22] Likewise the exchange of money for an ecclesiastical office was increasingly seen as simony rather than as an exchange of gifts, and beginning in the twelfth century such transactions were likely to be scrutinized or condemned.[23]

Of greatest interest here is the increasingly common twelfth-century custom of peasant laborers offering monetary payments to their lords in lieu of payments in agricultural commodities. Indeed, it is proper to speak of the institution of land rent in the twelfth century in those cases where the older exchange of "gifts" (land use for commodities) was displaced in favor of the payment of a fixed amount of cash. While some historians may see this shift as indicative of greater economic freedom for the landbound peasants, it seems proper to describe the shift to cash payments as a stage in the separation of the worker from the products of his or her work. Beginning in the twelfth century, both agricultural and craft labor were often performed under the obligation of creating a cash surplus, for wages rather than products, and in economically efficient but alienating, piecemeal fashion.[24] The introduction of money and the creation of a "profit economy" thus disrupted traditional forms of social interaction.

The creation of a technology that embodied abstracted value—and money must be considered one of the most significant of all technological innovations[25]—invited the reconsideration of the values that had for so long held European society together. The twelfth-century church was at first hostile to the implications of a profit-centered economy. Churchmen attacked merchants and emphasized the seriousness of the sin of avarice in their polemics against secular culture. As Lester K. Little has remarked, the twelfth-century church was largely unprepared for an urban and profit-centered economy; the "guardians of conscience" lacked an ideology with which to deal with the enormous changes that had occurred in secular society.[26] However, as an institution that had many times relied on its adaptability to changing social conditions, the "guardians of conscience" soon erected an ethic capable of coming to terms not only with urban society and its profit economy but also with the changing conditions under which labor was performed.

The period from 1100 to 1250, therefore, was a time of wide-ranging change within the institutional and liturgical structure of the church. During this century and a half, the Roman church redefined its relation to secular governments and rulers, created the system of canon law, reconceived its definition of the *vita apostolica,* and adapted to the infusions of Greek learning that revolutionized medieval education. Another aspect of this period of change was the church's formulation of new attitudes toward labor, trade, ownership, and the acquisition of wealth. The characterization of these attitudes should begin with what was one of the most important adaptations of the twelfth-century church—the establishment of reformed religious orders whose charters and practice specifically addressed the issues of labor and the wealth it created. These new orders embodied altered forms of piety and were manifestations of a persistent desire for personal reformation.

It is important to keep this continuity of spiritual purpose in mind when looking for evidence of social change within spiritual documents. A balanced approach to the secularization of labor in the twelfth century must acknowledge that the religious reform was inevitably influenced by events occurring in secular society, and then it must draw on the relevant literature in order to determine the meaning of these events for the changing status of labor and technology. In the remainder of this chapter, I will argue that part of the church's adaptation to economic and social change during the twelfth century was the creation of a new attitude toward manual labor. In particular, I would like to counter the view of Ernst Benz and Lynn White, Jr., that Christian theology catalyzed technological developments by suggesting that, in fact, the church reacted to changes in the social and productive order by removing labor and the mechanical arts from their association with the life of the spirit.

THE CISTERCIANS

The Cistercians were the most successful and influential of the new orders founded during the twelfth century, and a brief examination of their origins and early history illustrates the ideals and compromises of the reform movements of this period.[27]

The Cistercian Order was created in 1098 at Cîteaux by Robert of Molesme (circa 1027–1110). Although Robert was forced to return to Molesme, the small settlement at Cîteaux, which he envisioned as a return to the purity of the Benedictine Rule, survived. Like Cluny, Molesme was well endowed, powerful in church politics, and an uncongenial place for the saintly and austere Robert to cultivate the spirituality described by St. Benedict. The establishment of Cîteaux represents the most important event in the history of twelfh-century monastic reform, for it existed as a rebuke to the worldliness that dominated Cluniac monasteries.[28]

In 1112, Bernard of Clairvaux (1090–1153) came to Cîteaux, and his arrival, followed by the foundation (in 1115) of the daughter house at Clairvaux with Bernard as abbot, proved to be the crucial event in Cistercian history. The growth of the order was phenomenal—there were more than five hundred houses by the end of the twelfth century—and a great deal of the credit for this growth was owed to Bernard's energy and genius.[29]

In keeping with their desire to follow the letter of the Benedictine Rule, the Cistercians founded their communities apart from population centers; in fact, in their later history, the Cistercians depopulated villages in order to insure isolation; they therefore had to exert a considerable effort in land clearing and in creating habitable sites.[30] At their founding, the Cistercians held that the possession of any property by monks was forbidden. Bernard felt that the corrupt state of Christian spirituality could best be ascribed to the influence of material wealth, to an overly close association with the secular economy, and to a dependence on the labor of others.[31] In their desire to return to the ideals of primitive monasticism, the Cistercians renounced all the sources of revenue exploited by wealthy monasteries like that at Cluny, including revenues from churches and burial services, advowsons, gifts from wealthy patrons, tithes, ground rents, and fees for the use of mills. Furthermore, the Cistercians were to live by the labor of their own hands, as prescribed by the Benedictine Rule.

The issue of manual labor was the first source of difficulty for the Cistercians, for they quickly discovered what earlier Benedictines had learned, that economic self-sufficiency was incompatible with the perfor-mance of the Divine Office. At Cluny, the target of much of the reform-ers' general criticism of monastic practice, manual labor was not prac-ticed by the monks but by peasants who had no connection with the monastery.[32] In contrast, the Cistercians developed an economic plan to permit them to become materially self-sufficient without forcing individ-ual monks to devote too great a portion of their time to manual labor. The Cistercians established an order of lay brothers who performed the labor necessary for the maintenance of the community as a whole. These *conversi* were members of the order who had taken the same vows as the regular monks but whose status was lowered because they labored with their hands.[33] In fact, the *conversi* were monks who submitted themselves to the discipline of the abbot, who renounced possessions and family, but whose lives were focused on manual labor, craftsmanship, and (eventu-ally) commerce rather than on spiritual devotions.[34] These "half-monks" were drawn from the lower classes, and, at least in the early years of the Cistercian movement, there were many men willing to adopt this mode of life, presumably because the harshness of their lot outside the monastery would have far exceeded the difficulties of their lives as *conversi*. Thus the Cistercians temporarily solved the problem of economic self-suf-ficiency by instituting an economic plan that relied on the same division of labor between those who prayed and those who worked as existed among the Cluniacs. But they diminished the social distinctions between the two classes of monks by granting to the *conversi* a status and eco-nomic security not accorded ordinary peasants.

At Cîteaux and its daughter houses the monks denied themselves all of the trappings of manorial life—including serfs, trade with the outside world, and technological aids to agriculture.[35] The labor of the *conversi* was to free the monks from a great deal of work but not to free them from all labor whatsoever. Gradually, however, the Cistercians hired other laborers who supplemented the work of the lay brothers and who were also brought under the discipline of the abbot. While the duties of the *conversi* included carpentry, masonry, weaving, fulling, foundry work, beer and wine making, and land clearance, the tasks of the hired laborers demanded less skill and included plowing, harvesting, and the herding of the Cistercians' large flocks of sheep. In addition to these sources of labor, and despite the provisions of the Benedictine Rule against owning serfs, by the second half of the twelfth century the larger monastic establishments often did have control of serfs who came to the monastery in land grants.[36]

By the second half of the twelfth century the Cistercian ideal of self-sufficient and self-sustained marginal agrarian living had clearly failed. The monks had moved away from performing manual labor themselves, and they increasingly relied on hired labor when the number of *conversi* declined. Monasteries also owned and exploited mills, alienated villages by their expansive practices, engaged in profitable commerce, and, in general, experienced precisely the kind of economic success forbidden them in the *Exordium parvum*. In particular, the wool trade proved highly profitable for the Cistercians. Wool was a "cash crop," and while it was the lay brothers (under the supervision of the cellarer) who oversaw the production and sale of raw wool, by the thirteenth century the majority of English Cistercian monasteries were engaged in a lucrative commercial enterprise that clearly undercut the ideals of their foundation.[37] Naturally, the wealth of the Cistercians attracted the attention of the English kings: Richard I was ransomed from Holy Roman Emperor Henry VI in part with Cistercian money; King John fought a bitter battle to extract some of the white monks' income for his own use. In his criticisms of the Cistercians, Walter Mapes paid particular attention to their economic success and to the failures in discipline occasioned by this success.[38] Another effect of this wealth was that individual Cistercian houses became increasingly dependent on benefactors whose desire for both material and spiritual enrichment exerted an inappropriate influence on the monastery.[39]

Economically, both English and continental monastic granges were at first extraordinarily successful, supporting themselves, dependent houses, and charitable establishments; yet by the middle of the fourteenth century all but the wealthiest monasteries were in economic decline. The loss of a willing force of *conversi* was part of the problem; the unwillingness of the Cistercians to go as far as they had to go in introducing the most advanced business and financial practices was another.[40] Yet to call the Cistercian reform a "failure" is only to recognize that the ideal that inspired first Robert of Molesme and then Bernard of Clairvaux could not be realized in practice. The balance between seclusion and economic viability was no easier to attain in the twelfth century than it had been in the fifth or sixth. Whatever compromises the Cistercians may have been forced to make so as to survive as an order, the influence of the Cistercian model of monastic organization was important in shaping late-medieval spirituality. Yet the tension inherent within the Cistercian ideal was equally important. No one expressed this tension more clearly than Bernard of Clairvaux.

As one modern student of Bernard's work has noted, the influential abbot of Clairvaux stood apart from the mainstream of twelfth-century Scholastic thought. His opposition to Abelard is well documented, as are his quarrels with the "new philosophy" engendered by the recovery of Aristotelian texts.[41] Bernard's views also reflect a resistance to change and are a good indicator of the pressure a twelfth-century churchman felt from an increasingly powerful secular society. Bernard's writings stress the quest for inward perfection and are frequently dismissive of what he saw as misdirected attempts to rationalize the Christian faith.

In commenting on what is essential for salvation, Bernard, like Augustine, points out that personal simplicity may be preferable to knowledge of certain things, including the mechanical arts: "if you do not know the mechanical arts, either of the carpenter or the mason, what impediment would there be for your spiritual health? Even without all those arts that are called liberal, . . . how many men have been saved, giving satisfaction in their ways of life and their works?"[42] Bernard was not, however, opposed to all forms of the active life. In the *Sermones in Cantica Canticorum*, which have been carefully analyzed by Brian Stock, Bernard notes that activity and contemplation must be held in balance and that labor must reflect a carefully considered plan of living on the part of both the individual and the Christian community. The active pursuit of charity should incite the monk to learn how to balance material and spiritual labors. In a eulogy written to his brother Gerard, Bernard describes the perfect monk as one who masters "all the skills and jobs of the peasants," one who is a master of the work of the carpenter, the stonemason, the gardener, and the weaver.[43] Bernard deplores the dangers of *otium*, and he counsels his readers to engage in both spiritual and physical labor. Yet, of the two, spiritual labor is more important to the monk, and when he speaks of manual labor or craftsmanship, Bernard wants the reader to think of such activities as protections against the danger of leisure rather than as productive of material things. Yet, Bernard also considers labor to be a part of the Christian's social obligations, a means of bringing order to a world he characterizes as a "wilderness."[44] The labor of Christ's own life is for Bernard a model of the social necessity of work, and while the process of labor benefits the individual's soul the fruits of labor should be applied to the sustenance of those in need of charity. This charitable labor should be democratic in that everyone must share in the burden of providing society's needs.

The relation between the active and the contemplative life as expressed in the example of Christ is also a theme of the pseudo-Bernardine *De Jesu puero duodenni* included by Migne in Bernard's *Opera omnia*.[45] The author of this treatise informs the reader that the Christian must follow the example of Christ in "passing from Nazareth to Jerusalem, from toil to rest, from good works to contemplation." As was the case with Christ, the Christian must mix labor that produces opportunities for charity with the contemplation that provides the surest access to God.

Yet among the Cistercians, the ideals of personal manual labor, poverty, and communal simplicity were compromised by an economic success that was based on organizational skills, effective use of available technology, and the labor of *conversi*. Bernard of Clairvaux's idealized peasant-monk must surely have existed, but the order as a whole was unable to reconcile the call to labor in this world with the stronger call to worship God and to perfect the spiritual self. It is not an indictment of Cistercian spirituality to recognize the failure of their founders' ideal; it is, rather, a recognition of the difficulty faced by any community wishing to turn away from a world that offered increasingly greater scope for the kind of organizational and productive skills the Cistercians possessed. The Cistercians compromised with the world they sought to flee, and this was the direction taken by other religious orders as well.

THE PREMONSTRATENSIANS AND CARTHUSIANS

Like the Cistercians, the Premonstratensians were founded by an individual who wished to reform monastic practice in part by escaping from the pressures of urban and commercial life. Norbert of Xanten (died 1134) had a profound religious experience in the first decade of the twelfth century, became a hermit, and later set out to preach to and reform the canons at Xanten.[46] Norbert's fellow canons resisted his preaching and commented on the unsuitability of his behaving like a monk. Disappointed in this and other reformist missions, Norbert settled at Prémontré in 1120 with a small group of sympathetic hermits. This community grew quickly and adopted the Rule of Saint Augustine as its guide to religious practice. By the early 1130s, Hugh of Fosse, the first official abbot of Prémontré, had established a constitution detailing the organization of a federation of Premonstratensian houses; there were more than one hundred by the middle of the century.[47] The Premonstratensians were enjoined by their Rule and customs to wear coarse, undyed habits; to hold no material possessions of their own; and to perform daily manual labor. While they did not enjoy the same economic success as the Cistercians, they did gain papal support and were able to prosper through the fourteenth century. Like the Cistercians, they hoped to remain aloof from the secular and commercial life of the towns, and the apologists of the order, such as Adam of Dryburgh, stressed the necessity of a life lived apart from distracting urban centers. Nevertheless, the Premonstratensians were no more successful than the Cistercians in avoiding active involvement in the era's productive economy, nor were they able to realize the ideal of self-sustaining manual labor enjoyed by their Rule. Like the Cistercians, the Premonstratensians had to rely on an external work force to supply their material needs, so that by the middle of the century their apologists had created a theory of "appropriate labor" that rationalized the assignment of productive work to those thought best fitted to perform it, while leaving the remainder of the monks free to pursue the *opus Dei*.

Like the Premonstratensians and Cistercians, the Carthusians also thought of themselves as belonging to an order set apart from the mainstream of twelfth-century monastic practice. Their founder, Bruno of Cologne (died 1101), renounced his position as master of the episcopal school at Rheims to live in the wilderness with a small group of like-minded individuals. The seven original members of this order settled at

Chartreuse—a desolate spot high up in the Alps—and lived in meager huts that they constructed themselves.⁴⁸ Unlike the Cistercians and Premonstratensians, the Carthusians expanded very slowly—there were still fewer than forty monasteries at the end of the twelfth century. Likewise, the population of each house was kept deliberately small; indeed, the Carthusians pursued the *vita apostolica* directly by assigning twelve brothers to each house, in addition to a larger number of lay brothers who assisted them in the maintenance of the monastery.⁴⁹

More than any other reform order, the Carthusians attempted to follow the model of the original eremitical Fathers—they instituted a regime of strict silence, lengthy devotions, and rigorous mortifications. They did not, however, perform any manual labor. While most of the monks were actively engaged in copying manuscripts, the labor of physically maintaining the order was placed in the hands of the *conversi* who were attached to each monastery. The *conversi* performed the work of farming, cooking, and carpentry; they, in turn, hired secular workers to represent the monastery's interests at local markets. Guibert of Nogent, a visitor to the Grand Chartreuse in 1112, left us a vivid portrayal of the austere life led there by the Carthusians.⁵⁰ According to Guibert, the monks were pious, genuinely austere, and disinclined to have anything whatever to do with the secular world. In fact, the Carthusians went so far as to renounce the obligation to charitable labor or almsgiving so central to other monastic establishments because, as their *Consuetudines* puts it, they have left the world precisely because they are more concerned with the welfare of their own souls than with anyone's physical well-being.⁵¹ More than any other reformed order of the twelfth century, the Carthusians realized the ideal of isolation and economic self-sufficiency that lay at the heart of the new monasticism. They did so by rigidly observing their Rule and customs and by isolating themselves both physically and emotionally from the expanding urban world around them. The use of hired laymen as go-betweens with millers and merchants insured the monks' seclusion. By remaining small, the order could also hope to maintain a labor force of *conversi* who could see to their physical needs and thereby free them for a full commitment to the *opus Dei*.

The common theme of each of the three monastic reform orders was disengagement from the world and a return to the ideals of early eremitic or cenobitic practice. All three orders attempted to solve the problem of reconciling the active and the contemplative life by radically reducing their material needs and by providing for a separate group of manual laborers to take care of the needs that remained. All three orders recognized the supremacy of the contemplative life, though the Cistercians placed far greater emphasis on the necessity of personal manual labor than either the Premonstratensians or the Carthusians. Apologists or chroniclers of each order offered a variety of arguments for deemphasizing or abandoning personal manual labor; the most common argument was that the monk's labor is spiritual and that there are others better qualified to create and maintain the physical environment in which spiritual labor is performed.

By the end of the twelfth century, the ideal of the "well-rounded" monk portrayed in the Benedictine Rule—the monk who prays, labors with his hands, and studies Scripture—had been abandoned. By itself, this change is perhaps neither surprising nor especially significant; what is more important is that in recognizing that spiritual labor should be separated from physical labor, the theoreticians of the twelfth-century church established a distinction among the various "orders and callings" of those living in the world and acknowledged the legitimacy, if not the value, of a variety of occupations, professions, and classes. In coming to terms with the pluralism of a new urban society, theologians sought first of all to define the priority of the church's place within the new order; but they also defined the role of those who labored, traded, lent money, and invested. The effect of this division of social function—which was really nothing more than a recognition of what had already occurred—was the secularization of labor and its separation from the active concerns of the church. Manual labor remained part of the monastic ideal, but as the literature of the twelfth-century shows, the church, in coming to terms with urbanization and commercialism, redefined its role in secular society in such a way as to undercut the commitment to either productive or charitable labor. The next section looks at some of the texts that clarify this shift in attitudes about labor and about the relations between those who pray and those who work.

THE FORMULATION OF SECULAR LABOR

The most important confrontation of the later medieval church with the secular world was the series of struggles emanating from the Gregorian Reform movement and the Investiture Controversy. From this movement a wholly new relationship between the Church of Rome and Europe's secular rulers developed, which, the papal party claimed, was a return to the roots of apostolic Christianity because it established a papacy independent of secular authority. One consequence of the power struggle that grew out of the Gregorian Reform was the separation of spheres of authority within the church and the division of society into distinct classes defined by their relation to the emerging ecclesiastical bureaucracy.

Apart from the disputes between popes and emperors that occurred throughout the twelfth century, there were other, more subtle changes in the church's policies as it attempted to redefine itself in relation to an increasingly prosperous commercial economy. As we have seen, the emergence of reformed religious orders was one such change, and the attempts of these orders to create alternative economies based on strict observance of the Benedictine Rule shows how intense the pressure was to create new forms of spirituality with which to confront the changing conditions of twelfth-century life. The literature produced during the twelfth century was largely conventional—there were biblical commentaries, saints' lives, meditations, collections of glossed quotations from the Fathers, and so on—but there were also texts that reflect the preoccupation of twelfth-century writers with the need to redefine the practice of spiritual life in the light of the changing conditions under which this life was led. Thus there are new rules for monks and nuns as well as commentaries that reinterpret the old rules; there are texts written for the benefit of new orders, like St. Bernard's collection of advice for the Knights Templar; there are polemical works, bitter disputes within and between orders of monks and the secular clergy regarding the proper mode of living the Christian life; and there were also large-scale attempts to recreate the history of the Christian church in order to construct a rationale for the revised practice of a revolutionary century. Some of these texts contain reevaluations of the role of manual labor and craftsmanship in the religious life; many, in the face of great change, are content to repeat the old formulas from the *Rule* of St. Benedict or the *Conferences* of Cassian. What emerges from these texts is the sense that during the twelfth century, Christian theoreticians of culture attempted to fashion a pluralistic view of society and of social obligations, one that insisted on the primacy of the solitary spiritual life but also acknowledged that more public forms of spirituality, and a greater variety of professional occupations, could be integrated into the church. By verifying that, as Gerhoh of Reichersberg (died 1169) put it, "every profession . . . has a rule adapted to its character, and under this rule it is possible by striving properly to achieve the crown of glory" the church recognized the diversity of twelth-century society and defined its role as arbiter of society's spiritual life.[52]

Increasingly, the recognition of a pluralistic society meant that various classes or callings had wholly separate functions to perform and that while these functions might all be seen as part of God's plan, there were clear distinctions of value and utility among them. The religious life was, not unsurprisingly, maintained as the highest calling, and the acknowledgment of a plurality of "rules" by religious writers was first and foremost a way to insure the primacy of those men who lived according to the highest rule of all. What emerged from this literature was not just an apologetic for social diversity or a defense of the lowly tasks of the laborer, but also an insistence on the maintenance of clear distinctions between lower and higher callings.

An example of the twelfth-century attempt to reformulate the role of religious experience in a changing society is found in the polemical *Dialogus duorum monachorum* (*Dialogue Between a Cistercian and a Cluniac*). This tract, written by a German monk named Idung, is one of many texts in the prolonged debate between the defenders of two opposed monastic ideals.[53] This debate began with a letter written by Bernard of Clairvaux to his cousin Robert, who had been induced to leave Cîteaux in order to join the monks at Cluny. Bernard protested Robert's affiliation with Cluny and appealed to Rome for his cousin's release. Not only did Bernard lose his case, he also came face to face with the influence of the Cluniacs and their power in Rome. His letter to Robert sparked a vindictive exchange of public charges and countercharges, many of which severely distorted the real differences between the Cluniac and Cistercian ways of life.[54] Idung's *Dialogus* is one of the most effective documents produced by this controversy, perhaps because its author had been a *conversus* in a Cluniac monastery before becoming a Cistercian.

Idung was also clearly a careful student of patristic writings and the legal texts of the twelfth century, especially Gratian's *Decretum*. His central arguments in the *Dialogus* are that the Benedictine Rule is legally binding on the individual monk and that the monk's first duty is to the legal imperatives of the Rule rather than to the particular customs of any religious house. Idung's interest in the legal ramifications of the differences between Cluniacs and Cistercians reflects a widespread twelfth-century emphasis on the legal status of questions that were once informally decided on the basis of customary practice. It also reflects the church's desire to establish firm controls over its prerogatives by formalizing traditional relationships and by circumscribing secular authority over ecclesiastical matters.[55]

The thrust of Idung's argument is that the Cluniacs are guilty of having allowed their particular customs to undercut strict adherence to the legally binding precepts of the Benedictine Rule. What Idung had observed at Cluny was the identical ailment that later overtook the Cistercians: as Cluny became more powerful and wealthy, it abandoned the ideals of the Rule. The poor monks who once maintained themselves through manual labor became feudal lords who supervised the work of others and despised the degradation represented by manual labor. I suspect that this view of the status of manual labor reflected attitudes toward those who performed labor: the monks of Cluny saw themselves as belonging to a social class that was by natural right and legal precedent absolved from the labor counseled by the Rule.

In the *Dialogus,* the Cluniac monk accuses the Cistercian of inconstancy because he left Cluny for the "novelty" of Cîteaux. Idung defends the Cistercian by citing Anselm of Laon's legal argument (based on Augustine) that any monk, with the permission of his superior, may move from one monastery to another "in order to fulfill [his vow] fully."[56] The Cistercian then argues that in the Rules that preceeded Benedict's—the Rule of the Holy Fathers and the Rule of Macarius—it was commanded that peace exist between monasteries and that monks be permitted to seek the road to salvation that best suited them.[57]

His case for his own stability made, the Cistercian next turns to a discussion of the specific failings of the Cluniacs. The first issue discussed is the the fact that, as the Cistercian puts it, "above all, you [Cluniacs], in your practice and contrary to the precept of the *Rule* and of St. Paul [2 Thessalonians 3:10], have abandoned the time spent in manual labor." As we have seen, the Cistercian was right, the Cluniacs had virtually abandoned manual labor by the twelfth century and despised work as a distraction from their spiritual calling.[58] The Cluniac's habit of sitting idly with a book in hand and gossiping instead of doing manual labor is also cited.[59] The Cistercian paraphrases Augustine's *De opere monachorum* in defense of manual labor, including the exhortation to pray while laboring ("What is there to prevent God's servant from working with his hands while at the same time meditating on God's law and singing his praises?"). The unlearned Cluniac has not heard of Augustine's treatise, and he answers the Cistercian's charge by asserting that "the prostration of the whole body" required during the "long litanies" obviously cannot be accomplished if a monk is doing manual labor, and "it is in this prostration that the near perfection of our holy religion" exists.[60] The Cistercian quotes Cassian (*Institutes* 2, 7) to show that prolonged prostration is not sanctioned by the Fathers and is a custom that invites presumption—and sleep. Cluniacs upset the whole course of the monastic *horarium* by sleeping late, by celebrating Prime during the second hour rather than the first, and by generally ignoring the laws of monastic practice in favor of their own distorted customs. The Cistercian also accuses the Cluniac of belonging to an order that encourages (and pays) nuns to spin gold and silk cloth, an occupation that can only "feed the curiosity of the eyes."[61] By paying high prices for finely brocaded cloth, the monks of Cluny rob the poor, for "whatever you spend and waste is robbery of the poor." The Cistercian also finds waste and snobbery in the extravagant symbolism of the Cluniacs. Since, as the Cistercian says, "the Rule is law," these and other offenses of the Cluniacs prove that they live in violation of both the letter and the spirit of Benedict and the other Fathers.

The seriousness of the Cluniacs' breach with past monastic practice is revealed by the Cistercian as he continues his discussion of their failure to perform manual labor. The contemplatives of the desert, after all, labored daily, "while you [Cluniacs], who fancy yourselves contemplatives, do not do any manual labor. . . . No one may be said to be a contemplative if he refrains from works of mercy in order to meditate; manual labor furthers, rather than hinders, contemplation." The Cluniac answers rather weakly that even though he does not work in the fields, he and his brethern do read "and perform some work with our hands." But these are "empty labors," according to the Cistercian, because they are not productive or necessary. "What is the grinding of gold dust and the illuminating of large capital letters with that gold if not idle and useless work?"[62] The Cistercians, by contrast, do real work that is both communal and productive. "We work hard at farming, a labor which God created; we work in common [monks, lay brothers, and hired laborers], each according to his ability. And we make our living by our common labor."[63] The Cluniac responds that it is more profitable to sit in the spiritual reading, and to "be still and see that the Lord is sweet," as the Psalmist writes.

The argument remains unresolved. On the one hand, the Cistercian continues to support strict adherence to the traditions of the Rule, while on the other, the Cluniac argues for the superiority of Cluniac customs. Manual labor that is both productive and penitential, which gives the monks scope both for charity and for self-examination, remains central to the definition of religious life. For the Cistercian, work engenders humility and a spirit of cooperation in those who practice it; for the Cluniac, the contemplative life remains far superior to the active life, and work may properly be abandoned to those better suited to perform it.

These two views of manual labor are expressed continually throughout the twelfth century. For the Cistercians, personal manual labor remained a part of the monastic ideal—though not a part of monastic practice—while for the Cluniacs, Carthusians, and various members of the *ordo canonicus* personal labor was a distraction from spiritual concerns. Thus, in the *Life of Aelred* written by Walter Daniel after 1167, the Cistercian Aelred of Rievaulx is portrayed as a willing manual laborer who gladly performed those tasks required of him. Aelred, who was famous for piety and who, as we learn from the testimony of Walter Daniel and Gilbert of Hoiland, was learned, pleasant, and wise, was also willing "to strive to fulfill every order" and to labor with "an eagerness of spirit greater than his bodily strength."[64] Daniel continues: "Weak though he was in body, his splendid spirit carried him through the labors of stronger and more strenuous men. He did not spare the soft skin of his hands, but manfully wielded with his slender fingers the rough tools of his fieldtasks [*grossa utensilia rusticorum operum*] to the admiration of all."[65] Walter's *Life* is full of obvious exaggerations and distortions, but whether Aelred actually did work hard enough to inspire wonder is hardly the point; what matters is that spiritual perfection included a strong dose of "rustic labor" and that this work was noteworthy in being so obviously out of character for one like Aelred. One with soft hands and a quick mind is hardly to be expected to work like a peasant, yet this is precisely what the future abbot of Rievaulx did in his attempt to perfect his charitable spirit and his willing obedience. Manual labor, once an integral part of every devout life, becomes by the mid-twelfth century part of hagiography, an act of extraordinary devotion whose practice defines a religious ideal that, we may infer, is no longer the norm.

The theoretical dedication to a spiritualizing manual labor was also conveyed in the Rule Aelred himself wrote for recluses. Again, however, there are important qualifications. The *De institutione inclusarum* was composed early in the 1160s for his sister, about whom we know nothing more than what little we learn from Aelred himself. In this brief work, he instructs his sister, and all nuns who would live apart from the world, to follow the Benedictine Rule and to live by the work of their own hands.[66] If it is not possible for her to be materially self-sufficient—"the more perfect way"—then she should find a patron to provide her with the minimal necessities of life. If her constitution is not too delicate for manual labor and if she should succeed in providing herself with more than is needed for her own maintainence, then the recluse should turn her excess products over to the poor. Yet the recluse is not entirely alone, for Aelred cautions his sister to "limit the number of her attendants," restricting herself to a "strong girl who can do heavy work, like collecting wood and water . . . and sometimes to cook nourishing meals." The recluse, then, is provided for by one who is primarily a manual laborer, and while Aelred is explicit about the value of self-supporting work his principal point is that "idleness is the enemy of the soul . . . the mother of all evils that engender passion."[67] If the recluse is illiterate, she should spend additional time in manual labor—sewing and farming especially—but if she can read the Scripture, she should work from Prime to Tierce and from None to Vespars, filling the intervening time with prayer and meditation. Since literacy was still largely a function of social status in the twelfth century, the allocation of the recluse's time depends largely on her social standing.

Other twelfth-century writers echo Aelred's comments on manual labor as a weapon with which to fight the temptations of *accidia*. William of Saint Thierry writes in the *Speculum fidei* that "every vice has its own cure . . . [and] that what heals the head does not necessarily heal the foot." Manual labor is useful in suppressing temptations of the flesh, but it is reading and meditation that must be brought to bear on the temptations of the spirit.[68] The Premonstratensians were also enjoined to perform manual labor as a means to subduing the flesh and providing communal self-sufficiency. Anselm of Havelberg's *Liber de ordine canonicorum regularium* required the canons to work from Matins until Tierce or Sext, though this work includes both manual labor and the copying of texts. Anselm notes that no canon should "despise manual labor," which suggests that some did.[69]

Adam of Dryburgh was one such critic of labor. In his *Soliloquia de instructione animae,* Adam notes that "manual labor irritates me greatly" and that educated and ordained men should not be called upon to perform the work of peasants. Adam's view is that work might be of some indirect spiritual value, but that meditation and prayer are far more essential to the religious life; the work of providing for the canons' subsistence should, in any case, fall to those rustic men who are accustomed to harsh labor. Indeed, it is "detestable that one should expect to live well [e.g. idly] in the abbey when he knew hard times in the world."[70]

Adam's view that those who were accustomed to work in the secular world should continue to work in the abbey reflects the broader view that particular classes of individuals are naturally suited to particular occupations and should be allowed to pursue their inclinations rather than follow a single standard of conduct. While the virtues of manual labor in controlling human passions were extolled, the point was that monastic occupations should fit the inclinations of the particular monk or nun, thereby considerably softening the injunction to productive labor. Philip of Harvengt, for example, argues for some manual labor, but he also notes that study and contemplation are more essential to the spiritual life and should therefore be pursued by those who are so inclined.[71] A clear expression of the movement toward diversifying the requirements of monastic life in the interests of recognizing individual abilities may be found in the *Libellus de diversis ordinibus,* composed during the mid-twelfth century:

Our prayer is much helped by those who minister to us in external things, for it can hardly be offered if he who wishes to become perfect in prayer has also to occupy his mind with external matters and corporeal labours. And if anyone excels in doing this, for such perfect men are not lacking in the Church, let him praise God with the apostle, who worked with his hands lest he should be a burden to anyone (2 Thess. 3:8). . . . If anyone should be disturbed that many canons among those who, I say, live next to men do not work with their hands, we can first reply briefly with what the apostle said: "For bodily exercise is profitable to little, but godliness is profitable to all things." (1 Tim. 4:8) For when he says bodily exercise profits little, he shows that it is worth something, but not so much that he would impose more than this precept on anyone or would judge anyone who does not work physically to be inferior. . . . If they who remain in the cloister also wish to do some work with their hands, I declare this to be good, and I consider that idleness should be denied to them as it is to others, saying with the apostle: "If any man will not work, neither let him eat." (2 Thess. 3:10) *I understand that this was said not only of manual labor but of all work suitable for men of the church, that he who does nothing shall not eat.*[72]

This is the first interpretation of the often-quoted verse from 2 Thessalonians 3:10 to assert that labor need not be physical in order to be blessed. "Work suitable for men of the church" implies, of course, that manual labor is not always suitable for monks and canons and that, more broadly, different forms of work are better suited to different classes of men and women. Such an interpretation directly contradicts the injunction of the Benedictine Rule. It also implies that the performance of manual labor does not confer a higher status on a monk—"And let not him who works with his hands vaunt himself above the man who works seated, for there is labor in both." The anonymous author of the *Libellus de diversis ordinibus* affirms that the religious calling may be fulfilled in a variety of ways and that the mixture of the *opus Dei* with the *opus manuum* is not necessary for those whose inclination and temperament are not suited to one or the other.

This same point is made in the twelfth-century commentary on the Rule of St. Augustine written by Robert of Bridlington. Robert asserts that no servant of God many remain slothful because idleness feeds desire. However, he also maintains that the activity required of monks or canons need not be manual labor; indeed, "one is to be praised for being idle in contemplation."[73] Robert goes on to define a form of idleness that is conducive to the meditation on God's works, an idleness that detaches one from material concerns: "Idleness lifts the mind from outward cares that it may fix itself on God; activity involves the mind and weighs it down."[74] Robert next provides a list of acceptable monastic labors. In this list, contemplation comes first, writing and illuminating manuscripts comes next, sewing and other indoor domestic chores is third, and last is all outdoor work, including agriculture. The motive behind Robert's ordering of worthy labors is clear from his identification of manual labor with those of lower social status. He believes that physical labor is beneath the dignity of any Christian who has a sacrodotal calling: "There are some who think it unworthy and unfitting for those who are set apart for the service of the holy altar to be put to agricultural tasks, and especially to reaping, because of the danger to one's hands."[75] Like Adam of Dryburgh, Robert of Bridlington finds in manual labor a worthy ideal for some, but for others it is a distraction left to men and women whose harsh life or rough temperament better suits them to physical exertion.

Amalarius of Metz's *Institutio canonicorum* also acknowledges the paradox of manual labor central to the views of twelfth-century writers. On the one hand, the contemplative needs inactivity in order to relieve his or her mind from perturbations and to concentrate on Scripture; on the other hand, the dangers of such stillness are manifest and may best be countered by work of some kind. Like the apostles, those who have retired from the world should labor with their hands.[76] Indeed, the balancing of the active with the contemplative life was a constant topic of discussion in the twelfth century, but the twelfth-century writer was more likely to adopt the position that labor represents a distraction from the demands of the spiritual life, thereby separating what earlier monastic writers had sought to unite.[77] The monastic ideal was, as Amalarius noted, to realize the *vita vere apostolica*—the truly apostolic life—and for eleventh-century writers like Peter Damian the method whereby this ideal would be realized was reasonably easy to state. The clear goals expressed in Rupert of Deutz's early twelfth-century *De vita vere apostolica* were communal life; personal piety; adoption of simplicity in dress, diet, and behavior; and economic self-sufficiency through manual labor.[78] But this simple prescription for a truly perfect Christian life was not as well suited to the dynamic world of the twelfth century as it had been to the eleventh. One also recalls Abelard's well-known complaint in the *Historia calamitatum* that he was "incapable of working and ashamed to beg." In his case, the trade he knew best was teaching, so he "turned from manual labor to make use of [his] tongue."

Rupert of Deutz, commenting on the Benedictine Rule, was also willing to reinterpret the founder's call to personal manual labor in the life of the monastery. Like Robert of Bridlington, Rupert argues that the service of the altar takes precedence over any other form of monastic activity. He also asserts that Benedict had not intended labor to be essential to monastic life.[79] Rupert defended the idea of a division of responsibilities within the monastic establishment, with the *opus Dei* being a higher calling reserved for those with greater piety and the *opus manuum* reserved for those with a rougher, more worldly temperament. As more monks were ordained priests, more time was spent on liturgical celebrations at the expense of manual labor. Indeed, Rupert goes so far as to chastise those who put too great an emphasis on manual labor, asserting that excessive hope in labor is misguided and distracting.[80]

LABOR AND CHURCH REFORM

Rupert's interpretation of the role of the monk reflected the tendency of twelfth-century monastic writers to insist on divisions of social and liturgical function both inside and outside the monastery. The "truly apostolic life" was increasingly equated with the liturgical functions of the monastery, while the goal of the church after the Gregorian Reform was the recreation of the secular world after the model of the monastery. The "proliferation of new forms" of the religious life (to use Chenu's phrase), while upsetting to religious conservatives who, like Rupert of Deutz, placed their hope in the extension of the *vita communis* to the Christian world as a whole, was nonetheless an inevitable consequence of the social and political changes that occurred during the twelfth century. The plurality of orders and callings defended by the author of the *Libellus de diversis ordinibus* reflected an increasing plurality of spiritual needs in an urbanized and secular society. In particular, the orders of preachers founded in the closing decades of the twelfth century answered an acute need for activist-teachers who could both reject the enticements of newly wealthy urban centers and accept the valid spiritual needs of those who lived within these centers.[81] By the end of the twelfth century, the church had acknowledged the spiritual needs of merchants, farmers, and soldiers, and it proceeded to approve the mission of Franciscans and Dominicans in extending the *vita apostolica* to these various "orders and callings." Thus, while early in the twelfth century it was commonly understood that merchants, with their concern for profit, would find it nearly impossible to be saved, by the 1180s the value of the merchant's contribution to the Christian commonwealth was not only acknowledged but provided for by the church.[82]

The notion of the *ordo,* a division of society, was formulated in the twelfth century in recognition of the social pluralism of the age. By the thirteenth century, the concept of the *ordo* was fixed in church policy as a means of distinguishing among the occupations, powers, and responsibilities of Christian men and women: "This diversity of orders arises from the diversity of offices and actions, as appears in one city where there are different orders according to the different actions; for there is one order of those who judge, and another of those who fight, and another of those who labor in the fields, and so forth."[83] The orders of society reflect the facts of varying occupations and actions; in formulating the theory of the "three orders," the church recognized the complexity—Weber would say the "rationalization"—of Christian society and proceeded to secure for itself an authoritative position within the structure of these orders.

Georges Duby has argued that the "three orders" may be traced to the eleventh century in France, when the Church developed its concept of the "Peace of God."[84] By the twelfth century, Duby writes, the concept had spread throughout Christendom. The overt purpose of the Peace of God was to empower bishops to maintain order and to mete out justice. All members of the warrior class—the *bellatores*—were enjoined by the church under pain of excommunication to obey certain laws of "humane" warfare. But, Duby argues, the Peace of God had a deeper purpose. It was part of an attempt to submit all aspects of Christian social life—domestic, economic, and political—to the control of the church. While the Peace of God had as one of its direct purposes the externalization of the martial spirit through the institution of the crusade, it also proposed prohibitions designed to separate those who fought from those who prayed and those who labored from both of these groups. Thus, according to Duby, the real consequence of the Peace of God was the clarification of functional distinctions among the *oratores, bellatores,* and *laboratores.*

I would suggest that, economically speaking, there were really only two orders: on the one hand, those who managed and protected an increasingly "rationalized" society by means of ecclesiastical and military power, and on the other, those who were subject to this domination—the *laboratores.* As Duby has observed, the ideology of the Peace of God "presented a simple picture [of feudal society] in conformity with the Divine Plan thereby sanctioning social inequalities and all forms of economic exploitation."[85] Those who prayed were freed from economic distractions and made the recipients of great generosity. Indeed, the church encouraged gift giving by allowing oral bequests of land by those of the faithful who were inclined to be generous on their deathbeds. And in a work like St. Bernard's *In laude novae militiae* (circa 1129), one finds an explicit statement of the close relation between those who fight and those who pray. The Knights Templar are "chaste," they "dwell in one family," and they "shun idleness." Bernard continues by saying that, "I do not know if it would be more appropriate to refer to them as monks or soldiers, unless perhaps it would be better to see them as both."[86] This equation of monks and soldiers has been traced back to the "ritualized aggression" of Cluny and represents a point of contact between those whose duty it was to defend Christian society with prayers and those whose mission it was to defend it by force of arms.[87]

During the twelfth century, the relations between these two groups—and with the increasingly important classes of merchants and urban craftsmen—was codified into a legal form that gave de facto recognition to divisions of social class created by the commercial revolution. In support of the *oratores,* the *bellatores* fought against infidels and oversaw the control of the masses of men and women upon whose labor the empowered minority was dependent. We have seen how the burden of manual labor fell heaviest on the monks presumed least suitable for full engagement in spiritual life; by the twelfth century the informal custom of passing on labor obligations to secular laborers was sanctioned by regular custom as monks increasingly exempted themselves from the *opus manuum* in order to spend more time in spiritual activities. While the ideology and sanction for domination emanated from the church, the mechanics of power were exercised by a warrior class that continued to prey upon those whom it was enjoined to protect. So effective was this definition of Christian society that by the early thirteenth century Bonaventure could write with assurance of the three classes that compose Christian society, and he could state that while each of these classes is necessary for the proper functioning of the world, the call to perform manual labor is the lowest and least desirable calling of all.[88] Bonaventure was defending the right of the Franciscans not to perform manual labor, so he provided another defense of the pluralistic society—the society that is made perfect by the division of labor and by the recognition that spiritual occupations are the highest of all. The idea that the social world is made up of a variety of occupations was further developed by Thomas Aquinas into an apology for the labor of scholars and teachers. Aquinas writes that there are a number of appropriate modes of labor available to the Christian in general and to the monk in particular; not everyone needs to do manual labor to be saved.[89] Elsewhere, Aquinas expresses the view that what is done for the sake of knowledge is superior to what is done for the sake of utility, that in the world of work the architect is therefore superior to the laborer who implements his plans. In the Christian commonwealth, a diversity of forms of labor is needed, and these various forms are hierarchically arranged from the spiritual function of the contemplative, to the protective function of the warrior, down to the work of merchants, craftsmen, and, least of all, manual laborers.[90]

I suggest that the relation between the concept of the orders of society and the performance of manual labor emerged from revisions of monastic life and from redefinitions of apostolic life developed during the twelfth century. By recognizing the appropriateness of particular forms of social and spiritual action to various groups within society, the church provided a rationale for the detachment of manual labor from monasticism and from spiritual life in general. In an age of economic expansion and specialization, those who prayed could not be expected to perform sustaining labor. Work remained a part of an individual monk's or nun's calling insofar as it helped to undermine the temptations of *accidia,* but the ideal of self-contained monastic communities—an ideal born with Pachomius in the Egyptian desert—was surrendered as the boundaries between monastery and secular world disintegrated. The church came to recognize manual labor, craftsmanship, and technology as the proper sphere of the order of society called to them—the *laborantes*—and in so doing the church modified its millennium-old ideal of spiritualized, communal, and inner-directed labor. The continued placement of the mechanical arts at the bottom of the hierarchy of learning also reflected the doubts felt by twelfth-century writers about the value of labor. Since human ingenuity and ambition were preoccupied with the production of wealth, the church elected to adapt itself to the secular world by insisting on its own carefully delineated spiritual prerogatives. The Gregorian Reform movement, which established the bureaucracy of the Roman church as protection against secular power; the reformed religious orders with their revised description of spiritual life; and the ideology of the three orders of society, with its distribution of authority based on productive roles—all of these changes in church ideology were adaptations to a world that was being changed by the labor of human hands and the inventiveness of human minds. By the end of the twelfth century, this labor and its products were secularized, and the restoration of perfection was left to the mostly unknown men and women who were called to life in the world.

CHAPTER 6

Silent Workers: Craftsmen, Peasants, and Women

A S MANUAL LABOR and technology were secularized in the later Middle Ages, those for whom work was a way of life—that vast and mostly silent mass of men and women who produced the material goods that sustained, edified, and adorned medieval Europe—continued to make enormous progress in exploiting the land, in fashioning labor-saving devices, and in creating artistic monuments to the power of the *opus manuum*. What can be said about the status of manual labor, and the use of labor-saving technologies, among craftsmen and peasants? How did their world mesh with the picture of the world presented in the texts of the theoreticians, whose ample testimony leaves one with the sense that, whether as prayer or as penance, the labor of the hands remained an unattractive part of a life dedicated to higher ends? What was the role of women in the scheme of production that came to dominate European life in the later Middle Ages?

While the written record of Europe's educated elite suggests a certain ambivalence toward labor, its products, and its tools, until at least the twelfth century the church's official position was that the spiritual life of the individual Christian was enhanced by labor on three counts: first, labor helped to protect against the dangers of idleness; second, labor created opportunities for both charity and communal self-sufficiency; and third, labor was the means through which men exercised their stewardship over nature. Some writers dissented from one or another of these views, while others presented internally inconsistent arguments. For example, Augustine's prolabor arguments in *De opere monachorum* contradict the indifference to labor expressed in *De doctrina christiana*. I do not pretend that two clearly opposed and unambiguously described attitudes toward labor and technology can be extracted from the writings I have examined. Indeed, one of the clearest lessons to be drawn from a reconstruction of theologians' discussions of manual labor and the mechanical arts is that such activities were ambiguously placed within the hierarchy of medieval Christian values. God ennobled work by doing it himself;

God punished postlapsarian man by making him earn his bread in the sweat of his brow. Nature was intended for man's use; nature is to be cared for and emulated by man. Monks must labor with their hands; monks must be preoccupied with the *opus Dei*. Technical knowledge is a gift of God and a part of human wisdom; the mechanical arts are debased. Such ambivalent attitudes make every attempted generalization provisional. Yet this ambivalence is itself part of a general observation about labor and technology in the Middle Ages, namely, the observation that the "cultural climate" of the period was not nearly as favorable to the growth and development of Western technology as some writers have suggested. The fact that the theoreticians of medieval culture could maintain diverse and often contradictory attitudes toward those human activities we associate with technological progress suggests that their speculations were in good measure reactive rather than generative; that is, they wrote in response to changes in the "structures of everyday life" that were being created by others. I have suggested that by the twelfth century these changes became too great to ignore and that the creation of a new view of the classes and labors that make up society was undertaken. What remain in the shadows, however, are the men and women whose material labors provoked this reconstruction and secularization of labor.

In order to learn a little of these hidden lives, I will take up the question of the look and feel of the laborers' and craftsmen's world in the first part of this chapter; in the second part I will look specifically at the work of women and at the role their work played in the construction of the medieval world. In neither case can I offer more than an overview of the material that might be included in a reconstruction of the lives of the "people without history."[1]

We know, certainly, that an enormous gap separated the scholars who theorized about labor and the craftsmen, villeins, and serfs who actually worked. The size of this gap may be perceived in the following well-known text of Gervase of Canterbury:

> In the year 1174, by the . . . judgment of God, [the choir of] Christ Church at Canterbury was burned . . . for five years [the monks] remained in the nave of the Church in grief and sadness, divided from the layfolk by a long wall. In the meantime, the brother sought counsel how and by what means the burnt church might be repaired, but they were unsuccessful. The columns of the Church, ordinarily

termed the pillars, were so weakened by the great heat of the fire, with pieces falling off and hardly able to stand, that they put it beyond even the wisest to make any useful suggestions. So they called together both French and English architects, but they disagreed among themselves. Some said that they could repair these columns without risk to the upper part of the building; others, contradicting their arguments, said that the whole church must be pulled down if the monks wished to live in safety. It is not surprising that this view, though correct, shocked the monks, for they could hardly hope that in their days so great an undertaking might by completed by the ingenuity of man.[2]

Eventually, the monks of Canterbury retained William of Sens to undertake the reconstruction of the choir, a man who was "a very clever artist in wood and stone." William, who perceived exactly what he must do in order to repair the church, at first "avoided saying what would have to be done, in order not to shock [the monks] too severely in their enfeebled state of mind." In eight years time, the "ingenuity of man" in the person of William of Sens and his army of nameless masons, stonecutters, carpenters, haulers, and drudges (the latter group no doubt including some women), had reconstructed the church, much, we may imagine, to the astonishment and gratification of the skeptical and "enfeebled" monks.

There is a timeless quality to this famous story: men of God, contemplatives and scholars, at a loss when faced with a serious practical problem; enter the artisan-engineer who can survey the damage and prepare a rational plan for its repair that appears nothing short of miraculous. The culture implicit in Gervase of Canterbury's anecdote—a culture of laborers, craftsmen, and engineers—must surely have felt differently about the purpose and value of manual labor than the intellectuals whose writings have thus far concerned us.

Unfortunately, but not unexpectedly, few opinions on the status of manual labor and the mechanical arts written by workers survive. The reasons for this silence are not difficult to perceive. For one thing, most craftsmen and manual workers (male and female) were illiterate during the course of the Middle Ages—that is, they lacked the ability to read and write Latin. It was not until the sixteenth century that a significant body of technical literature written in the vernacular languages by and for workers and engineers began to appear in Europe. The work of Michael

Clanchy and M. B. Parkes on the question of lay literacy suggests that while some peasants may have been "pragmatically literate"—that is, able to decipher business documents and simple charters—they were not broadly familiar with Latin. Clanchy also describes the complex relations that existed between oral and written language during the later Middle Ages, for while many laborers and craftsmen might not be able to read or write Latin, they might have possessed the ability to understand the spoken language and might have had far more opportunities to listen to Latin than to read it.[3] None but the most affluent peasant would have been able to afford the high price of even the simplest book.[4] In any case, while peasants were aware of the value of literacy, as a bitter remark by Walter Mapes suggests (*"servi*, whom we call peasants [*rustici*], are eager to educate their ignominious and degenerate children in the [liberal] arts"), they had few opportunities to develop their language skills much beyond the minimum required for the fulfillment of ordinary religious and labor obligations.[5]

A second reason for the silence of laborers and craftsmen during the Middle Ages can be stated very briefly: craft skills continued to be associated with the menial functions of manual labor, and, as we have seen, while this labor was idealized by the members of the educated elite who discussed the ordering of monastic life, the fact remains that both labor and craftsmanship were thought to confer, and to possess, little value. Thus few details of the lives and contributions of laborers have survived from the Middle Ages, and much of our evidence for these lives is indirect and speculative.

In addition to the limitations placed on the recording and dissemination of laborers' attitudes by the narrowness of literate culture in the Middle Ages, it is also important to recall that the education of workers took place within a context defined by tradition and practice. A craftsman instructed his sons in the skills of his craft, and there was no need for any training beyond what could be offered on an informal and personal basis. The example of a mason's training and education can perhaps illustrate this point. A master mason would learn some Latin grammar and study some Latin literature in grammar and primary school—that is, if he was able to attend school at all. No mason would attend a university because no university taught anything remotely related to the building crafts.[6] Nor would any mason need to study any textbook or technical treatise relating to the performance of his craft; of the books available, only Vitruvius's *De architectura* would have been of value to a mason, but there is no evidence to suggest that this text was widely known to any audience during the Middle Ages.[7] Villard de Honnecourt's thirteenth-century book of drawings, including drawings of mechanical inventions and information on building techniques, was by no means thorough enough to have served as a handbook for a practicing mason.[8]

Furthermore, as the studies of Douglas Knoop and G. P. Jones suggest, this oral education probably began in the family, with a father or brother instructing a young man in the rudiments of the craft at the same time as the apprentice worked in an unskilled capacity. This informal mode of instruction did not involve indenture of the apprentice until at least the thirteenth century. Thus, oral instruction, supervised practice, and long years of "hands-on" training constituted the preparation of medieval masons and other craftsmen. The paucity of written documents about the labor of craftsmen is therefore attributable to the function of education as a means of preparing young men for careers in the church (and later in law and medicine), the attitudes of the educated elite toward those who worked with their hands, and the existence of informal networks of oral training in craft skills.

In order to reconstruct the attitudes of laborers and craftsmen toward the work they did, and in order to understand the role this labor played in the social and moral world of the Middle Ages, I would like to examine some of the evidence available to us for describing the roles of craftsmen, peasants, and women. Specific texts include a twelfth-century technical treatise and two documents composed for the guild of masons, which focus our attention on the attitudes of craftsmen toward their crafts; some literary texts that help us to reconstruct the lives of peasants; and, since the work of women has been most neglected, a variety of sources that reveal something of women's work in the Middle Ages.

THE LABOR OF CRAFTSMEN

One of the most important sources of information we have for the attitudes of craftsmen toward their labor is *De diversis artibus* of Theophilus. "Theophilus" was the pseudonym of a twelfth-century German Benedictine monk, and his book is a compendium of practical recipes for such crafts as paint making, metal casting, glazing, gold plating, machine design, and dozens of other specialized tasks associated with the creation of artworks intended for the ornamentation of churches.[9] While the contents of Theophilus's recipes and technical descriptions are intrinsically interesting, of greater importance for my purposes are the three prefaces that he appended to his discussions of specific crafts. Lynn White, Jr. has argued that Theophilus wrote these prefaces as a means of refuting Bernard of Clairvaux's charges against the ornamentation of churches, and one certainly should read *De diversis artibus* against the background of Cistercian attacks on the distracting beauty of gold-plated chalices and intricately colored windows. White has also argued, perhaps less convincingly, that Theophilus's defense of craftsmanship in the service of divine beauty should be taken as part of a wider twelfth-century "theology of labor, the earliest phase of a basic mutation in Europe's view of the relation between the theoretical and the practical."[10] The difficulty with this view, as I have argued in chapter 5, is that alongside of Theophilus's praise of craftwork and labor one must line up an enormous number of qualifications and objections that undermine the clarity of any twelfth-century "theology of labor." Indeed, the tone of Theophilus's prefaces suggests that the defenders of craftsmanship and labor were still embattled in the twelfth century and that objections to the kind of work Theophilus describes were made on grounds broader than the aesthetics of the liturgy.

In the first preface, Theophilus repeats the Benedictine argument for the utility of manual labor: through work one may slay "the sloth of mind and the wandering of the spirit." Labor occupies the hands, and it also creates new and beautiful objects. Theophilus's arguments for the value of manual labor and craftsmanship extend the Benedictine ideal at precisely this point: the products of work are both spiritual and physical, for while it is the duty of the monk or nun to be busy, it is the duty of all who have been created in God's image to exercise intelligence and skill in the various arts and thereby to participate in the creativity of God himself.

Theophilus does not hesitate to find pleasure as well as edification in craftsmanship. It is "sweet and delightful" to practice the various arts, and this pleasure may be communicated to others through the creation of beautiful objects.[11] For Theophilus, labor is clearly not penance; but, of course, he is writing about craftsmanship—bronze casting and painting glass—and not about hewing out a living from the soil. Theophilus's argument for the dignity of manual labor hinges on the observation that in using one's hands and head one is utilizing gifts given by God, so that the obligation to labor is implied by the ability to perform it. Such an argument, by looking at the post-subsistence products of the *opus manuum*, extends Hugh of Saint Victor's idea that work remedies bodily deficiencies by creating products specifically intended to praise the original Craftsman.

Theophilus also writes that, as the bearer of knowledge concerning the "diverse arts," he is obliged to communicate what he knows to others. "I, an unworthy human being, almost without a name, freely offer to all those who, in humility, desire to know that which God has given freely to me."[12] Those who, upon reading Theophilus's text and committing it to memory, are themselves drawn to "the useful occupation of the hands," must in turn enhance and pass on this freely given inheritance to others. In so doing, the student of Theophilus's book fulfills the author's purposes, the "giving of aid to man in his need" and the honoring of God. Theophilus describes the transmission of the knowledge he has laboriously acquired in terms that approximate the brotherly and corporatist educational methods of the guilds, and he makes it clear that this craft knowledge exists not for individual profit but for the betterment of the Christian community as a whole.

Theophilus also tells his readers that his own initiation into the diverse arts, while initially stimulated by the desire to avoid sloth and to cultivate God-given reason, was sustained by laborious experiment and practice:

"But rather let him labor, working with his hands the thing which is good, that he may have to give to him that needeth." Therefore, longing to be an imitator of this man, I drew near to the forecourt of holy Wisdom, and I saw the sanctuary filled with a variety of all kinds of differing colors, displaying the utility and nature of each pigment. I entered it unseen and immediately filled the storeroom of my heart fully with all these things. I examined them one by one with careful experiment, testing them all by eye and by hand, and I have committed them to you in clarity and without envy for your study.[13]

The mixing in this account of transcendental and empirical forms of knowledge—measuring the utility of that which is found in the "forecourt of holy Wisdom"—may strike the modern reader as yet another proof of the confusions obfuscating medieval approaches to practical knowledge. Yet I would prefer to see in this brief passage a paradigmatic description of precisely the way medieval technology came to grow. There can be no doubt that Theophilus did handle the materials he describes so well, and that he was well versed in such complex crafts as glazing and casting. Nor is the accuracy or usefulness of the techniques he describes in doubt. What we may not understand is that these practical matters—tested, observed, and passed on by a twelfth-century monk—were derived from the contemplation of divine wisdom and pursued for the glory of God and the perfection of the self. These medieval notions, which we moderns have reified into "R and D" and "profits," define an alternative technology that is itself a tool for clarifying the complex relations between the individual soul, the natural world, and the Creator. That Theophilus envisioned labor's products in this way is clear from his description of the "seven-fold Spirit" of labor:

> Through the spirit of wisdom you know that created things proceed from God and that without Him nothing is.

> Through the spirit of understanding, you have received the capacity for practical knowledge of the order, the variety, and the measure that you apply to your various kinds of work.

> Through the spirit of counsel you do not hide away the talent given you by God, but, working and teaching openly and with humility, you faithfully reveal it to those who desire to learn.

> Through the spirit of fortitude you shake off all the apathy of sloth, and whatever you commence with quick enthusiasm you carry through to completion with full vigor.

> Through the spirit of knowledge that is given to you, you are the master by virtue of your practical knowledge and you use in public the perfect abundance of your abounding heart with the confidence of a full mind.

> Through the spirit of piety you set a limit with pious consideration on what the work is to be, and for whom, as well as on the time, the amount, and the quality of work, and, lest the vice of greed or cupidity should set in, on the amount of the recompense.

> Through the spirit of the fear of the Lord you bear in mind that of yourself you are nothing able and you ponder on the fact that you possess and desire nothing that is not given to you by God, but in faith,

trust, and thankfulness you ascribe to divine compassion whatever you know or are or can be.[14]

One may detect in this craftsman's credo many of the strands of thought discussed in previous chapters of this book. Theophilus asserts the craftsman's belief in the primacy of God's creative act; in the importance of labor as a means of self-perfection; in the usefulness of labor as a antidote to sloth; in the social utility of constructive crafts; in the concern for retaining pure motives when confronted by monetary rewards; and in the ultimate purpose of labor as a means of recognizing personal spiritual goals. The craftsman so described may surely be creative and open to the possibility of technical innovation, but only insofar as creativity and innovation further spiritual goals that are primary.

While it is true that Theophilus, as a monk, might be expected to express such a view of labor and craftsmanship, similar sentiments may be found in the secular masonic poem contained in the Cooke manuscript.[15] This fourteenth-century poem, written to provide masons with a history of their craft and with a survey of the guild's rules and rituals, begins with an argument for the divine origins of useful objects: "Thonkyd be god / our glorious /Fadir and foun-/ der and former of heuen / and of erthe. and of alle. / thyngis that in hym is / that he wolde fochesaue of / his glorious God-hed for to / make so mony thyngis of di / uers vertu for mankynd" (lines 1–10). This invocation notes God's production of useful things for mankind; the next lines develop this idea by evoking the theme of human sovereignty through the practice of crafts and labor:

> For he made alle thyngis for / to be abedient & soget to man / For alle thyngis that ben comes- / tible of holsome nature he / ordeyned hit for manys susty- / nauns. And all-so he hath yif / to man wittys and connynge / of dyuers thyngys and craf- / tys by the whiche we may / trauayle in this worlde to / gete with our lyuyng to make / diuers thingys to goddis ple- / sens [glory] and al-so for our ese and / profyt. (lines 11–24)

The "diverse things" created by the labor of human beings are a form of praise as well as a source of "ease and profit" because, as Theophilus noted, these things are born of human wit just as surely as any other product of the human world. One may see in this description of labor and crafts a defense of the spiritual values of menial occupations, and, in the face of the scholars' qualified admission of the value of labor for some classes of men, a demonstration of the divine sanction given to the works of the hands.

In the case of the masonic poem, the argument for the value of labor goes further than Theophilus does, in that the poet demonstrates that masonry is founded on the scientific principles of geometry, the ultimate science: "Mervile ye not that I/seyd that alle sciens lyuen/alle only by the sciens of Geme-/try. For there is none artifici-/alle ne hond-craft that is wro3the/by manys hond bot hit is / wrou3ght by Gemetry" (lines 100–105). All work done with the hands is done with tools, and all tools are designed according to the rules of geometric proportions, "and propor-cion is mesure / the tole er the instrument is erthe. / And Gemetry is said the mesure of erthe where- / fore I may sey that men lyuen / all by Gemetrye. For alle / men here in this worlde lyre / by the laboure of here hondys" (lines 117–126). Of course, the last clause is literally untrue— neither the clerics, who would have argued that theology rather than geometry is the ultimate science, nor the nobles, whose hands never knew work, would have agreed that "all men live by the labor of their hands." But in a figurative sense the assertion is quite true, because what the poet is really saying is that to be human is to work, for this is the consequence of the Fall. In this attempt to recount the anthropology of human work, that is, to connect labor with human origins and divine intentions, the social realities of class and exploitation are irrelevant. All human beings must work in order to live; that some do not should not lessen the value placed on the contributions of those who do.

PEASANT LABOR

In attempting to recapture the feeling of medieval labor, and especially in attempting to locate some expression of the lives of those who actually worked at maintaining medieval society, one is drawn to a variety of sources. Iconography can be an especially rich source of information in this regard, since late-medieval manuscripts—books of hours, medical texts, and literary works especially—are often illustrated with scenes of peasant's and craftsmen's labor. The Index of Christian Art is a particu-larly rich source for illustrations depicting medieval labor and craftsman-ship.[16] Likewise, texts that are chosen for illustration can provide us with glimpses into the lives and the labor of the men and women whose personal histories are otherwise lost. Thus, for example, the *Roman de la Rose,* a thirteenth-century romance often copied and often amply illustrated, provides us with a description of a wall constructed with "mortar mixed of lime and vinegar" that is strong enough to withstand the shock of ballistas, arbalests, or any other instrument of warfare. This structure is designed by "A master mason of such handicraft / . . . no better keep could ever be." An illustration of this passage in one manuscript shows workmen armed with shovel and pick digging a moat, while Jealousy—looking rather like a master mason—stands nearby.[17] This text also celebrates the craft of stonecarvers (in the story of Pygmalion) and condemns the laziness and ineptitude of monks and friars—a condemnation that one may find in fully developed form in Chaucer's Parson's Tale.[18]

Other medieval texts, which one would perhaps be most inclined to read for their depiction of chivalry, courtly love, or bawdy humor, also yield details of the lives of men and women who, because of their social status, are peripheral to the story but who fill the background against which the story unfolds. Coarse peasants hacking at clods of earth give directions to Arthurian knights, while women, endlessly spinning woolen thread or embroidering their lord's garments, are the object of noble infatuations and valient rescue attempts. Since most medieval literature is concerned with the lives of the rich, highborn, and privileged, the picture of peasant culture that occasionally intrudes on the narratives is scanty and unsympathetic: Chrétien de Troyes refers to "the rough and vulgar crowd," contrasting unruly country folks to courtly knights and damsels.[19] Poor people are physically grotesque and appear only as a means to advance the mindless wanderings and incessant warfare of the more glamorous men at the center of the tale. When Lancelot needs to find his lady the queen and is without a horse he stops a cart—a symbol of shame—and asks the "miserable and low born dwarf" who drives it for directions. Like all churlish dwarfs, this one refuses to answer, and instead invites Lancelot to debase himself by riding on the cart. For the order of knights and the order of religious men, no shame was greater than this descent down the hierarchy of class and occupation.[20]

Peasants are sometimes compared to animals. Thus Andreas Capellanus's influential *De arte honeste amandi,* composed late in the twelfth century, describes the love of peasants in this way: "We say that it rarely happens that we find farmers serving in Love's court, but naturally, like a horse or a mule, they give themselves up to the work of Venus, as nature's urging teaches them to do. For a farmer hard labor and the uninterrupted solaces of plough and mattock are sufficient."[21] Any man of the middle classes or aristocracy may freely partake of the dubious pleasures of peasant women; Andreas's advice is to be direct and "embrace them by force," for rape effectively cures a lowborn woman's shyness. Whether he was being ironic or not, Andreas's discussion of the rituals of twelfth-century love reveals something about the status of peasants in high medieval culture.

Saints' lives also contain information on labor, though for the most part hagiography concerned itself with the careers of men and women of noble birth. Thus the life of St. Bernwald (died 1022), chaplin to Emperor Otto III and bishop of Hildesheim, demonstrates the interest of an influential churchman in metalworking, painting, and glazing.[22] William of Hirschau (died 1091), a founder of the institution of the lay brotherhood, was also a skillful craftsman, though William's interests ran more to astronomy and clockwork.[23] However, Bernwald's and William's interest in labor and craftwork was unusual; more typical, especially after the twelfth century, was the attitude of St. Philip Benizi (died 1285), a pious and energetic man, propagator of the Servite order in Italy, who debased himself by becoming a lay brother at St. Buonfiglio and working with his hands.[24] A great number of saints were born into wealthy families, had a conversion experience, divested themselves of all their property, and then lived lives of extreme asceticism—often as hermits or beggars. Indeed, in the hagiographic literature, sanctity attaches itself to mendicancy more often than to labor. When Elizabeth the Good (died 1420), a Franciscan tertiary, was apprenticed to a poor woman weaver, it was clear enough to her biographer that she had willingly endured an unenviable fate.

Not all literary sources ignore the poor and despised worker, however. A poem in MS Landsdowne 762, though late (circa 1500), reflects the timeless predicament of those who labored, especially those who labored on the land.[25] The narrator of this short poem walks over a field and sees husbandmen at work plowing and sowing "the londe that was so tough." A husbandman replies that it is needful to pray that "God spede wele the plough" for "all the yere we labour with the [lande] / With many a comberous clot of [claye], / To mayntayne this world yf that we may" (lines 11–13). The need to ask God's help is made all the more imperative because of the many exactions faced by those who plow and sow and reap; kings (who pay for their exactions with blows), lords, parsons (who extract a "tithe shefe of the lande"), friars, monks, "poore obserua-untes," summoners, priests, and scholars all claim their share of the fruits of the husbandman's labor. Indeed, the poem shows the whole hierarchical structure of medieval society—from kings and priests to prisoners and minstrels—demanding sustenance from those who struggle with the land (lines 17ff.). Religious obligations, royal prerogatives, legal charters, and simple charity are combined to create a compelling rationale for extracting the products of peasant labor. The husbandmen, "And all tho that laboreth with the londe, / And them that helpeth them with worde or dede" are blessed by the narrator, praised for their clear consciences, and commended to their just reward in heaven—certainly the only solace for those whose lives were indelibly bound to a social system that despised the labor (and the laborers) that sustained it.

The most fully developed literary expression of the hidden lives of peasants is William Langland's *Piers Plowman*—an enormously complex allegorical poem of the fourteenth century.[26] One of this work's main themes is that the search for truth, for forgiveness, and for redemption is not personal but social; men and women struggle together through the burdens of labor and injustice to discover a higher form of life.[27] Langland's allegory incorporates the idea of the interrelated orders of society; society is the product of each order's attempt to discover the form of spiritual perfection appropriate to it.

The poem begins with the narrator's dream of "A faire felde ful of folke . . . alle maner of men the mene and the riche, / Worchyng and wandryng   as the worlde asketh." Life in the world demands work of all kinds: "Somme putten hem to the plow   pleyed ful selde / In settyng and in sowyng   swonken [labored] ful harde." What some men and women labor to produce, others—the "wastours"—destroy through their gluttony. Langland thought that the world was out of balance: peasants were obliged to fulfill their social duties, but the other orders of society—the priests and friars, monks and knights—failed to fulfill theirs. "Alle the foure ordres" of religious preached for their own profit and neglected both their own souls and the souls of the poor men who could not pay for the comforts of religion. Langland's revolutionary fervor was diffused in *Piers Plowman* into millennialism: the end of history would bring with it a renewal of social justice and a regeneration of those who do the world's work. When the world ends in revolution, the plowman, along with all those who labor, will at long last emerge from the silence of history.

WOMEN'S WORK IN THE EARLY MIDDLE AGES

The situation of women laborers in the Middle Ages is complex enough to warrant special treatment, particularly since I detect in the history of women themes that illuminate the general history of medieval labor and its cultural climate.

First of all, the persistence of myths about "women's work" is astonishing. In her book *Labor of Love, Labor of Sorrow*, Jacqueline Jones shows that black women living in the rural South after their "emancipation" continued to be regarded by their white male bosses (who were often their former overseers) as lazy, unreliable, untrainable, impractical, and promiscuous. While black women felt that the primary purpose of their menial occupations should be the sustenance and improvement of their families and communities, their former masters and the government bureaucrats sent to help them adjust to freedom felt that a far more profound loyalty should bind these women to their employer and to the economic unit—farm or factory—for which they toiled. While these women were valued as workers and as bearers of children, they had no value as human beings, as wives, or as members of a community. Their "rights," circumscribed to begin with in a world of mostly racist men, were protected only insofar as they had a bearing on the women's ability to be productive. Jones's narrative shows these unknown women struggling to create a better life for themselves and for their families within the context of an economic freedom that was little better than slavery.[28]

Apart from the crucial element of racial prejudice, Jones's eloquent description of the labor of black women and of the myths that kept them isolated from economic and political power might be taken to describe the condition of women laborers during the Middle Ages. In medieval Europe, as in post-Civil War America, women's work was indispensable to the domestic economy; yet, in both cases, the workers themselves were denied social and political status. The invisibility of women during the Middle Ages is trebled by the circumstances of their lives: they lived in a remote age, separate from our own in almost every way; they lived as laborers and were therefore as mute as their male coworkers; and finally, being women, they lived their lives at the very bottom of the hierarchy of human beings. It is no wonder that the reconstruction of their lives has proved a difficult task.

The position of women during the early Middle Ages was largely a continuation of their position during the later Roman Empire. As Sarah Pomeroy has shown, during the Roman Republic women were regarded as "perpetual minors" (*alieni iuris*) who lived under the authority of their husbands, fathers, or elder brothers. When Emperor Augustus exempted women who had borne three children from the restrictions of this subservient legal status, he was merely acknowledging what had long been the case—that a woman's value could be precisely measured on three axes: the ability to bear children, the ability to satisfy men's sexual needs, and the ability to perform domestic labor. Only after fulfilling her biological debt to the state could a woman inherit property or seek the protection of Roman law.[29]

During the imperial period, women who had reached the age of twenty-five could control their own property; before that age they were entitled to inherit equal shares of property with their male relatives and to give their consent to a marriage, they were, in fact, subject in every way to the will of their male guardians. Furthermore, the late empire institutionalized a sexual double standard that allowed men to enter into adulterous relationships without penalty but that penalized women for the same behavior; a woman convicted of adultery lost half her dowry and was exiled.[30] Men, meanwhile, could be divorced for their adulterous relationships only with women of their own social class—hence the Roman male penchant for liaisons with slaves and freedwomen, a form of recreational sex that carried with it no penalty whatsoever. Of course, the servile and slave women who were the objects of this amorous attention could not be legally married, so that, in effect, every woman who was not free was potentially a concubine.

With the coming of the Germanic tribes and the gradual adoption of Christianity, the role of women improved, but only temporarily and only within limited social contexts. Tacitus's description of the structure of the Germanic family accords women (wives and daughters) an important economic role as well as a degree of respect nowhere found in the late empire. In particular, a woman's reproductive function was critical in a culture whose expansionism required constant reinforcements, and whose disdain of manual labor required strong female backs and skillful female hands. Indeed, a woman's *wergild* or "life price" was twice that of a man's, and, as Tacitus tells us, a woman's advice was often heeded in male counsels: "They even believe that the sex has a certain sanctity and prescience."[31]

The "aboriginal" tribes of Germanic men appear loutish in Tacitus's account; when they are not engaged in warfare and rapine, they either hunt or "lie buried in sloth, a strange combination in their nature that the same men should be so fond of idleness, so averse to peace." But the combination appears less perplexing when one realizes that in their women they possessed an efficient work force, so that they were free to pursue full-time the masculine dream of domination, tainted by physical risk, but elevated above every mundane concern.

The Germanic family seems praiseworthy to Tacitus, perhaps because it existed in such stark contrast to the loose alliances fashionable in the late empire. The mostly monogamous Germanic family begins with equal exchanges of gifts between the man and the woman, and the ritual of espousal ends with the woman's acceptance of her equal partnership in toil and danger. Tacitus writes that adultery was not tolerated by the Germanic tribes, and this surely seems a piece of social criticism on his part. This alleged fidelity was later held up by the National Socialists as a salubrious model of Aryan purity.[32] In any case, the role of women in Germanic society was narrowly circumscribed by their reproductive functions, by the perpetuation of sexual double standards (a Germanic husband could have more than one wife), and by the attitude of Germanic men toward manual labor.

Similarly, early Christianity did not fulfill the promise of equality between the sexes promised either by the scriptural tradition or by the first generations of its social practice. By insisting on the sanctity of monogamous and binding marriage, and by finding in women the same potential sanctity to be found in men, Christianity allowed women to perceive themselves in new ways. St. Paul's seemingly unambiguous insistence on the spiritual value of both men and women seemed likewise to promise women a status they had not previously enjoyed. The spiritual equality expressed in Galatians 3:28 ("There is neither Jew nor Greek: there is neither bond nor free: there is neither male nor female. For you are all one in Christ Jesus") may have given women converts the hope that Christianity, as one among many religions available to the men and women in the "age of anxiety," would offer a source of social and spiritual hope. Women died as martyrs and fled to religious communities in the Egyptian desert; they also formed the nucleus of the new faith's adherents, as the circle of Jerome and the life of Augustine illustrate.[33]

Yet the hope of equality offered by Christianity was quickly withdrawn. The hermaphroditic God implied by Genesis 1:26–27 ("And God created man in the image of himself: in the image of God he created him, male and female he created them") became God the Father, and beginning with Tertullian and continuing through Augustine, Jerome, Ambrose, and Gregory the Great, antifeminism and outright misogyny displaced the democracy of genderless souls. By the third century, women were denied the right to preach or to hold any office in the church but the diaconate; by the fourth century, ecclesiastical prohibitions on sexual intercourse institutionalized the dread of women expressed in a work like Tertullian's *On the Apparel of Women*.[34]

In this work, Tertullian warns women not to be an occasion of sin; a beautiful woman, in particular, must try to subdue rather than enhance her beauty. The only person a woman must please is her husband, and since "every husband demands that his wife be chaste," he is not likely to want his wife to be attractive to others. Any form of personal adornment appears to Tertullian to be the work of the devil; God has made all creatures as beautiful as they should be, and for a woman to paint her face or wear attractive clothing is a form of "adultery in appearance." Tertullian characterizes the mutual attraction of the sexes as "a defect of nature," and he warns both men and women that even the desire to please each other is a form of lasciviousness. In a very interesting passage, Tertullian reveals that while it was God who taught men how to dye wool, it was the fallen angels who introduced artistic skills and elaborate workmanship. Since these angels were condemned by God, one may fairly assume that their idolatrous abilities are to be condemned as well. Tertullian thereby turns his condemnation of women's attractiveness into a general condemnation of any alteration of the natural or human world: "These condemned angels revealed well-hidden substances and numerous arts that were only partially revealed, for it was these fallen angels who showed an ignorant age the secrets of metallurgy, the natural properties of herbs, the power of charms, and, indeed, who looked into everything, including the powers of the stars. Then they granted to women the special abilities of feminine vanity." Women are copartners with the fallen angels in revealing the secrets of technology, and they share with devils a blasphemous curiosity, which probes the hidden secrets of nature for the purpose of modifying what is intrinsically good. This association of women with the forbidden arts and with a technology that threatens the natural order of the world was subsumed into the literature of magic and witchcraft.[35] In view of the dangers women represent, they must "bow their heads to their husbands" (Tertullian cites Ephesians 5:22–23) and remain at home, "busy with spinning," chaste, and out of the eyes of men. For "the curse of God on this [female] sex continues even into our own time, and so it is necessary that their guilt live on as well; for it was [a woman] who first deserted the divine law, plucked the forbidden fruit, and opened the door to the devil. It was you who destroyed man, made in the image of God."[36]

Tertullian's text illustrates the problem faced by theologians who would banish women from the eyes of men, for how could this removal of women be accomplished without the loss of their economic and reproductive value? The institution of celibacy as a requirement of the religious life was one way, for it had the effect of taking from women the status they had gained as bearers of children. Women who wished to live a religious life had to renounce their reproductive function and enter a world whose rules of work and prayer were set by men and whose structure denied them any access to spiritual power. Since women could neither preach nor be priests, they could merely serve as chaste recipients of a faith preserved and distributed by men.

At the Council of Elvira, convened in 309 as a means of asserting the authority of the bishops of Spain at a moment that saw the transformation of ancient Christianity from a sectarian to an imperial religion, one of the primary issues addressed was that of the relation between "power and sexuality."[37] Nearly half of the eighty-one canons drawn up at Elvira deal with sexuality and with the rights, or rather limitations on the rights, of women. Central to the canons is the circumscription of sexual transgressions, especially the elimination of sexual intercourse from clerical marriages. In asserting that "Bishops, presbyters, and deacons and all other clerics having a position in the ministry are ordered to abstain completely from their wives and not to have children," the council made explicit the essential difference between those called to the religious life and everyone else. As Georges Duby has noted, the denial of the flesh was not a means of controlling the clergy but of extending their power over the concupiscent laity.[38]

The penitential handbooks—which served as guides to confessors by providing discussions of various sins and the penances appropriate to them—reflect the same attitudes toward women. The only legitimate use of sexuality, as formulated by Augustine and repeated throughout the Middle Ages, was procreation. Handbooks of penance composed in Ireland and England from the sixth to the ninth centuries severely limit the number of occasions on which a husband and a wife may have intercourse: forbidden periods include the forty days preceding Christmas and Easter and following Pentecost; Saturdays and Sundays (in preparation for Communion); and Wednesdays and Fridays (traditional days of penance). Indeed, St. Paul's recommendation that even married couples refrain from sexual relations, and his suggestion that unmarried men and women as well as widows remain chaste (1 Corinthians 7:1–9), become in some of the pentitentials an implicit suggestion that married men and women avoid intercourse if at all possible.[39] Also included are taboos on intercourse during the menstrual period, during pregnancy, and for a fixed period after childbirth—though it is important to note that there is considerable variation within the penitential tradition regarding the exact times of required abstinence. While some of the handbooks of penance also circumscribe women's access to the church and its sacraments—perhaps following purification traditions outlined in Leviticus—other sources, including Pope Gregory the Great's letter to Augustine of Canterbury, reproduced in book 1 of Bede's *Ecclesiastical History,* are more lenient toward women.[40]

Furthermore, the canons of Elvira and of other councils specify the limited sphere that women could occupy within the church, both by eliminating them from any clerical office and by emphasizing that the real danger posed to the religious man is female sexuality; indeed, as Payer remarks, "the Christian theologian was as much ashamed to be a bodily man as was the Neoplatonic philosopher a century before him." This rejection of sexuality evoked "narcissistic reactions" in the various spiritual movements that arose during the last centuries of the Roman Empire. All of these movements—Neoplatonism, Manichaeism, Gnosticism, Montanism—preached the rejection of sexuality, and they all had in common the provision of "an escape from direct, concrete relationships" between men and women "by creating a metaphysical abstraction, by objectifying and spiritualizing sexual language, or by treating women as if they were asexual or in a presexual stage of life." Yet despite these provisions of the early church that were designed to remove women from any active involvement in its affairs, women were nonetheless central to the economic and social life of Christian Europe.

Women in the early Middle Ages exercised control over the "inner economy" of their households. Furthermore, while men were engaged in warfare, women oversaw their husbands' property and attended to its "outer economy" as well. Women whose husbands were killed in battle appear in charters as heads of families and managers of estates.[41] Economically, the principal function of Merovingian and Carolingian women was the maintenance of the household, but one must be careful not to conceive of this "huswifery" in too narrow a sense. Duties of the "inner economy" included baking, brewing, animal husbandry, water portage, home repairs, and the cultivation of small plots of land. The maintenance of a household thus presumed that a woman could practice a wide variety of tasks associated with an agrarian economy, some of which required the cultivation of craft skills. This labor was punctuated by frequent childbearing and often terminated, despite the perceptions of clerical writers, by early death; indeed, the shortened lives of laboring women led to the institution of male dowries during the early Middle Ages.[42]

As the nonagricultural sector of the medieval economy began to expand in the ninth and tenth centuries, the emergence of domestic industries—especially the cloth industry—improved somewhat the prospects for laboring women. Spinning and sewing—the tasks most consistently associated with "women's work" in the Middle Ages—freed some women from agricultural drudgery. The etymological connection of the Anglo-Saxon words *weras* and *wifas* with "weaving" suggests the depth of this association, while the fact that women working in the domestic cloth industry had to master the various tools of their trade—spindles, distaffs, reels, shears, and combs—indicates the extent to which the growing cloth industry drew women into the mainstream of the medieval craft traditions.[43] Of course, it must be recalled that not all women labored at the same tasks; while the tedium of spinning and weaving cloth fell to poorer women, the finishing of expensive cloth was the work of those who were not necessarily obliged to work at all. The economic status of women throughout the Middle Ages was as much a matter of class as of gender, although it remains true that all women had their economic and political autonomy circumscribed in a male-dominated world.

Nowhere is this circumscription clearer than in the church. During the Carolingian period, women's roles in the life of the religious community shifted drastically and in unexpected ways. Thus, when Charlemagne's son Louis the Pious made divorce illegal and argued for the indissolubility of marriage, he protected some women from the contingencies of the sexual double standard that had been the norm in the late classical and

Merovingian periods. Yet, this legislation also permitted fewer women access to men and to the economic power that they possessed. Thus a far greater number of women were left unmarried and drawn into the religious life. At the same time, the Frankish clergy narrowed the role of women within the church by reinforcing the male-dominated hierarchy and by removing women from their local functions in the diaconate.[44] Within the church, women continued to be undervalued, mere supernumeraries of male priests and monks, the subject of sexually biased canons and the rich patristic tradition of misogynist attack. Furthermore, as we learn from various letters written by Boniface to two Northumbrian kings during an earlier period, women in monastic establishments were subject to sexual harassment and attack, though Boniface is inclined to blame "loose women" as much as immoral men for these distasteful episodes.[45]

One of the few sympathetic voices of support for women and for women's roles in the early church was that of Caesarius of Arles. His sermons reveal a great deal about the kinds of attacks that were being made on women during the Carolingian period, and his Rule for nuns shows us something of the lives lived by religious women during the early Middle Ages.

In his sermons, Caesarius (470–543) took up the whole range of topics treated in the pedagogical traditions of the early church: there are sermons on the lives of the saints, on Scripture, on moral questions, and on the duties of monks. In his sermons on the moral obligations of Christians, Caesarius denies the sexual double standard that had bound women to fidelity but permitted men to take concubines: "Whatever is unlawful for women is likewise unlawful for men," Caesarius writes, and he goes on to say that men and women should both endeavor to be chaste before marriage and, once married, only to have intercourse when there is a desire for children.[46] Unlike Tertullian, Caesarius does not blame women for the sexual transgressions of men; indeed, he strongly condemns the male concupiscence that leads bachelors, husbands, soldiers, and traveling merchants to take up with slaves, prostitutes, and concubines. At the same time, he repeats Old Testament admonitions against intercourse with a woman who is menstruating or pregnant; he also warns that children conceived on a Sunday will be born as lepers, epileptics, or demons.[47] Women are warned not to seek out medical remedies for sterility, or to attempt to abort unwanted children: "If a woman does not wish to bear children, she should enter into an agreement with her husband, for only abstinence is chastity."[48] Yet in Caesarius's account, the victim of sexual transgressions is the man or woman who sins, not, as in Tertullian, the (male) human race as a whole; women are not singled out for their weakness or for their role in destroying men's holiness. The broad brush of concupiscence touches everyone in Caesarius's sermons—men and women, priests, noblemen, slaves, soldiers, and merchants. While the archetypical woman for Tertullian is Eve, for Caesarius she is Mary.[49]

In his Rule for nuns, written first in 512 and then revised for the community of nuns at Arles in 534, Caesarius shows a degree of concern for the religious life of women shared by few of his contemporaries. His Rule was based on a text he had composed for monks, the various Rules of St. Augustine, and the writings of John Cassian. In his text, Caesarius says that he will take into account the fact that monasteries of women differ from those of monks, yet much of what he writes is identical to what one finds in the various Rules for monks.

Thus no woman may choose her own manual labor but must submit to the wishes of her superior; food and drink are to be apportioned to each nun's bodily needs and according to her labor; the daily "wool work" is to be performed with humility and devotion, but without expecting or taking any reward other than that granted to the whole community. All of the nuns must learn how to read; while engaged in communal labor, one of the nuns shall read a lesson aloud for the edification of her sisters.[50] The principal form of manual labor as described by Caesarius was in the manufacture of cloth and clothing. Other forms of labor, such as repairs to the monastery buildings and grounds, were to be entrusted to skilled workmen and slaves, but only with the permission and under the supervision of the mother superior; Caesarius was aware of the temptations incited by the presence of men, and he reminded his readers of these dangers and of the steps needed to attenuate them.[51] Likewise, the nuns must not dye any of their clothing, wear embroidered garments, or furnish their sleeping quarters with any but the most simple provisions. Because Caesarius had provided for the financial self-sufficiency of the monastery at Arles through a permanent endowment, the labor of the nuns in the wool trade was supplemental, and the obligation to perform other types of sustaining work did not interfere with the nuns' devotions. Indeed, the description of the Divine Office to be recited by the nuns leaves little doubt that worship left little time for any other occupation.[52] Still, the framework and model created by Caesarius made possible the existence of communities of women who could live together in moderate physical safety, with communal support, and, once free of the demands of men and childbearing, in pursuit of personal spiritual goals. Few women in any stratum of early medieval society enjoyed similar opportunities.

The influence of Caesarius's Rule may be traced through the intervening years to the life of St. Radegund (died 587), whose famous letter to the bishops of Gaul describes the lives of both Merovingian and Carolingian nuns:

> Some time ago, when I found myself freed from earthly cares, with Divine Providence and with God's grace to inspire me, I turned of my own volition, under Christ's guidance, to the religious life. I asked myself, with all the ardour of which I am capable, how I could best forward the cause of other women, and how, if our Lord so willed, my own personal desire might be of advantage to my sisters. Here in the town of Poitiers I founded a convent for nuns. Lothar, my lord and King of glorious memory, instituted this and was its benefactor. When it was founded, I made over to it by deed of gift all the property which the King in his munificence had bestowed upon me. For the community which, with Christ to help me, I had myself assembled, I accepted the Rule in accordance with which Saint Caesaria [sister of Caesarius of Arles] had lived, and which in his loving care Saint Caesarius had drawn up from the writings of the holy Fathers to suit her very needs. . . . The other nuns and I followed the example of the Apostles in making over to her [the Mother Superior] by deed whatever earthly property we possessed at the moment we entered the nunnery, reserving nothing at all for ourselves.[53]

St. Radegund's letter was a plea for protection and for the continued observation of the promises of maintenance originally made by King Lothar. "May it never be allowed to come about that our Mother Superior . . . shall be molested or harassed by any man, or that anything pertaining to this nunnery should in any wise be alienated or changed": only the "Defender of the poor" and the "Husband of all nuns" can assure that Radegund's petition would be granted, for like all medieval women she lived in the perilously narrow space accorded the supplicant.

The existence of the nunnery as a refuge from the world that offered women few options could only be assured by men, with their grants of land, money, and protection.

In the life of St. Macrina, written by Gregory of Nyssa, another aspect of women's lives is clearly illustrated. The beautiful and intelligent Macrina was taught to recite the Psalms (also to avoid the temptations of secular literature) and to be skillful in working wool. When the suitor chosen for Macrina died, the young girl expressed the wish to remain unmarried; to insure that her wish was respected, she attached herself to the protection of her mother. The young virgin shared all of her widowed mother's woes, which included the management of her properties. Eventually Macrina persuaded her mother to abandon her wealth and servants in order to live together with her maids "as sisters and equals." Gregory describes the feminine communal life that resulted from this decision of Macrina and her mother as a perfect life, divorced from all envy, anger, and vanity. All the women remained chaste and detached from material concerns; "prayer was their only labor," though Macrina is also described as working ceaselessly with her hands and never taking anything from any man. Macrina's pious life and tranquil death embody an idealized Christian life—as seen through the eyes of a man. Like Radegund, Macrina left the world of men behind and sought comfort in the company of other women; only their wealth and the protection of men allowed these women to pursue this form of life in a world made by men.[54]

WOMEN'S WORK IN THE LATER MIDDLE AGES

Generally speaking, while from the eleventh through the fourteenth centuries the economic position of women improved, their social status remained unchanged. The gradual diversification of the medieval economy and the emergence of nonagricultural forms of labor offered working men and women opportunities denied them in a purely rural environment. While peasant women continued to perform the kinds of labor that had always defined agrarian life—plowing and planting, reaping and gleaning, husbandry, food preparation, and child care—townswomen often worked for their craftsman-husbands or as independent craftswomen in various parts of the textile industry but also in brewing, baking, small-scale metalwork (the manufacture of needles), net making, shoemaking, bookbinding, goldsmithing, butchering, candlemaking and, occasionally, as merchants, copyists, and moneylenders. While women were generally excluded from certain occupations, especially the highly skilled building crafts and some of the specialized textile crafts, overall they were well represented in the craft guilds. Indeed, a reading of medieval English guild regulations reveals that many thirteenth- through fifteenth-century guilds had women as members—often as founding members—but that women did not hold offices within these organizations, did not receive equal pay for their labors, and were often prohibited from training apprentices.[55] In 1297, the fullers of Lincoln were forbidden to work with any women but their wives; at Norwich, women were represented in the barbers guild but held no offices in the organization. Yet, despite these exclusions, the craft guilds, conceived as sources of mutual aid and expressions of corporate life within the towns, provided a model of communal harmony based on the division of labor. Aquinas expressed the communal ideal in this way: "It is natural to man that he live in partnership with many. . . . It is therefore necessary, if man is to live in association, that one should be helped by another, and that different people should be occupied in discovering different things through reason."[56] Unfortunately, this communal ideal was not powerful enough to displace gender stereotypes or antidemocratic sentiments; Marsiglio of Padua's idea of a society based on the guild principles of mutual aid and communal cooperation had no influence on contemporary politics.[57]

During the later Middle Ages, "women's work" was broadly defined, but its definition centered on crafts that were domestic rather than professional. Women worked for their husbands and learned trades from their brothers and fathers; if they were single or widowed they could practice their craft under the same regulations as a man.[58] Yet women could not easily labor in highly specialized trades like medicine; they were permitted to be midwives, and they also worked as barbers and surgeons.[59] Once medicine became an academic subject in the thirteenth century, however, women were generally excluded from advancing to the highest stage in the healing profession. Likewise, in other crafts that were deemed highly skilled, or which necessitated the separation of a woman from her domestic duties, exclusionary rules were employed to insure male control. Women's work in the Middle Ages was largely supplementary; the wives of guildsmen worked for their husbands; poor women worked alongside their husbands in the fields or in the cloth and food trades; widows assumed the responsibilities of their husbands in many of the craft guilds, while unmarried women entered nunneries if they were relatively well off and became shopkeepers or laborers if they were not.

In the later Middle Ages, as now, women were largely a part of the "shadow economy" that existed alongside the male-dominated institutional economy. While men occupied positions of authority in the church, state, and army and exercised power over the lives of women and propertyless men, women derived their status from the narrower confines of the local community. In the Castilian towns studied by Heath Dillard, women performed domestic chores like food preparation and childrearing while at the same time laboring as laundresses, wetnurses, or cloth makers to earn supplemental income. Women in twelfth- and thirteenth-century Castile also worked as shopkeepers, often selling the products produced by their craftsmen husbands.[60] Other townswomen, presumably freed of some responsibility for child care, labored in the trades; there are records of women working as tailors, furriers, jewelers, drapers, and shoemakers, though the actual extent of their involvement in these occupations is unknown. In some cases, as in Seville in the fourteenth century, there are records of women working in the building trades as masons, carpenters, and laborers—at wage rates far lower than those of men.[61] Among laboring women, as among men, there were clear-cut variations in economic reward. Thus rural women were paid far less for agricultural work than any townswoman was paid for either domestic or craft work, and this fact precipitated a shift in population toward the towns.[62] In the towns themselves, domestic labor, including child care and wetnursing, was far less remunerative than craft work or shopkeeping. While women in every occupation earned less than men, their wage-earning abilities varied according to their level of skill, usually measured by their distance from purely domestic work.

Yet domestic work—as wives and as servants—remained the province of women throughout the later Middle Ages. Since the wages of a servant were so low, even relatively low-status craftsmen could afford to hire a woman to attend to the menial chores of household maintenance. Young women who had escaped from rural hardship by emigrating to towns often found themselves employed at domestic drudgery with little prospect of achieving economic self-sufficiency.[63] These servants worked at cooking, cleaning, and husbandry, though the exact nature of their responsibilities, as well as their treatment and remuneration, depended on the attitudes of their employer.

For those women who escaped into nunneries during the later Middle Ages, the achievement of economic independence and social status was equally problematic. From the sixth century onward, houses of nuns were either attached to, or otherwise dependent on, male monastic establishments. The *monasteria duplicia,* in which a group of priests administered to the spiritual needs of a group of mostly highborn women, had its origin in the time of Pachomius. Of course, these early double monasteries all practiced strict sexual segregation. Monks assisted nuns in both manual and spiritual labor, but always under careful supervision. Although Pachomius wrote a Rule for nuns that encompasses many of the attributes of his Rule for monks, his relatively liberal allowance of regulated contact between monks and nuns was exceptional. Both the Council of Agde (506) and the Justinian *Codex* (529) forbade all such contact; the latter document permitted elderly priests to administer to the spiritual needs of nuns.[64] In seventh-century Gaul, nuns were also ministered to by priests but otherwise kept separated from men, often including their own relatives. In Spain in the eighth century, monks were allowed to perform manual labor for nuns but were denied any other communication with them.

In the later Middle Ages, the general tendency to separate nuns strictly from monks was continued. The reformed orders, particularly the Cistercians and Premonstratensians, either forbade or severely limited all contact between their monks and related orders of nuns. The Cistercians were especially harsh on women. As one modern historian has put it, "the whole tenor of several of the early Cistercian statutes was that women were to be avoided at all costs."[65] Women had been drawn to the ascetic rigors of the Cistercian order from the time of Robert of Molesme, and Bernard of Clairvaux's sister, Humbelina, was one of the first prioresses of Jully, near Cîteaux. In the twelfth-century *Dialogue between a Cistercian and a Cluniac,* the Cistercian mentions the women who imitate his order; women worked in the fields at Clairvaux and otherwise followed the lives of the monks there.[66] Yet the women who gathered together near the centers of Cistercian monastic culture were not considered a part of the order, and the monks were unwilling to commit themselves to providing either spiritual or material care for them until the middle of the thirteenth century.

The Premonstratensians, by contrast, had at first welcomed women. By 1150, there were over a thousand women attached to the Church of Prémontré, and, according to a canon of Laon, over ten thousand women belonged to the Premonstratensian order overall.[67] While these numbers may be exaggerated, the fact is that there were so many women drawn to this new ascetic discipline that the double monastery was revived and extended. Yet, as R. W. Southern has noted, even as this enormous outpouring of female devotion to an antiworldly religious discipline was taking place, the "same anti-feminine criticisms" were being voiced by "common religious opinion"—by the monks themselves presumably, as well as by bishops and others within the hierarchy of the church.[68] Thus by the end of the twelfth century, the General Chapter of Prémontré had declared that no more nuns could be admitted to the order, and the reasons for this decision were clearly tied to the fear that proximity to women would lead the monks into sins of concupiscence. As the re-formed orders of Cîteaux and Prémontré solidified their position within the structure of the Christian church, they, like their earlier counterparts in the Frankish church, detached themselves from the world of women and sexuality. The women who remained in religious orders were supported by bequests of land, by the labor of serfs and peasants, and sometimes by their own labor as well.

But it became increasingly difficult for religious women to maintain themselves in orders that lacked connections to monasteries, with their resources for material and spiritual sustenance. The alternative to the double monastery and dependence on men was the religious organization of self-reliant and mutually dependent women. The Beguines were one such order.[69] Gregory IX recognized the Beguine way of life as an authentic form of religious expression in a bull published in 1233; the Beguines had been organizing in the area around Liège since the beginning of the thirteenth century. Originally, the Beguines and Beghards were pious laywomen and men who wished to live an evangelical life outside of the established religious orders and, often, outside the doctrinal rigidities of the church. The Beguines sometimes lived together in loose organizations that approximated nunneries, and they also continued to support themselves by working in the world. Not all Beguines lived under the discipline of a rule or in a beguinage, however; it was these independent religious women who drew the most criticism from the church.[70] In the thirteenth-century letters of Hadewijch of Antwerp to a young Beguine, the pressures felt by those who lived this life are evident. Hadewijch warns her correspondent to persevere in her faith no matter what others say; to live a life of service to God and to suffer gladly the contempt of others.[71]

There were also considerable regional variations in the Beguine movement. Thus, while in places like Bruges and in the Netherlands in general, beguinages became large enough to establish independent parishes of two to three hundred women, in other places, like Frankfurt and Cologne, the beguinages remained small, with at most a dozen members. There were also regional variations in the degree of support for, or animosity toward, these independent religious women. In the case of France, Louis IX supported a beguinage near Paris that housed both rich and poor women. In the Rhineland, the movement did not enjoy this kind of support and therefore did not develop to the same extent.

In any case, the Beguines generally held certain convictions in common no matter what their geographic location or status within the regional church hierarchy. For one thing, individual Beguines retained whatever property they possessed when they joined a beguinage, and many of them worked in the outside world, most often in the textile industry, in order to support themselves and their sisters. Unlike the orders of nuns associated with the Cistercians and Premonstratensians, the Beguines did not separate themselves from secular society or disdain the contributions of wealthy men and women who made endowments to the order. The "ambivalent" attitude of the Beguines toward wealth—since they were women they were for the most part unable to earn much money by their labor, and it would not be wrong to construe their life as one of apostolic poverty—enabled them to support women from diverse socioeconomic backgrounds. While nuns generally came from the nobility, beguinages were likely to have among their numbers women from the nobility as well as from the "middle class" of knights' and merchants' daughters and wives; there was also a lesser number of members from poor families.[72] Those women who joined a Beguine order and submitted to the discipline of a head mistress were taught some Latin, given manual labor to perform, and given the opportunity to indulge their predilections for penance, prayer, and poverty. The Beguines also preserved their chastity, though they were allowed to leave the order to marry.

The importance of a movement like that of the Beguines—or the Humiliati or the Cathars—was that it created a context within which religious impulses left unsatisfied by the established orders of nuns and monks could be expressed. These orders, which were variously tolerated and encouraged (like the Beguines) or persecuted (like the Cathars) also attracted women (and men) of varying socioeconomic groups, especially poorer women, who were able to fulfill their desire for intensive, often mystical, religious experience in exchange for a certain amount of manual labor and adherence to a set of communal practices. The economic repression of medieval women and their exclusion from anything but a subsidiary role in the church made more appealing the relatively democratic world of apostolic or mystical (orthodox or heretical) religious movements. Lacking free access to the mainstream of late-medieval economic, political, and religious life, women of the twelfth through the fourteenth centuries increasingly chose to express themselves through lives of great spiritual achievement, much as unempowered black women in nineteenth- and twentieth-century America found self-affirmation in their churches.

THE "PEOPLE WITHOUT HISTORY"

Although I have surveyed only a small sampling of the available evidence here, I would like to attempt to make some general statements about the status of women and their relations to labor and technology during the Middle Ages. The enormous social, economic, and theological changes that occurred during the eleventh through the thirteenth centuries invite this attempt at a summing up, especially since I detect in the condition of medieval women evidence for the confluence of many of the other changes that I have discussed in this book.

First of all, the principal sphere of woman's work throughout the Middle Ages was unquestionably the home. While women, like men, came increasingly to labor in industries located within urban centers, the majority of medieval men and women worked the land with traditional tools in order to obtain a meager living for themselves and their children.[73] Women's extradomestic work was traditionally centered in the textile industry, though there is evidence from the later Middle Ages to suggest that women worked in some of the same trades as men. In any case, women were paid less than men, were excluded from some specialized crafts, and were responsible for the care of their homes and families. Although women of the nobility were often able to read and write and sometimes to own books, thereby becoming "ambassadors of culture," they were less often literate than men. Thus, except for women in nunneries or women of leisure, the opportunity to live the life of the mind was not available to medieval women.[74] In any case, even a woman who was literate and well educated bore the burdens of masculine disapproval. Thus in the twelfth century, Hildegard of Bingen, one of the most learned individuals of her time, nonetheless felt that "woman is weak, and [must] look to man for strength just as the moon receives its strength from the sun. Thus women are subject to men and must always be prepared to serve them. . . . Man therefore rules over the world, is lord over all creatures, while woman is under his mastery and subject to him."[75]

My second point focuses on women in religious life. Beginning as early as the fourth and fifth centuries, female piety was consigned to the periphery of Christian spirituality. Women were denied the right to preach or to participate in the Mass; they were excluded from holding ecclesiastical office, and, in holy orders, were dependent on the spiritual attentions of male counterparts. More often than not female piety took ecstatic forms—visions and great acts of self-abrogation were common—and was given scope only in the apostolic sphere that existed outside the established religious orders. The careers of women like Margery Kempe or, later, Teresa of Ávila, illustrate both the institutional distrust of unrestrained female piety and the sincerity of women's commitment to an emotionally charged Christianity. The studies of "affective Spirituality" and the "feminization of religious language" written by Caroline Walker Bynum reveal clearly the extent to which women influenced the content of twelfth-century Christianity. Late-medieval hagiography included stories that emphasized the relativity of gender distinctions in the face of great devotion: St. Bernard's lactating breasts, Christ's intimate physical association with the Virgin, the devotion to Mary herself, and the general circulation of the image of "God as Mother" all point to the influence of women on late-medieval piety.[76] At the same time, the medieval church insisted on the dangers of female sexuality and stressed that those (male) Christians who would be saved must separate themselves from women both physically and spiritually.

The fact is that the contributions of medieval women to European culture, like those of black women to American culture, are largely invisible. History has described public lives and has therefore concerned itself with the institutions created by the actions of men. Indeed, the discipline of history is itself a product of "outward-directed" lives, created by men who themselves share in the institutional identities that have been their subject. Women mother and create men, while men have created governments, economies, technologies, and ideologies that have removed women from history. The question is why this has been so. Why did the West come to devise a sexual division of labor that relegated the inner economies of childrearing and the maintenance of the home to women and the outer economies of governance and world building (and destroying) to men? The simple answer—that women care for children because women bear children—is inadequate because we know of societies in which either men care for children exclusively or child care is shared. Indeed, anthropology confirms that patterns of child care and labor, and the relations of inner and outer economies, are not biologically determined but culturally chosen.[77]

Unfortunately, no twelfth-century writer undertook the kind of socio-psychological analysis that might help us to understand directly the diminished status of women. This is especially unfortunate because I suspect that it was in the later Middle Ages that women's historical position in the West was defined.[78] Comparative anthropological analysis cannot provide us with a satisfactory answer, for while there are many societies both historical and "primitive" in which women's roles are subordinated to men's, none is enough like the commercial, protocapitalistic society of the late Middle Ages to offer a convincing analogy.

There is, however, one possible answer to this question, and it is one that touches both on the question of women's roles in late-medieval society and on the cultural context of medieval technology that has been the subject of this book. During the twelfth and thirteenth centuries, Europeans fashioned economic, social, and technological tools for the domination of the natural world. I would like to suggest that the subordination of women in the later Middle Ages was one of the goals of the reforms that took place in theology, social theory, politics, and the history of technology during this critical period. Women, as possessors of a sexual power that men can only emulate through the prosthesis of technology or invert through the domination of the natural world, are part of the generative forces that lie outside of masculine control and serve as a constant reminder of the limitations of male power.[79] At the same time that men directed their interest toward subduing nature, including their own, they began in earnest the immense task of subduing the natural world by destroying or domesticating those creatures who lived outside the bounds of masculine "rationality." The medieval church—which is to say, the small group of men empowered within medieval Europe—likewise sought to strengthen their control over the rest of society: over those who labored, those who fought, and those others, like women, whose work was essential, but who nonetheless existed on the margins of the economic and social order.

The project of excluding women from economic and political power did not begin during the later Middle Ages, nor did it cease then; but this exclusion took on new meaning during those centuries when technology and rational theology were constructing a carefully circumscribed world dominated by a particular kind of man, a man whose character embodied piety, rationality, and a disdain for the physical and emotional.[80] The project of securing political, economic, and intellectual hegemony reached its climax during the eleventh and twelfth centuries when the Gregorian Reform movement, the Peace of God, the Crusades, the Inquisition, and the initiation of large-scale commercial ventures set into place the basic structures of centralized and rationalized control that have characterized Western society ever since. The three "orders" were successfully defined, with an elite of churchmen and warriors sharing power over the masses of working men and women. Labor and the mechanical arts, while admitted into the classification of knowledge as meaningful forms of human activity, were at the same time denigrated as activities for those men who would experience spiritual illumination. At the same time, women were pushed farther away from direct contact with the active life of the church, which was still the main authority in the new order of European power.

During the later Middle Ages, then, women were progressively excluded both from the mainstream of economic life and from the official life of the church. These dual exclusions were linked, and their common element was the sexual puritanism of the period that began with the Gregorian Reform movement. Although the church had supported sexual abstinence since the fourth century, the enforcement of celibacy as a central tenet of the religious life of Christian Europe did not occur until the eleventh and twelfth centuries. At the same time, the theoreticians of the church tried to come to terms with the problems created by wealth, by the appearance of occupations and phenomena like simony, which threatened to undermine the otherworldly spirituality that had always been the implicit core of Christian ideology. Put simply, sexuality and money threatened to destroy the source of the late-medieval church's moral hegemony over the laity. This is why one finds in the literature of the reformed orders—the Cistercians and Carthusians, the Franciscans and the Dominicans—a zealous rejection of both the temptations of the flesh and the enticements of lucre. As Alexander Murray has shown, simony blurred the distinctions between the flesh and the spirit by allowing unworthy men to advance their careers in the church. The fear of simony reflected the desire of those in power to exclude men of lesser social status from authority in the church.[81] As we have seen, the material prosperity that was in part created by technical innovations and reevaluations of labor made it essential for churchmen to construct a theory of the social order and of economic responsibility that would ensure that increases in wealth would not create realignments of power. Simony posed a threat to the political status quo, and it was therefore bitterly denounced.

Similarly, a concern with sexual pollution, which led to a succession of prohibitions against women's participation in the religious life of the church—women were forbidden to approach the altar during Mass or to touch the chalice, to preach, or to administer to their own spiritual needs within monastic establishments—reflected a masculine distrust of women's economic and spiritual power. As Mary Douglas has shown, the fear of sexual pollution increases whenever there is a discrepancy between the lowly role assigned to women and the importance they actually possess.[82] As the economic status of women improved during the later Middle Ages and as independent movements of religious women assumed greater importance in the spiritual life of the church, the need to reassert masculine authority over women became imperative. Prohibitions against sexual intercourse and clerical marriage insured the removal of churchmen from the domestic sphere and also reflected a disdain for procreation among men whose theology had always insisted on the proximate ending of the world rather than its continuation.

But more to the point was the fact that celibacy separated women from the places where power was exercised, from the "outer world" of politics, education, and social management. This separation continued to exist, and its importance increased as the "outer world" expanded and grew more powerful.[83] Women, peasants, and slaves provided the reserves of muscle necessary to initiate and sustain the "European miracle" of economic growth and geographic expansion, but their importance remained unnoticed and their lives invisible. Medieval technology, which collected human power over nature into a rationalized system that was subordinated to economic expansion, could not displace these invisible workers; neither did its inventors and propagators seek to use machines as a means of ameliorating labor. That some should labor seemed just, a reasonable provision in a world created by a form of divine labor. And if the arbiters of medieval culture were never quite able to accept labor's intrinsic value, they did believe in its ability to edify, even when they themselves were willing to forego such edification. To those who labored and practiced crafts was left the task of sustaining the imperfect world, a circumstance that has not altered in any appreciable way since the twelfth century.

CONCLUSION

The Loss of Perfection

B Y THE END of the thirteenth century, one may find in the writings of the theoreticians of medieval culture a complex and often inconsistent attitude toward labor, its tools, and its products. Twelfth-and thirteenth-century theologians continue to subscribe to the Augustinian view that work and its products assist man in realizing God's providential intentions; the world is the stage of personal and collective self-discovery and perfection, and the tools through which the individual's apotheosis is realized include both the disciplines of the cloister and the work of the hands. Thinkers like Hugh of Saint Victor and Thomas Aquinas believed that manual labor is redemptive, a protection against sloth and a source of humility. At the same time, these and other writers propagate the view that clear distinctions must be maintained between sacred and secular labor and that a pious man is fully justified in sacrificing the *opus manuum* in order to advance the *opus Dei*. In the twelfth century, the idealized Benedictine view of a mixed life of work and prayer is qualified in important ways, primarily as part of a campaign to clarify the means whereby the sacred sphere dominates the secular sphere. Twelfth- and thirteenth-century theologians acknowledged the existence of an order of workers, the *laborantes,* whose calling included the provision of material support for those engaged in spiritual pursuits. Thus the adaptation of Christian theology to the Christian commonwealth began with a specification of appropriate "callings" and of hierarchically arranged "orders." The meaning of work was expanded to include a far broader spectrum of activities, so that the occupations created by protocapitalism (like merchandising) as well as by the expansion of the church (like university teaching) had a place in the new social order.

The attitude of the church toward manual labor and its products was neither univocal nor even consistent during the Middle Ages, and I hope that some of its richness (and bafflements) have been revealed in my discussions of particular traditions of thought. Despite the polysemous nature of medieval Christian attitudes toward manual labor, I think that some conclusions can be drawn on the basis of the texts studied here, and

Conclusion

I would like to summarize these conclusions by reinvoking the interpretations of the modern writers I discussed in my introduction.

First of all, I think that the study of the history of labor and technology must begin with the acknowledgment that a modern, progressivist bias obscures the contribution of the European Middle Ages to this history. Typical accounts of technological history, focusing on "hardware," skewed toward the perspective of "managers" rather than that of workers, of men rather than of women, preoccupied with products rather than processes, and instrumentalist in their conception of the relationship between technology and culture offer meager assistance in our attempts to understand the contributions of the Middle Ages to material life. Instead, we must be prepared to think of progress as culturally relative and as a function of the broader intellectual, ethical, and social goals of a particular society. For the Middle Ages, progress was to be discovered in the working out of God's providential design for human beings; material and technological advances merely reflected more significant changes in the spiritual life of men and women.

Second, with regard to the status of manual labor during the Middle Ages, the evidence suggests the coexistence of two traditions. On the one hand, Ernst Benz is correct in supposing that some writers (notably Augustine and Cassian) argued for the centrality of manual labor to the realization of human spiritual aspirations; on the other hand, virtually every medieval commentator subordinated the *opus manuum* to the *opus Dei,* described manual labor in idealized, often ritualistic rather than productive terms, and—especially beginning in the twelfth century—subscribed to the idea that particular classes of Christians are naturally suited to particular types of labor. Classification of learning reinforced the idea that while work was theoretically blessed, the mechanical arts were tainted by their concern with worldly ends.

Third, the medieval Christian attitude toward nature was not exploitative, and its anthropocentrism arose in part out of a concern for human beings' spiritual well-being. Postlapsarian human beings have much to learn from the creation and the creatures of the Earth, not least being the responsibility that they have to acknowledge, and live in cognizance of, the providential design of the Creation.

Fourth, the Benedictine tradition of combining prayer with labor—a tradition central to the description of the Middle Ages found in Weber and Mumford—turns out to have been rather more complex than these modern writers led us to believe. Above all, the literature of monasticism suggests that manual labor was far less important than individual spirituality during the early centuries of monasticism's existence, and that beginning no later than the twelfth century, the monastic commitment to manual labor was further eroded in the church's redefinition of its relationship with the secular world. The idealized worker-monk, most memorably portrayed in Thomas Carlyle's *Past and Present,* combined the virtues of spiritual commitment and practicality prized by the Victorians; in truth, the writings of monks suggest that all forms of practicality were subject to the demands of the spirit.

After these general observations, what remains to be explained is the significance of these attitudes toward labor for the history of the West. As Peter Brown and others have noted, one of the critical changes that began in the twelfth century was the "redrawing of the boundaries between the sacred and the profane."[1] As the church and the secular world divided responsibility for governance between them, Brown says, "a whole middle distance of conflicting opportunities for the deployment of talent" was created. In my view, one of the things that filled the "middle distance" was a conception of labor divorced from personal or communal spiritual goals, a conception that cleared the way for an emphasis on productivity and profitability at the expense of the Benedictine ideal of an edifying subsistence economy. It would be far too simple to assume that at some specific moment late in the fourteenth century the attitudes of men and women toward labor changed; that somehow, in a second, a profit economy replaced a gift economy; or that capitalism, that Gorgon of history, suddenly arose from the ashes of feudalism. The immense labors of historians like Fernand Braudel and Immanuel Wallenstein, who have traced patterns of continuity in European economic and social life from the fifteenth through the eighteenth centuries, make a mockery of such easy generalizations. Yet my reading of medieval texts and of astute modern students of the period strongly suggests that some important change in both material and intellectual life did occur during the eleventh, twelfth, and thirteenth centuries; I have chosen to characterize this change as the secularization of labor, that is, as the abandonment of a commitment to the balanced life of physical, intellectual, and spiritual work best described in the *Rule* of St. Benedict. I count this abandonment as a loss, not because I see the monastery as a model for a perfect world but because, like Lewis Mumford, I see that in the late Middle Ages labor, which once was a tool for cultivating individual moral values and for sustaining a community's collective life, began to be controlled by the purveyors of "megatechnics," by managers and middlemen. Even at the end of the Middle Ages, the majority of men and women did not lose their ties to the land, their respective tools, their religious ideals, or their terrible bondage.[2] The world changed very slowly over the next three centuries, but some of the most important things that changed in the West can be traced back to the Middle Ages.

It was, for example, sometime during the eleventh and twelfth centuries that the status of women was altered for the worse. Although much more needs to be done in order to understand exactly what effects the realignments of sacred and secular culture had on women, I suspect that one reason for the increased pressure to eliminate women from participation in both sacred and secular public life must be traced to the broader project of subduing the natural world through technology.[3]

It was during the twelfth and thirteenth centuries that a whole new tradition of classical learning, based on Aristotle and located in the newly founded universities, was introduced into the West. One consequence of this introduction was the creation—or the clarification, depending on one's point of view—of the differences between liberal and mechanical arts, between the work of the mind and the works of the hands.

It was during the twelfth, thirteenth, and fourteenth centuries that economic expansion and technological innovation helped to create distinctions among orders or classes of men and to create wholly new professions, both sacred and secular, devoted to the service of these classes.

New technologies, new alignments of men, new learning. And the new, we are taught, is the source the progressive, so that the story we have been asked to believe is that sometime near the end of the Middle Ages, secularism freed men (always men) from the bondage of theology, piqued the curiosity of a few precursors of modernity, and set the West on the road to the conquest of nature. Few objected to these changes in social alignments, educational goals, and productive techniques. Indeed, the author of a just-published book on early modern technology assures me that "everyone" greeted the invention and use of the mechanical clock with approval. What more suggestive symbol of modernity could we find, aside perhaps from the printing press, to convince ourselves that it was surely then, late in the thirteenth century, that mankind first began to use those "true helps" Francis Bacon referred to in order to free the mind for the clock's greatest feat—the invention of history.

Yet one might construct an altogether different story from the insights about labor and technology that we can assemble from the Middle Ages. We might begin by noticing that all of the important changes that occurred during the latter part of our period had to do with the establishment of new divisions among men (and between men and women). The secular world is derived from an increasing tension within the sacred; the self-contained peasant village becomes the interdependent town; the master of tools (that are themselves biomechanically exact projections of a worker's body) becomes the specialized laborer, employed by another; men and women become *laborantes,* a status understandable only in terms of the classes that rule them; learning and teaching become specialized and professionalized, while the world that is studied becomes itself dualistic, one part ruled by divine law, the other by chance.[4] This is not the description of a perfect world. Prelapsarian Eden was, of course, a perfectly whole place; man and woman lived, though briefly, as complements to each other, like two hands holding a hoe or working a distaff. These two human beings knew a benign and cooperative nature, the pleasure of labor, and the promise of immortality.

Adam and Eve squandered perfection after a verse or two because they were curious about evil (and possibly also about good). But their shame and banishment were at least only a personal loss, and their world of difficult labor and certain death was surely no worse than the lives led by 99 percent of all the men and women who have come after them. The first real tragedy—because tragedy is always social rather than personal—came at the moment Cain slew Abel, because it was then that the pattern of domination of one human being by another began.

Those who have told the story of benign progress have never assessed the effects that the loss of human and communal unity have had on the project of restoring perfection through labor and technology. Neither have those who have worked so hard at making over the imperfect world—the scientists, engineers, investors, and developers—told us very much about what the perfect world will look like when their business is done. What we also have not heard enough about are the ideas of those who have dissented from the progressivist instauration—a group that has included technophobes, religious zealots, magicians, witches, heretics, and political radicals, as well as all the ordinary men and women who have had more sensible views on how they should live their lives.

For those who have questioned the course of Western technological progress, one alternative social model in particular has been especially attractive. Monasticism, with its communalism, its simplicity, its self-sufficiency, its emphasis on the wholeness of men and women, and its commitment to a material life that sustains spiritual values, has been attractive to utopians, social reformers, and the disenchanted. Perhaps those who wish to contribute to the process of restoring the world to its perfect and original condition should search for their true helps in precisely the place Francis Bacon warned them against, namely, the Middle Ages. In any case, both the faint hope of restoring perfection, and the somewhat greater hope of making the world reflect broad-based and humane values, depend on our ability to understand that the means of restoration lie now, as they always have, in our own hands.

Notes

PREFACE

1. For this concept, and much else besides, I am indebted to Lynn White, Jr., "Cultural Climates and Technological Advance in the Middle Ages." *Viator* 2 (1971), 171–201.

2. Eric Wolf, *Europe and the People Without History* (Berkeley, 1982) has been of great assistance to me.

INTRODUCTION

1. See, for example, Arnold Pacey, *The Maze of Ingenuity* (Cambridge, Mass., 1976) for an account of the history of technology that demonstrates the continuity of technical development from the European Middle Ages to the present. As Pacey says in his preface, "To achieve progress is to thread a maze, not to follow a straight highway."

2. Karl Marx, *Capital,* trans. Ben Fowkes (New York, 1977), 1.283. Marx writes in this same section that "nature becomes one of the organs of [man's] activity, which he annexes to his own bodily organs, adding stature to himself in spite of the Bible. As the earth is his original larder, so too is it his original tool house" (285).

3. Karl Marx, "Economic and Philosophical Manuscripts (1844)," in *Early Writings,* trans. Rodney Livingstone and Gregor Benton (New York, 1975), 325, 343–344.

4. See Jane Goodall, "Tool-Using and Aimed Throwing in a Community of Free-Living Chimpanzees, *Nature* 201 (28 March 1964), 1264–1266; Gordon Hewes, "An Explicit Formulation of the Relationship Between Tool-Using, Tool-Making, and the Emergence of Language," *Visible Language* 7 (1973), 101–127; Leslie White, "On the Use of Tools by Primates, *Journal of Comparative Psychology* 34 (1942), 369–374; Jane B. Lancaster, "On the Evolution of Tool-Using Behavior," *American Anthropologist* 70 (1968), 56–66.

5. For a well-documented analysis of tool use from a Marxist perspective see Charles Woolfson, *The Labour Theory of Culture* (London, 1982), 34–43.

6. Ibid., 67.

7. Donald MacKenzie, "Marx and the Machine," *Technology and Culture* 25 (1984), 473–478 and Richard W. Miller, *Analyzing Marx* (Princeton, 1984), 174–181 for two recent discussions of Marx's alleged technological determinism.

8. Karl Marx, *A Contribution to the Critique of Political Economy,* trans. S. W. Ryazanskaya (Moscow, 1970), 3–4.

9. Karl Marx, *The German Ideology,* in *Selected Writings,* ed. and trans. David McLellan (Oxford, 1977), 161. Also 164: "The production of ideas, of conceptions, of consciousness, is at first directly interwoven with the material activity and the material intercourse of men, the language of real life. . . . Men are the producers of their conceptions, ideas, etc.—real, active men, as they are conditioned by a definite development of their productive forces and of the intercourse corresponding to these." On the concept of alienation in Marx, see Bertell Ollman, *Alienation: Marx's Conception of Man in a Capitalist Society* (Cambridge, 1971), 99–105.

10. See Karl Marx, *The Eighteenth Brumaire of Louis Bonaparte,* in *The Marx–Engels Reader,* ed. Robert C. Tucker (New York, 1972), 437.

11. Raymond Williams, *Marxism and Literature* (Oxford, 1977), 83–89.

12. Marx, *Capital,* 1.493; my emphasis. See Miller, *Analyzing Marx,* 188ff.

13. Max Weber, *General Economic History,* trans. Frank Knight (New Brunswick, N.J., 1981), 310.

14. Ibid., 313.

15. Ibid., 356.

16. Max Weber, *The Protestant Ethic and the Spirit of Capitalism,* trans. Talcott Parsons (New York, 1958), 124.

17. Weber, *General Economic History,* 361–365.

18. Lewis Mumford, *The Myth of the Machine,* vol. 1: *Technics and Human Development* (New York, 1967), 8.

19. Ibid., 1.9.

20. Ibid., 1.188–190, 273.

21. Ibid., 1.264–267.

22. Langdon Winner, *Autonomous Technology* (Cambridge, Mass., 1977).

23. Lynn White, Jr., "The Study of Medieval Technology, 1924–1974: Personal Reflections," *Technology and Culture* 16 (1975), 519–530, esp. 522–523; repr. in *Medieval Religion and Technology* (Berkeley, 1978), xi–xxiv.

24. Ernst Benz, "I fondamenti cristiani della tecnica occidentale," in *Technica e casistica,* ed. Enrico Castelli (Rome, 1964), 241–263; discussed by Lynn White in "Study of Medieval Technology," 527.

25. Ernst Benz, "The Christian Expectation of the End of Time and the Idea of Technical Progress," in *Evolution and Christian Hope: Man's Concept of the Future from the Early Fathers to Theilhard de Chardin* (Garden City, N.Y., 1966), 121–142.

26. Lynn White, Jr., "The Historical Roots of Our Ecological Crisis." in *Dynamo and Virgin Reconsidered* (Cambridge, Mass., 1968), 75–94 (repr. from *Science* [10 March 1967]).

27. Ibid., 86.

28. Lynn White, Jr., "Cultural Climates and Technological Advance in the Middle Ages," *Viator* 2 (1971), 171–201.

29. Lynn White, Jr., "The Iconography of *Temperantia* and the Virtuousness of Technology," in *Medieval Religion and Technology*, 181–204, repr. from *Action and Conviction in Early Modern Europe: Essays in Memory of E. H. Harbison*, ed. Theodore K. Rabb and Jerrold E. Seigel [Princeton, 1969]).

30. White, "Iconography of *Temperantia*," 201–202.

31. Jacques Le Goff, "Labor, Techniques and Craftsmen in the Value Systems of the Early Middle Ages (Fifth to the Tenth Centuries)," in *Time, Work, and Culture in the Middle Ages* (Chicago, 1980), 71–86, esp. 75. Also valuable is Le Goff's essay from the same book, "Techniques and Professions as Represented in Medieval Confessors' Manuals," 107–121.

1. PROGRESS AND PROVIDENCE IN THE MIDDLE AGES

1. See Ludwig Edelstein, *The Idea of Progress in Classical Antiquity* (Baltimore, 1967); E. R. Dodds, *The Ancient Concept of Progress* (Oxford, 1973), 1–25.

2. Cornelius Agrippa, *Of the Vanity and Uncertainty of Artes and Sciences*, (London, 1569), fol. 4r. "[Knowledge] is the very pestilence that putteth all mankinde to ruien, the which chaseth awaie all innocence."

3. William Ames, *Technometry*, ed. and trans. Lee Gibbs (Philadelphia, 1979), 118–119: "Now these less dignified faculties . . . are called sordid, lucrative, ignobile, mechanical, manual, and productive, insofar as many are commonly required . . . for the sake of common gain." For the "radical Enlightenment," see Margaret C. Jacobs, *The Radical Enlightenment: Pantheists, Freemasons, and Republicans* (London, 1981), 215ff.

4. One such recent exploration of an alternative view of the history of progress is to be found in David F. Noble, *Forces of Production* (New York, 1984), 324–353; also Arnold Pacey, *The Culture of Technology* (Cambridge, Mass., 1983), 13–34.

5. Examples of the continuity view in the history of science include William Wallace's studies of Galileo's intellectual debts, collected in *Prelude to Galileo* (Dordrecht, 1981) and in *Galileo and His Sources* (Princeton, 1984); see also I. B. Cohen, *Scientific Revolutions* (Cambridge, Mass., 1980) for the articulation of a theory of "transformation" as opposed to "revolution."

6. Francis Bacon, *Works*, ed. Basil Montagu, 3 vols. (Philadelphia, 1842), 334.337. For useful background on seventeeth-century ideas of the role of experience and the changing attitude of manual labor, see Rodolfo Mondolfo, *Alle origini della filosofia della cultura* (Bologna, 1956), 125–149.

7. Francis Bacon, *Works*, 3.345; italics mine.

8. Ibid., 3.346.

9. Giordano Bruno, *Expulsion of the Triumphant Beast*, ed. and trans. Arthur Imerti (New Brunswick, N.J., 1964), 205.

10. See Paolo Rossi, *I filosofi e le Macchine* (Milan, 1962); trans. as *Philosophy, Technology, and the Arts in the Early Modern Era* by Salvator Attanasio (New York, 1970), 1–62.

11. Francis Bacon, *Works*, 3.351.

12. Francis Bacon, *Preparation for a Natural and Experimental History*, in *Works*, 3.428–429. The observation that the mechanical arts contribute to scientific knowledge was also made by Descartes in *Discourse on the Method*, trans. by Elizabeth S. Haldane and G.R.T. Ross, in *The Philosophical Works of Descartes*, 2 vols. (Cambridge, 1911), 1.119 (part 6); Descartes speaks here of how "practical philosophy," like the crafts of artisans, allow human beings to become "the masters and possessors of nature." Furthermore, the "invention of an infinity of arts and crafts" would "enable us to enjoy without any trouble the fruits of the earth and all the good things which are to be found there."

13. For the dangers of the mechanical arts, see Bacon's *The Wisdom of the Ancients*, in *Works*, 1.300–301; for the "illiberal" nature of these arts see *Preparation for a Natural and Experimental History*, 3.428.

14. Joseph Glanville, *Plus ultra, or The Progress and Advancement of Knowledge Since the Days of Aristotle* (London, 1668; repr. Gainesville, Fla., 1958), 122–128. On the program of late seventeenth-century science in general, see Michael Hunter, *Science and Society in Restoration England* (Cambridge, 1981). On the mechanical arts in seventeenth century thought see Rossi, *Philosophy, Technology, and the Arts*, 100–136; Rossi is an essential source for any study of this issue.

15. See Paolo Rossi, *Francis Bacon: From Magic to Science*, trans. Sacha Rabinovich (Chicago, 1968), 1–35.

16. Glanville, *Plus ultra*, 11.

17. See Francis Bacon, *Novum organum* 1.64, in *Works*, 3.351; also Rossi, *Philosophy, Technology, and the Arts*, 146–173.

18. Thomas Sprat, *History of the Royal Society* (London, 1667), 1–2.

19. Ibid., 11–12.

20. Ibid., 14.

21. Ibid., 35.

22. William Wotton, *Reflections upon Ancient and Modern Learning* (London, 1694), xiv–xvii. Richard F. Jones, *Ancients and Moderns: A Study of the Rise of the Scientific Movement in Seventeenth Century England*, 2d ed. (St. Louis, 1961) remains valuable, though his Baconianism sometimes causes him to overestimate the progressivism of the seventeenth century (e.g. 268–269).

23. Wotton, Reflections, 1–3.

24. Ibid., 18.

25. See, for example, R. S. Crane, "Anglican Apologetics of the Idea of Progress." Modern Philology (1934), 273–306.

26. Anne-Robert-Jacques Turgot, On Progress, Sociology, and Economics, ed. and trans. Ronald L. Meek (Cambridge, 1973), 41.

27. Ibid., 45.

28. John Ray, The Wisdom of God as Manifested in the Works of Creation (London, 1691), frequently reprinted, presents the clearest argument for design in nature. For a lucid presentation of the arguments for design and their impact on both natural and social history, see Peter Bowler, Evolution: The History of an Idea (Berkeley, 1984), 48–54.

29. Turgot, On Progress, 55.

30. Chesterton's remark is recorded in Carl Becker, Progress and Power (Stanford, 1936), 9; the relation of progress and providence is an inference drawn with help from José Ortega y Gasset, Toward a Philosophy of History, trans. Helene Weyl (New York, 1941), 102–111 and passim.

31. Condorcet, Esquisse d'un tableau historique des progrès de l'esprit humain (Paris, 1822), 108; 115–148: "Dans cette époque désastreuse [le Moyen Âge], nous verrons l'esprit humain descendre rapidement de l'hauteur ou il s'etoit élève, et l'ignorance trainer après elle" (115).

32. Condorcet, Esquisse, 67.

33. William Whewell, History of the Inductive Sciences, 3d ed., 3 vols. (London, 1857), 1.41–51.

34. Ibid., 1.55.

35. Ibid., 1.58.

36. Ibid., 1.333.

37. Thomas Thompson, Sketch of the Progress of Physical Science (Glasgow, 1843), 10–12.

38. John Tyndall, Advancement of Science [includes articles by Tyndall and Henry Thompson "On Prayer"] (New York, 1874), 28.

39. Ibid., 29–35.

40. See Jacques Le Goff, "The Several Middle Ages of Jules Michelet," in Time, Work, and Culture in the Middle Ages (Chicago, 1980), 15; while Le Goff's essay is specifically about the views of Michelet, he in fact presents a chronicle of the changing fortunes of the Middle Ages in the nineteenth century.

41. J. B. Bury, The Idea of Progress (New York, 1920; repr. 1932), 20–21, 23, 27–28, 30; on Bury, see R. G. Collingwood, The Idea of History (New York, 1956; orig. Oxford, 1946), 147–150.

42. Gerald Heard, The Ascent of Humanity (New York, 1929), 154ff.

43. Carl Becker, *Progress and Power* (Stanford, 1936), 2ff.

44. Michael M. Postan, "Why Was Science Backward in the Middle Ages?" in *The History of Science: A Symposium* (Glencoe, Ill., 1951), 25–33.

45. Sidney Pollard, *The Idea of Progress* (New York, 1968), vi, 6, 13–15. See also Charles Van Doren, *The Idea of Progress* (New York, 1967), 4–6.

46. L. Houllevigue, *The Evolution of the Sciences* (New York, 1910), 21–23.

47. Ernest W. Brown et al., *The Development of the Sciences* (New Haven, 1923), 43–44.

48. W. T. Sedgwick and H. W. Tyler, *A Short History of Science*, rev. ed. by H. W. Tyler and R. P. Bigelow (New York, 1958; orig. 1939), 202.

49. Thomas Goldstein, *The Dawn of Modern Science* (New York, 1980), 77.

50. See in particular, Edgar Zilsel, "The Genesis of the Concept of Scientific Progress," *Journal of the History of Ideas* 6 (1945), 325–349; also "The Sociological Roots of Science," *American Journal of Sociology* 47 (1942), 544–562.

51. Studies by most of these key figures have been already cited; see Lynn White, Jr., "The Study of Medieval Technology, 1924–1974: Personal Reflections," in *Medieval Religion and Technology*, xi–xxiv for other citations; for R. S. Lopez, see *The Commercial Revolution of the Middle Ages* (Englewood Cliffs, N.J., 1971); for E. L. Jones, see *The European Miracle* (Cambridge, 1981).

52. For the deforestation of Europe, see H. C. Darby, "The Clearing of the Woodland in Europe," in *Man's Role in Changing the Face of the Earth*, ed. William L. Thomas (Chicago, 1956), 1.183–216.

53. For technological change in the cotton industry, see Maureen F. Mazzaoui, *The Italian Cotton Industry in the Later Middle Ages, 1100–1600* (Cambridge, 1981), 73–86; for the tin industry, see John Hatcher, *English Tin Production and Trade Before 1550* (Oxford, 1973).

54. See F. van Steenberghen, *Aristotle in the West,* trans. Leonard Johnston (Louvain, 1955); also, Bernard G. Dod, *"Aristoteles latinus,"* in *The Cambridge History of Later Medieval Philosophy,* ed. Norman Kretzmann et al. (Cambridge, 1982), 45–79.

55. An account of the Scholastic use of Aristotle may be found in Anneliese Maier, " 'Ergebnisse' der spatscholastischen Naturphilosophie," *Scholastik* 35 (1960), 161–188; texts bearing the specific case of impetus theory are in Marshall Clagett, *The Science of Mechanics in the Middle Ages* (Madison, 1961), 505–540, which includes Clagett's analysis of the Scholastic criticism of Aristotelian dynamics. For an example of the use of Aristotle, see William of Ockham, *Philosophical Writings,* ed. and trans. Philotheus Boehner (London, 1957), 2–16.

56. For the continuity of Aristotelianism, see Charles B. Schmitt, *Aristotle and the Renaissance* (Cambridge, Mass., 1983), especially, 10–33; for a consideration of the extent to which Aristotelian influence did not impede instruction in the mathematical sciences during the sixteenth and seventeenth centuries, see

Mordechai Feingold, *The Mathematicians' Apprenticeship* (Cambridge, 1984), 2–4, 102–103, and passim.

57. My view of the medieval use of Aristotle has been influenced by John Murdoch, in particular, "The Development of a Critical Temper: New Approaches and Modes of Analysis in Fourteenth-Century Philosophy, Science, and Theology," in *Medieval and Renaissance Studies* 7, ed. Siegfried Wenzel (Chapel Hill, 1978), 51–79.

58. For evidence from the visual arts see Lynn White, Jr., "Natural Science and Naturalistic Art in the Middle Ages," in *Medieval Religion and Technology*, 23–42. See also Antonia Gransden, "Realistic Observation in Twelfth-Century England," *Speculum* 47 (1972), 29–51.

59. For the detachment of natural philosophy from nature, see John Murdoch, "The Analytic Character of Late Medieval Learning," in *Approaches to Nature in the Middle Ages*, ed. Lawrence D. Roberts. (Binghamton, N.Y., 1982), 171–213. The same volume contains another paper—Robert A. Koch, "The Origin of the Fleur-de-lis and the *Lilium candidum* in Art," 109–130—which illustrates precisely the opposite point—that the observation of nature was undertaken during the Middle Ages.

60. For the "unacknowledged revolution" of printing, see Elizabeth A. Eisenstein, *The Printing Press as an Agent of Change*, 2 vols. in 1 (Cambridge, 1979), 3–42 and 520–574.

61. See Leonardo Olschki, *Geschichte der neusprachlichen wissenschaftlichen Literatur*, esp. vol. 1, *Die Literatur der Technik und der angewandten Wissenschaften vom Mittelalter bis zur Renaissance* (Heidelberg, 1919). For specific craftsman-scholars, see Emmanuelle Poulle, *Jean Fusoris, un constructeur des instruments astronomiques du XVe siècle* (Paris, 1963), and J. D. North, *Richard of Wallingford* (Oxford, 1976).

62. Vern L. Bullough, "Status in Medieval Medicine," *Journal of Health and Human Behavior* 2 (1961), 204–210.

63. Nancy G. Siraisi, *Taddeo Alderotti and His Pupils* (Princeton, 1981), 147–202: "The reconciliation of philosophers and physicians was a task that seemed urgent to Taddeo [Alderotti] and his associates. . . . The physicians of Taddeo's day could have ignored Aristotelian natural philosophy only at the risk of taking medicine out of the mainstream of learned scientific activity" (201).

64. Theophilus, *De diversis artibus,* C. R. Dodwell, ed. (London, 1961); for St. Bernard's attack on the ostentation of Cluniac churches, see his *Apologia and Guillelmum*, in *S. Bernardi Opera*, ed. Jean Leclercq et al., 8 vols. to date (Rome, 1957–), 3.81–108. Suger's defense can be found, with much useful analysis, in Erwin Panofsky, *Abbot Suger* (Princeton, 1946).

65. Roger Bacon's well-known technological ruminations are in the *Epistola Fratris Rogerii Baconis de secretis operibus artis et naturae, et de nullitate magiae,*

ed. J. S. Brewer, vol. 1 of *Opera hactenus inedita Rogeri Baconi* (London, 1859), 532–533.

66. Konrad Kyeser, *Bellifortis*, ed. G. Quarg, *Facsimile-Ausgabe der Pergamenthandschrift, Cod. Ms. philos. 63 der Universitätsbibliothek, Göttingen*, vol. 2 (Dusseldorf, 1967).

67. I am indebted here to William Eamon, "Technology as Magic in the Late Middle Ages and the Renaissance," *Janus* 70 (1983), 171–212.

68. See Maurice Vignes, *Saint Bernard et son temps*, Association Bourguignonne des sociétés savantes (Dijon, 1928), 259ff. Also, O. Martin-Larber, "L'Exploitation d'une grange Cistercienne à la fin du XIVe et au debut du XVe siècle," in *Annales Bourgogne* 29 (1957), 161–180. Also instructive is the history of particular inventions; for example, the *churka*, a set of wooden rollers used in the ginning of cotton which was adapted by Italian workers from an Indian model. In cases like these, one sees the extent to which the needs of laborers and the availability of practical solutions to technical problems informed questions of the acceptability of technological change. See Mazzaoui, *Italian Cotton Industry*, 73ff.

69. Langdon Winner, *Autonomous Technology* (Cambridge, Mass., 1977), 44–100, discusses the unforeseen consequences of technological change.

70. Robert Boyle, *Of the Usefulness of Experimental Philosophy*, in *Works*, 6 vols. (London, 1772).

71. For particular cases of the continuity of concerns, see Steven Dick, *The Plurality of Worlds* (Cambridge, 1982) and Paolo Rossi, *The Dark Abyss of Time*, trans. Lydia G. Cochrane (Chicago, 1984), which examines the history of the questions of the Earth's age and the mechanics of creation.

72. Arnold Pacey, *Culture of Technology*, esp. 13–34.

73. See Jack Goody, *Technology, Tradition and the State in Africa* (Cambridge, 1971), 22–38. Otto Mayr's *Authority, Liberty and Automatic Machinery in Early Modern Europe* (Baltimore, 1986), seems to offer the kind of study of "cultural context" that I have advocated here.

74. Marx makes this argument in the *Gundrisse*: "In no respect is the machine the means of labour of the individual worker. Its distinctive character is not at all, as with the means of labour, that of transmitting the activity of the worker to its object; rather this activity is so arranged that it now only transmits and supervises and protects from damage the work of the machine and its action on the raw material. With the tool it was quite the contrary. The worker animated it with his own skill and activity; his manipulation of it depended on his own dexterity. The machine, which possesses skill and force in the worker's place, is itself the virtuoso, with a spirit of its own in the mechanical laws that take effect in it" (*Selected Writings*, trans. David McLellan [Oxford, 1977], 375).

75. See Pacey, *Culture of Technology*, 20–22; for additional discussion of the

complexity of technological change, see David Landes, *The Unbound Prometheus* (Cambridge, 1969), 80–88 (dealing with the cloth industry).

76. David F. Noble, *Forces of Production* (New York, 1984), 324–353.

77. So argued by Lynn White, Jr., *"Temperantia* and the Virtuousness of Technology," in *Medieval Religion and Technology,* 201–202.

78. See John Fitchen, *The Construction of Gothic Cathedrals* (Chicago, 1961), 9–41; for remarks on lifting devices, see 303–306: "Until the timber-work of the great roof came into use, however, it would seem that very simple and relatively slight hoisting apparatus was all that could be employed for raising stone and beams onto the thin and lofty walls of the towering, skeletonized churches of Gothic times" (306).

79. Tertullian, *Apologeticum,* CCSL 1, Chap. 40, 13.

80. Eusebius, *The Ecclesiastical History,* ed. and trans. Kirsopp Lake, 2 vols. (Cambridge, Mass., 1926), 391 (bk. 4, chap. 26).

81. Lantantius. *Divinae institutionis,* in *Opera omnia,* ed. Samuel Brandt, CSEL 19 (Vienna, 1890), bk. 2, chap. 2, 100–102; bk. 5, chap. 19, 465–467; bk. 6, chap. 2, 481–485.

82. Paulus Orosius (b. ca. 380–390), *Historiarum adversus paganos libri septem,* PL 31, cols. 985–991.

83. Tertullian, *Apologeticum,* bk. 10, chap. 6, 105–107.

84. Arnobius, *Adversus nationes,* ed. Augustus Reifferscheid, CSEL 4 (Vienna, 1875), bk. 2, chaps. 66–67, 101–102. For a general discussion of the idea of reform and its relationship to the idea of Christian progress, see Gerhart B. Ladner, *The Idea of Reform* (Cambridge, Mass., 1959).

85. Ambrose, *Epistolae,* PL 16, col. 1015, Epist. 18, 7; see Ladner, *Idea of Reform,* 149.

86. Ambrose, *Epistolae,* PL 16, col. 1020 (epist. 18, 23).

87. Tertullian, *De anima,* ed. J. H. Waszink (Amsterdam, 1947), ch. 30, 370.

88. On the development of the linear conception of time and its impact on Christian thought, see Oscar Cullman, *Christus und die Zeit* (Zurich, 1946) and Jean Guitton, *Le Temps et l'éternité chez Plotin et Augustin* (Paris, 1933).

89. Augustine, *Confessiones,* CCSL 27 (Turnhout, 1981), bk. 11, chap. 14.

90. Central to this discussion of Augustine is Theodor E. Mommsen, "St. Augustine and the Christian Idea of Progress: The Background of *City of God,*" in *Medieval and Renaissance Studies,* ed. Eugene F. Rice, Jr. (Ithaca, N.Y., 1959), 266ff.

91. Augustine, *De civitate Dei,* ed. Bernard Dombart and Alphonse Kalb, CCSL 48 (Turnhout, 1955), bk. 12, chap. 14.

92. See Mommsen, "St. Augustine," 295–297.

93. Augustine, *De civitate Dei,* bk. 10, chap. 14; trans. by Henry Bettenson, *City of God,* ed. David Knowles (Harmondsworth, 1972).

94. Ibid., bk. 22, chap. 24.

95. See Marie-Dominique Chenu, "Tradition and Progress," in *Nature, Man, and Society in the Twelfth Century,* trans. Jerome Taylor and Lester K. Little (Chicago, 1968), 310–330.

96. Adelard of Bath, *Die Questiones naturales,* ed. Martin Müller, Beiträge zur Geschichte der Philosophie und Theologie des Mittelalters, 31.2 (Muenster, 1934), 4–5.

97. That an "intellectual context" exists in a particular culture is, of course, an assumption. I am speaking here of what an anthropologist might call an "invariant point of reference," and I conceive of this framework of ideas, rituals, and beliefs in terms described by Clifford Geertz in *The Interpretation of Cultures* (New York, 1973), 40–41 and especially the essay entitled "Religion as a Cultural System," 87–125. An "anthropology of technology," which described the techniques devised to assist human beings in exercising a reassuring (and therefore a quasi-religious) control over the environment, would go a long way toward releasing the history of technology from the limitations of its Western-progressivist bias. Geertz's essays suggest directions for such a study, as do the writings of Jack Goody.

98. Apart from Weber's own *Wirtschaft und Gesellschaft,* ed. J. Winckelmann (Tubingen, 1956), available as *Economy and Society,* trans. E. Fischhoff et al. (Berkeley, 1968, repr. 1978), one of the better surveys of Weber's thought as it touches religion and society is an essay by Wolfgang Schluchter, "Die Paradoxie der Rationalisierung: Zum Verhaltnis von 'Ethik' und 'Welt' bei Max Weber," *Zeitschrift für Soziologie,* 5 (1976), 256–284.

99. For the possibility of a reactionary technology, see Jeffrey Nerf, *Reactionary Modernism: Technology, Culture, and Politics in Weimar and the Third Reich* (Cambridge, 1984), esp. 189–216.

2. God as Craftsman and Man as Custodian

1. For an overview of the tradition of seeing God as a craftsman, see "Création" in *Dictionnaire de théologie catholique,* ed. A. Vacant et al., vol. 3, pt. 2 (Paris, 1938), cols. 2,034ff.

2. Frank E. Robbins, *The Hexaemeral Literature* (Chicago, 1912), 2–7.

3. "Benedixitque illis Deus, et ait: Crescite et multiplicamini, et replete terram, et subiicite eam, et dominamini piscibus maris, et volatilibus caeli, et universis animantibus, quae moventur super terram" (Genesis 1:28) and "Tulit ergo Dominus Deus hominem, et posuit eum in paradiso voluptatis, ut operaretur, et custodiret illum: Praecepitque ei dicens: Ex omni ligno paradisi comede" (Genesis 2:15–16) are the key texts, quoted here from *Biblia sacra,* ed. Alberto Clunga and Laurentio Turrado, 5th ed. (Madrid, 1977).

4. See Dorothy Glass, "*In principio:* The Creation in the Middle Ages," in *Approaches to Nature in the Middle Ages,* ed. Lawrence D. Roberts (Binghamton, N.Y., 1982), 72.

5. See Glass, "*In principio,*" 68, and notes 11–14, 98–99 for sample illustrations.

6. Jean Gimpel, *The Cathedral Builders* (New York, 1984), 91.

7. Philo Judaeus, "On the Creation of the World," in *Philo,* ed. F. H. Colson, 10 vols. (Cambridge, Mass., 1929–1962), 1.15–16. For the creation through the imitation of a pattern, see also Plato, *Timaeus,* 28a.

8. Philo Judaeus, "On the Creation," 1.19–20.

9. Ibid., 1.24.

10. Basil of Caesarea, *Homiliae in Hexaemeron,* in *Opera Sancti Basilii,* PG 29, homily 1, 3 (cols. 10–11).

11. Ibid., homily 1, 11 (col. 26).

12. Ibid., homily 1, 5 (col. 14).

13. Ibid., homily 1, 7 (cols. 18–19) for God as Craftsman.

14. Ibid., homily 2, 2 (col. 31) and 2, 3 (col. 34): "God is not only the inventor of the shapes of things but the creator of the essence of all that exists."

15. Ibid., homily 2, 7 (col. 46).

16. Robbins, *Hexaemeral Literature,* 58 for Basil's influence on Ambrose; I would dissent from Robbins's view that Ambrose's version "has little value" as a work independent of Basil's *Homilies.* For Ambrose's *Hexaemeron* see *Sancti Ambrosii opera,* ed. K. Schenkl, CSEL 32.1 (Vienna, 1897); for the creation of the world and time through the divine will, see hom. 1, 2, 5 (pp. 6–7).

17. Ambrose, *Hexaemeron,* homily 1, 8, 31 (pp. 31–33).

18. Ibid., homily 1, 5, 17 (p. 14).

19. Ibid., homily 1, 6, 22 (pp. 18–19).

20. Augustine, *De Genesi ad litteram libri duodecim,* in *Sancti Aureli Augustini,* ed. Joseph Zycha, CSEL 28.1 (Vienna, 1894), bk. 4, 12 (pp. 108–109); see also Bede, *Hexaemeron,* PL 91, col. 34, and Peter Abelard, *Expositio in Hexaemeron,* PL 178, col. 769.

21. Augustine, *De Genesi,* bk. 1, 4 (pp. 7–8).

22. Bernardus Silvestris, *Cosmographia,* ed. Peter Dronke (Leiden, 1978), bk. 1, chap. 1 (p. 97).

23. Augustine, *De Genesi,* bk. 5, 23 (pp. 167–169): "Sicut autem in ipso grano inuisibiliter erant omnia simul, quae per tempora in arborem surgerent, ita ipse mundus cogitandus est, cum deus simul omnia creauit, habuisse simul omnia, quae in illo cum illo facta sunt, quando factus est dies, non solum caelum cum sole et luna et sideribus, quorum species manet motu rotabili, et terram et abyssos, quae uelut inconstantes motus patiuntur atque inferius adiuncta partem alteram mundo conferunt, sed etiam illa, quae aqua et terra produxit potentialiter

atque causaliter, priusquam per temporum moras ita exorerentur, quomodo nobis iam nota sunt in eis operibus, quae deus usque nunc operatur" (168).

24. Ibid., bk. 2, 5 (p. 39).

25. John the Scot, *Periphyseon* (*De divisione naturae*), ed. and trans. I. P. Sheldon Williams (Dublin, 1981). All translations are taken from this edition.

26. Ibid., 26.

27. Ibid., 184.

28. Ibid., 190.

29. Ibid., 194.

30. Ibid., 220–221.

31. Ibid., 230.

32. Ibid., 230–231.

33. See Augustine, *De Genesi*, bk. 1, 18: "Sed ante amnia meminerimus, unde iam multa diximus, non temporalibus quasi animi sui aut corporis motibus operari deum, sicut operatur homo uel angelus, sed aeternis atque incommutabilibus et stabilibus rationibus coaeterni sibi uerbi sui et quodam, ut ita dixerim, fotu pariter coaeterni sancti spiritus sui" (p. 26).

34. Alcuin of York, *Interrogations et responsiones in Genesim*, PL 100, col. 519.

35. For the modern background to this ongoing debate see Neal C. Gillespie, *Charles Darwin and the Problem of Creation* (Chicago, 1979), esp. 82–108; David Hull, in *Darwin and His Critics* (Chicago, 1973) presents nineteenth-century creationist responses to the theory of evolution—responses that illustrate the continuing debate over the mechanisms of God's Providence.

36. Honorius Augustodunesis, *Clavis physicae*, ed. Paolo Lucentini (Rome, 1974), 4–5.

37. For a summary of Lull's views and of his relation to Eriugena, see Frances A. Yates, "Ramon Lull and John Scotus Erigena," in *Collected Essays: Lull and Bruno* (London, 1982), 1.78–125, esp. 82.

38. Cudworth's "Digression" is published in *The Cambridge Platonists*, ed. C. A. Patrides (Cambridge, Mass., 1970), 293.

39. Anne Conway, *The Principles of the Most Ancient and Modern Philosophy*, ed. Peter Loptson (The Hague, 1982), 79.

40. Arnold of Bonneval, *De operibus sex dierum*, PL 189, cols, 1515–1517.

41. Bernardus Silvestris, *Cosmographia*, 98–99.

42. Thierry of Chartres, *De sex dierum operibus*, ed. Nicholas M. Häring, in "The Creation and the Creator of the World According to Thierry of Chartres and Clarenbaldus of Arras," *Archives d'histoire doctrinale et littéraire du Moyen Âge*, 30 (1955), 137–216, esp. 185; see also Alan of Lille, *De planctu Naturae*, PL 210, col. 445.

43. Bede, *Hexaemeron*, col. 39.

44. Robbins, *Hexaemeral Literature*, 79, n. 2.

45. Hugh of Saint Victor, *Adnotationes elucidatoriae in Pentateuchon*, PL 175, cols. 33–34.

46. Peter Abelard, *Expositio in Hexaemeron*, cols, 746–747.

47. William of Conches, *Philosophia mundi*, PL 172, col. 56.

48. See Marie-Dominique Chenu, "Nature and Man: The Renaissance of the Twelfth Century," in *Nature, Man, and Society in the Twelfth Century*, trans. Jerome Taylor and Lester K. Little (Chicago, 1968), 11 and n. 21. For God as workman, see Bede, *Hexaemeron*, col. 15 and William of Conches, *Glossae super Platonem*, ed. Edouard Jeauneau (Paris, 1965), 104.

49. Thomas Aquinas, *Summa theologiae*, pt. 1, q. 44, arts. 2 and 3.

50. Ibid., pt. 1, q. 45, art. 1 and q. 66, art. 1.

51. Thomas Aquinas, *Summa contra gentiles*, bk. 2, 17–19.

52. Lynn White, Jr., in *Dynamo and Virgin Reconsidered* (Cambridge, Mass., 1968), 86.

53. Lynn White, Jr., "Cultural Climates and Technological Advance in the Middle Ages," in *Medieval Religion and Technology* (Berkeley, 1978), 235–242.

54. John Passmore, *Man's Responsibility for Nature*, 2d ed. (London, 1974), 20, 111–118, 209ff.

55. F. B. Welbourn, "Man's Dominion," *Theology* 78 (1975), 564.

56. William Coleman, "Providence, Capitalism, and Environmental Degradation—English Apologetics in an Era of Economic Revolution," *Journal of the History of Ideas* 37 (1976), 27–44.

57. Lewis W. Moncrief, "The Cultural Basis for Our Environmental Crisis," *Science* 170 (1970), 508–512.

58. Robin Attfield, "Christian Attitudes Toward Nature," *Journal of the History of Ideas* 44 (1983), 386.

59. See, for example, Clarence Glacken, *Traces on the Rhodian Shore* (Berkeley, 1967), 187ff.

60. See R. H. Hilton and P. H. Sawyer, "Technical Determinism: The Stirrup and the Plough," *Past and Present*, 24 (1963), 90–100.

61. Philo Judaeus, "On the Creation, 1.111. (sect. 48).

62. Ibid., 1.112–117. (sects. 48–52).

63. Basil of Caesarea, *Homiliae in Hexaemeron*, homily 5, 1 (cols. 94–95).

64. Ibid., homily 5, 4 (col. 102).

65. Ibid., homily 5, 5 (col. 103).

66. Ibid., homily 5, 9 (cols. 114–115).

67. Ibid., homily 7, 5 (cols. 158–159).

68. Ibid., homily 8, 2 (col. 167).

69. Ibid., homily 9, 2 (col. 190).

70. Ibid., homily 9, 5 (cols. 199, 202).

71. Ambrose, *Hexaemeron,* homily 7, 2, 5 (pp. 143–144).

72. Ibid., homily 7, 5, 12 (pp. 148–149). Ambrose repeats many of Basil's examples of "moralized nature" verbatim.

73. Ibid., homily 7, 10, 27 (p. 161).

74. Ibid., homily 8, 15, 52 (pp. 179–180).

75. Ibid., homily 9, 2, 3 (pp. 205–206).

76. Ibid., homily 9, 3, 9 (p. 209).

77. Ibid., homily 9, 5, 30–34 (pp. 223–227).

78. Ibid., homily 9, 8, 45 (p. 236).

79. Ibid., homily 9, 9, 54–74 (pp. 247–260).

80. Augustine, *De Genesi,* bk. 3, 11 (p. 75).

81. Ibid., bk. 3, 11 (pp. 75–76).

82. Ibid., bk. 3, 18 (pp. 83–84).

83. See Robbins, *Hexaemeral Literature,* p. 5, n. 4 for examples.

84. Augustine, *De Genesi,* bk. 6, 12 (pp. 185–186).

85. Étienne Gilson, *History of Christian Philosophy in the Middle Ages* (New York, 1955), 74.

86. Augustine, *De Genesi,* bk. 3, 21 (p. 88).

87. Ibid., bk. 3, 22 (pp. 88–89).

88. Augustine, *De civitate Dei,* ed. Bernard Dombast and Alphonse Kalb, CCSL 48 (Turnhout, 1955), bk. 13, chap. 21.

89. See Robbins, *Hexaemeral Literature,* 77.

90. Bede, *Hexaemeron,* col. 27.

91. Ibid., cols. 29–30.

92. See Bede, *Opera exegetica: Libri quatuor in principium Genesis,* ed. C. W. Jones, CCSL 118A (Turnhout, 1967), 51; Bede takes this from Augustine's *De Genesi.*

93. Bede, *Hexaemeron,* col. 50.

94. Alcuin of York, *Interrogationes,* cols. 521–522.

95. See *The Book of Jubilees,* ed. R. H. Charles (Oxford, 1902), 46–51 for another account of prelapsarian labor.

96. John the Scot, *Periphyseon,* 284ff.

97. Ibid., 288.

98. Ibid., 298.

99. Ibid., 300–301.

100. For citations see Ambrose, PL 14, col. 245; Bede, PL 91, col. 29; Rabanus Maurus, PL 107, col. 460; Rupert of Deutz, PL 167, col. 267; Peter Comestor, PL 198, col. 1063.

101. Bernardus Silvestris, *Cosmographia,* bk. 2, chap. 10.

102. Ibid., bk. 2, chap. 10.

103. Ibid., bk. 2, chaps. 13–14.

104. See Nicholas M. Häring, "The Creation."

105. Arnold of Bonneval, PL 189, col. 1534.

106. Robert Grosseteste, *Hexaemeron,* ed. Richard c. Dales and Servus Gieben (London, 1982), xix–xxv for Grosseteste's sources.

107. Ibid., 248.

108. Ibid., 260–261.

109. Thomas Aquinas, *Summa theologiae,* pt. 1, q. 96, art. 1.

110. Ibid., pt. 1, q. 96, art. 2.

111. Passmore, *Man's Responsibility,* 6–8.

112. See Sherwood L. Washburn, "Tools in Human Evolution," *Scientific American* 203 (1962), 63–75; Kenneth Page Parkley, *Man the Tool-Maker* (Chicago, 1976); and Charles Woolfson, *The Labour Theory of Culture* (London, 1982), which summarizes recent literature on tool use and culture in chapters 2 and 3.

113. Lewis Mumford, *The Myth of the Machine,* vol. 2, *The Pentagon of Power* (New York, 1970), 155.

114. In addition to Mumford, see Langdon Winner, *Autonomous Technology* (Cambridge, Mass., 1977), 109.

115. Cited by, and commented upon, by William Leiss, *The Domination of Nature* (New York, 1972), 51; my emphasis.

116. Paolo Rossi, *Francis Bacon: From Magic to Science* (Chicago, 1968), 20–21, 54.

117. For the legacy of the more important domination—of human beings by other human beings—see chapter 6 below as well as Georges Duby, *The Three Orders; or, Feudal Society Imagined,* trans. Arthur Goldhammer (Chicago, 1980), 157–166 and passim.

3. Labor and the Foundations of Monasticism

1. Herbert Workman, *The Evolution of the Monastic Ideal* (London, 1913), 219–220.

2. Ibid.

3. Max Weber, *The Protestant Ethic and the Spirit of Capitalism,* trans. Talcott Parsons (New York, 1958), 118–119.

4. Lewis Mumford, *The Myth of the Machine,* vol. 1, *Technics and Human Development* (New York, 1967), 263.

5. Ibid., 1.264; my debt to Lewis Mumford's extraordinary analysis in the chapter "Pioneers in Mechanization" (263–294) is very great.

6. Also informative is Clarence Glacken, *Traces on the Rhodian Shore* (Berkeley, 1967), 176–273.

7. See Lynn White, Jr., "Cultural Climates and Technological Advance in the

Middle Ages," *Viator* 2 (1971), 187, 191–192. See also idem, "What Accelerated Technological Progress in the Western Middle Ages?" in *Scientific Change,* ed. A. C. Crombie (New York, 1963), 286–288; also idem, "The Iconography of *Temperantia* and the Virtuousness of Technology," in *Medieval Religion and Technology* (Berkeley, 1978), 182–183.

8. See, for example, Robin Attfield, "Christian Attitudes Toward Nature," *Journal of the History of Ideas* 44 (1983), 369–386; also idem, *The Ethics of Environmental Concern* (New York, 1983); John Passmore, *Man's Responsibility for Nature,* 2d ed. (London, 1974); and Keith Thomas, *Man and the Natural World* (New York, 1983).

9. For Philo's account of the *Therapeutae* see his *De vita contemplativa* in *Philonis Alexandrini Opera quae supersunt,* ed. L. Cohn 7 vols. in 6 (Berlin, 1896–1930), vol. 4; Eusebius records Philo's account of this sect in the *Historia ecclesiae,* PG 20, bk. 2, chap. 17 (col. 175).

10. Athanasius, *Vita Antonii,* PG 26, cols. 915 and 919. It is important to note that Anthony also stressed that devotion to the spirit must always take precedence over any labor done for the sake of the body; see col. 910.

11. *Apophthegmata patrum,* PG 65, cols. 205–206: John's brother says to him, "Homo es, necesse est ut iterum opereris, unde alas te."

12. Tertullian, *De testimonia animae,* in *Opera,* CSEL 20, ed. Georg Wissowa and August Reifferscheid (Vienna, 1890), 135–136; also *De idololatria,* ibid., 34–35: "Pateat igitur ecclesia omnibus, qui manibus et suo opere tolerant, si nulla exceptio est artium quas dei disciplina non recipit." Also Lactantius, *Divinae institutiones,* in *Opera omnia,* ed. Samuel Brandt, CSEL 19 (Vienna, 1890), 446; Minucius Felix, *Octavius,* ed. H. A. Holden (Cambridge, 1853), 54–56.

13. *Apophthegmata patrum,* cols. 219–220.

14. For Jerome's labor in the desert, see Jerome, *Epistulae,* CSEL 54, ed. I. Hilberg (Vienna, 1910), pt. 1, epistle 17, 72: "Nihil alicui praeripui, nihil otiosus accipio. Manu cotidie et proprio sudore quaerimus cibum scientes ab apostolo scriptum esse: qui autem non operatur, nec manducet." See also J. N. D. Kelly, *Jerome* (New York, 1975), 47–48.

15. For the varieties of manual labor undertaken in the desert see Palladius, *The Lausiac History,* ed. Dom Cuthbert Butler, in Texts and Studies, Contributions to Biblical and Patristic Literature 6.1, 2 vols. (Cambridge, 1898–1904), vol. 2, esp. 17, 43–45, 100–106. For a summary of the forms of communal labor, see Dewas Chitty, *The Desert a City* (Oxford, 1964), 40 and n. 45 for additional texts.

16. *Apophthegmata patrum,* col. 418: "Dixit abbas Serenus: Tempus meum peregi metendo, consuendo, plectendo; atque in his omnibus, nisi manus Dei cibasset me, non potuissem nutriri."

17. For Pambo, see *Apophthegmata patrum*, cols. 367–370: "Bona quidem sunt ea opera; sed si custodieris conscientiam erga proximum, ita servaberis" (col. 370); for additional information on Pambo, see Palladius, *Lausiac History*, 2.29–31.

18. For the mix of the *opus Dei* and *opus manuum*, see the life of John of Lycopolis, in the *Historia monachorum in Aegypto*, trans. Rufinus, PL 21, cols. 398–399.

19. The histories of Paesius and Isais are told by Palladius, *Lausiac History*, 2.37–38.

20. Ibid., 2.33–34.

21. *Vita S. Pachomii*, trans. Dionysius Exiguus, PL 73, col. 270.

22. Palladius, *Lausiac History*, 2.87–96; see also *Vita S. Pachomii*, col. 236.

23. *Vita S. Pachomii*, cols. 242–243, 253.

24. For Jerome's remarks, see *Pachomiana latina*, ed. A. Boon, Bibliothèque de la Revue d'histoire ecclésiatique 7 (Louvain, 1932), 3–6; or PL 23, col. 66: "sintque pro numero fratrum triginta, vel quadraginta domus in uno monasterio, et ternae, vel quaternae domus in unam tribum foederentur, ut vel ad opera simul vadant, vel in hebdomadarum ministerio sibi succedant per ordinem."

25. *Apophthegmata patrum*, col. 375: "Quid agam, quia angustiis urgeor in vendendo opere manuum mearum? [Pistamon answers] Etiam abbas Sisoes et reliqui vendebant quae ipsi confecerant. In hoc noxia non est. Sed cum vendis, semel profer vasis pretium; deinde si volueris aliquid pretii minuere, in tua potestate est. . . . Quantumvis habeas, ne dereliqueris opus tuum: pro viribus fac; duntaxat absque conturbatione."

26. For the terminology of monastic contemplation, see Jean Leclercq, *Otia monastica: Études sur le vocabulaire de la contemplation au Moyen Âge*, Studia Anselmiana 51 (Rome, 1963).

27. Basil of Caesarea, *Regulae fusius tractatae*, PG 31, cols. 927–934.

28. Ibid., cols. 1010–1011.

29. For a summary of these rules, see Adalbert de Vogüé, "The Cenobitic Rules in the West," *Cistercian Studies* 12 (1977), 175–183; for labor in Western monastic rules see E. Delaruelle, "Le travail dans les règles monastiques occidentales du IVᵉ au IXᵉ siècle," *Journal de psychologie normale et pathologique* 41 (1948), 51–62, and Émile Levasseur, "Le travail des moines dans les monastères," *Séances et travaux de l'Académie des sciences morales et politiques* 154, n.s. 60 (1900), 449–470.

30. Jerome's preface is included in *Pachomiana latina*, 6; also PL 23, col. 67: "Fratres eiusdem artis in unam domum sub uno praeposito congregantur: verbi gratia, ut qui texunt lina sint pariter; qui mattas, in unam reputantur familiam; sarcinatores, carpentarii, fullones, gallicarii seorsum a suis praepositis gubernantur: et per singulas hebdomadas ratiocinia operum suorum ad Patram monasterii referunt."

31. Jerome, *Epistulae*, CSEL 56, epistle 125 (p. 132): "Aegyptiorum monasteria hunc morem tenent, ut nulum absque opere ac labore suscipiant, non tam propter uictus necessaria quam propter animae salutem."

32. See Kelly, *Jerome*, 47–48.

33. See Jerome, in *Pachomiana latina*, 5; also see H. Bacht, "Antonius und Pachomius: Von der Anachorese zum Conobitentum," in *Antonius Magnus eremita*, ed. B. Steidle, Studia Anselmiana 38 (Rome, 1956), 66–107 for an overview of the transformation of monasticism under Pachomian influence.

34. Augustine, *De opere monachorum*, PL 40, col. 550.

35. Ibid., cols. 553–554.

36. Ibid., col. 565: "Cantica vero divina cantare, etiam manibus operantes facile possunt, et ipsum laborem tanquam divino celeumate consolari."

37. Ibid., cols. 558–559.

38. See Augustine, *La règle de Saint Augustin*, ed. Luc Verheijen, 2 vols. (Paris, 1967), 1.61, 150, and 439–441.

39. Ibid., 1.429–430.

40. Cassian, *Conlationes*, ed. Michael Petschenig, CSEL 13 (Vienna, 1886), bk. 24, chap. 12 (686–687): "Nam utique omne hominum genus absque illo tantum genere monachorum, quod secundum praeceptum apostoli cotidianis manuum suarum laboribus vivit, agapem alienae miserationis expectat. Unde non solum eos, qui ali semet ipsos vel parentum facultatibus vel famulorum laboribus vel fundorum suorum fructibus gloriantur, sed ipsos etiam reges mundi huius agape certum est sustentari. Hoc denique maiorum nostrorum definitio habet, qui quidquid ad necessitatem cotidiani victus insumitur, quod opere manuum nostrarum effectum partumque non fuerit, ad agapem referri debere sanxerunt secundum apostolum, qui otiosis penitus interdicens opem largitatis alienae qui non, inquit, operatur, nec manducet [2 Thessalonians 3:10]."

41. Cassian, *De institutis coenobiorum*, ed. Michael Petschenig, CSEL 17 (Vienna, 1888), bk. 2, chap. 14 (29): "Et idcirco eas cum adiectione operis exsequuntur, ne uelut otiosis ualeat somnus inrepere."

42. Cassian, *De institutis*, bk. 2, chap. 14; also bk. 10, chap. 12 (p. 184): "ita ut, quid ex quo pendeat, haud facile possit a quoquam discerni, id est utrum propter meditationem spiritalem incessabile manuum opus exerceant, an propter operis iugitatem tam praeclarum spiritus profectum scientiaeque lumen adquirant."

43. Ibid., bk. 10 (23): "Hinc est quod in his regionibus nulla videmus monasteria tanta fratrum celebritate fundata quia nec operum suorum facultatibus fulciuntur, ut possint in eis jugiter perdurare, et si eis suppeditare quoquo modo valeat sufficientia victus alterius largitate, voluptas tamen otii et pervagatio cordis diutius eos in loco perseverare non patitur."

44. Sulpicius Severus, *Vita Sancti Martini*, ed. C. Holm, CSEL 1 (Vienna, 1866), 120: "cui tamen operi minor aetas deputabatur: maiores orationi uacabant."

45. See Joseph T. Lienhard, *Paulinus of Nola and Early Western Monasticism* (Cologne and Bonn, 1977), 42.

46. See Ansgar Mundo, *Les Anciens Synodes abbatiaux et les "Règulae SS. Patrum,"* Studia Anselmiana 44 (Rome, 1966), 107–125.

47. A critical edition is "Règle des IV pères et seconde Règle des pères," ed. Jean Neufville, *"Revue bénédictine,* 77 (1967), 47–95; for this passage, see 82: "A tertia uero usque ad nonam quidquid fuerit imperatum sine murmuratione perficiatur."

48. "Règle des IV pères," 85: "Hoc autem obseruandum est ut in nullo uoluntatem suam faciat."

49. Edited in *Les Règles des saints pères,* ed. Adalbert de Vogüé, 2 vols. (Paris, 1982), 1.374.

50. Ibid., 1.389: "Illud etiam addendum fuit, ut intra monasterium artificium non faciat ullus, nisi ille, cuius fides probata fuerit, qui ad utilitatem et necessitatem monasterii faciat, quid poterit facere."

51. *La règle du Maître,* ed. Adalbert de Vogüé, Sources chrétiennes 105–107 (Paris, 1964–1965); the literature on the controversy concerning the influence of the Rule of the Master on Benedict is immense: see B. Jaspert, *Regula Magistri, Regula Benedicti: Bibliographie ihrer Erforschung 1938–1970,* Subsidia Monastica 1 (Montserrat, 1971) for a bibliography up to 1970.

52. *La règle du Maître,* chap. 50 (236–238): "Ad laborem uero operis terreni uel missiones uiarum hii fratres deputentur, qui artes nesciunt aut discere nolunt aut non possunt. Artifices uero, deputato ad diem et experimentato artis suae penso, artibus cottidie sedeant. Qui tamen cum aliqua necessitas laboris terreni aut uiarum pro monasterii utilitate perurserit, tunc relictis artibus, aut fratrum adiutoriis aut uiarum necessitatibus occupentur. Fratribus delicatis et infirmis talis labor iniungatur, ut nutriantur ad seruitium Dei, non occidantur. Duricordes uero et simplices fratres uel qui litteras discere nolunt et non possunt, ipsi gurdis operibus intricentur, tamen cum temperamento iustitiae, ne soli iugiter diuersis opprimantur laboribus."

53. *La règle du Maître,* chapt. 86 (p. 351): "Casas monasterii oportet esse locatas, ut omnem agrorum laborem, casae sollicitudinem, inquilinorum clamores . . ut hae res, quae migrantibus nobis de hac uita saeculo remanent et animam nostram post mortem sequi non possunt digne non debemus de eis nostros cogitatos occupare." Monkish distaste for those immersed in the world is made especially clear in this chapter of the *Rule of the Master.*

54. *La Règle de saint Benoît,* ed. Adalbert de Vogüé, Sources chrétiennes 181–186 (Paris, 1971–1972), is the critical edition; chap. 48 (pp. 599–604): "quia tunc vere monachi sunt si labore manuum suarum vivunt, sicut et patres nostri et apostoli." Interestingly, Benedict adds immediately after this sentence the following qualification: "Omnia tamen mensurate fiant propter pusillanimes."

Notes to Pages 103–112

55. See Columbanus, *Opera,* ed. G.S.M. Walker, Scriptores latini Hiberniae 2 (Dublin, 1957), 138, also 78.

56. Adalbert de Vogüé, "Travail et alimentation dans les règles de saint Benoît et du Maître," *Revue bénédictine* 74 (1964), 242–251.

57. *La Règle de saint Benoît,* chap. 57.

58. For the influence of monasticism on the history of utopian thinking, see J. C. Davis, *Utopia and the Ideal Society* (Cambridge, 1981), 58–59, 72, 79–80, 371.

4. THE MECHANICAL ARTS IN THE ORDER OF KNOWLEDGE

1. For Plato's scheme of the classification of knowledge see the *Republic,* 509d6–511e5, along with the other texts cited in my discussion; see also Henri Marrou, *A History of Education in Antiquity,* trans. George Lamb (New York, 1956), 61–115.

2. See *Metaphysics* 1025b–1026a; for the theoretical underpinnings of this division, see *Nicomachean Ethics,* 1139b15–1141a7; for Aristotle's critique of Plato's view of the organization of knowledge, see *Metaphysics* 987a30–988a15. For a schematic presentation of Aristotle's views and the views of other writers discussed here, see James A. Weisheipl, "The Nature, Scope, and Classification of the Sciences," in *Science in the Middle Ages,* ed. David Lindberg (Chicago, 1978), 468; another work by Father Weisheipl, "Classification of the Sciences in Medieval Thought," *Mediaeval Studies* 27 (1965), 54–90 has also been of great value to me.

3. Although I have not discusssed it directly here, the Stoics' division of knowledge into logic, ethics, and physics indirectly affected the Middle Ages through Augustine, who used this division thinking that it came from Plato. See *De civitate Dei,* bk. 8, chap. 4; also Weisheipl, "Nature, Scope, and Classification," 469.

4. For Varro, see Friedrich Ritschl, *Questiones Varronianae* (Bonn, 1845).

5. Martianus Capella, *De nuptiis Philologiae et Mercurii,* ed. Adolf Dick (Leipzig, 1925). For Martianus's sources, see William H. Stahl, *The Quadrivium of Martianus Capella* (New York, 1971), 41–54.

6. Gregory of Tours, *Historia francorum,* ed. W. Arndt and Bruno Krusch, Monumenta germaniae historica, Scriptores rerum Merovingicarum 1 (Hanover, 1885, repr. 1961), bk. 10, chap. 31.

7. Martianus Capella, *De nuptiis,* bk. 9, 890.

8. See Rabanus Maurus, *De universo,* PL 111, col. 413 and passim for a division of learning that also includes mechanics and medicine: "Dividitur autem Physics in septem partes, hoc est, Arithmeticam, Astronomiam, Astrologiam, Mechaniam, Medicinam, Geometriam, et Musicam.... Mechania est peritia fabricae artis in metallis et in lignis et lapidibus."

9. Boethius, *In Isagogen Porphyrii commenta,* ed. Samuel Brandt, CSEL 48 (Vienna, 1906), 135–169.

10. Boethius, *De trinitate,* ed. Samuel Brandt, CSEL 48 (Vienna, 1906), 27–32.

11. Cassiodorus, *Institutiones,* ed. R.A.B. Mynors (Oxford, 1937), 91: "Ars vero dicta est, quod nos suis regulis artet."

12. James Feibleman, "Pure Science, Applied Science, and Technology: An Attempt at Definition," in *Philosophy and Technology,* ed. Carl Mitcham and Robert Mackey (New York, 1972), 33–41 attempts to sort out the distinctions between science and technology (understood on both a formal and informal level). His discussion of the theoretical issues is helpful, but he neglects the social and cultural distinctions one can make between technology and "applied science."

13. Cassiodorus, *Institutiones,* bk. 1, chap. 30 (77–78): "Paravimus etiam nocturnis vigiliis mechanicas lucernas conservatrices illuminantium flammarum, ipsas sibi nutrientes incendium, quae humano ministerio cessante prolixe custodiant uberrimi luminis abundantissimam claritatem; ubi olei pinguedo non deficit, quamvis flammis ardentibus iugiter torreatur."

14. Ibid., bk. 1, chap. 28 (73): "adest enim cum desideratur, et cum vota compleverit remotus abscedit."

15. Ibid., bk. 1, chap. 30 (79–80).

16. Cf. Augustine, *De doctrina christiana,* ed. Joseph Martin, CCSL 32 (Turnhout, 1962), 65.

17. Weisheipl, "Classification of the Sciences," 63.

18. Isidore of Seville, *Etymologiarum sive originum, libri xx,* ed. W. M. Lindsay, 2 vols. (Oxford, 1911), vol. 1, bk. 2, sect. 24.

19. See, for example, Isidore's account of farming and agricultural practice in vol. 2, bk. 17.

20. Weisheipl, "Classification of the Sciences," 65.

21. Rabanus Maurus, *De universo,* cols. 413–414 (see note 8 above).

22. Ibid., col. 416.

23. John the Scot, *Periphyseon* (*De divisione naturae*), ed. and trans. I. P. Sheldon-Williams, Scriptores latini Hiberniae 2 (Dublin, 1981), 27.

24. Ibid., 222–224.

25. Ibid., 230.

26. Roger Baron, *Science et sagesse chez Hugues de Saint-Victor* (Paris, 1957), 73–74.

27. Hugh of Saint Victor, *Didascalicon de studio legendi: A Critical Text,* ed. Charles Henry Buttimer, Studies in Medieval and Renaissance Latin 10 (Washington, D.C., 1939), 22.

28. Ibid., 38–39; the question of which sciences are subordinate and which are subordinating, considered by Plato in *Republic,* 528b, was central to Aristotle's

classification of knowledge (see *Posterior Analytics,* 75b15). For an overview of this matter of subordination, see Richard D. McKirahan, Jr., "Aristotle's Subordinate Sciences," *British Journal for the History of Science* 11 (1978), 197–220.

29. "Ex quibus tres ad extrinsecus vestimentum naturae pertinent, quo se ipsa natura ab incommodis protegit, quattuor ad intrinsecus, quo se alendo et fovendo nutrit, ad similitudinem quidem trivii et quadrivii, quia trivium de vocibus quae extrinsecus sunt et quadrivium de intellectibus qui intrinsecus concepti sunt pertractat." *Didascalicon,* 39.

30. Translation is by Jerome Taylor, *The Didascalicon of Hugh of Saint Victor* (New York, 1961), 75. Taylor's edition and especially his extensive notes have been very valuable to me.

31. For Hugh's concept of the "adulterate" mechanical arts see *Didascalicon,* 16 and 39; see also his earlier *Epitome Dindimi philosophiam,* in "*Epitome Dindimi in philosophiam:* Introduction, texte critique, et notes," ed. Roger Baron, *Traditio* 11 (1955), 112, line 210.

32. M. I. Finley, "Technical Innovation and Economic Progress in the Ancient World," *Economic History Review* 2d ser. 18 (1965), 43–45; and Lynn White, Jr., "The Iconography of *Temperantia* and the Virtuousness of Technology," in *Medieval Religion and Technology* (Berkeley, 1978), 181–204.

33. Marc Bloch, "The Advent and Triumph of the Watermill," in *Land and Work in Medieval Europe* (Berkeley, 1967), 145.

34. See chapter 3, above.

35. Jacques Le Goff, "Labor, Techniques and Craftsmen in the Value Systems of the Early Middle Ages (Fifth to Tenth Centuries)," in *Time, Work, and Culture in the Middle Ages,* trans. Arthur Goldhammer (Chicago, 1980), 75.

36. Roger Bacon, *Opus maius,* ed. J. H. Bridges, 3 vols. (Oxford 1897–1900), 1.23; for more on the relationship of "clerks" and artisans, see Guy Beaujouan, "L'interdépendance entre la science scholastique et les techniques utilitaires (XIIe, XIIIe, XIVe siècles), in *Les Conférences du Palais de la Découverte,* ser. D, 46 (Paris, 1946), 10–15.

37. *Didascalicon,* 6; translation is by Taylor, *The Didascalicon of Hugh of Saint Victor,* 47.

38. See L. M. De Rijk, "Some Notes on the Twelfth-Century Topic of the Three (Four) Human Evils and of Science, Virtue, and Techniques as Their Remedies," *Vivarium* 5 (1967), 8–15.

39. Hugh of Saint Victor, *Didascalicon,* 23; for another statement of this view see his *De arca Noe morali,* PL 176, col. 619.

40. Augustine, *De doctrina christiana,* bk. 2, chap. 39.

41. Godefroy of Saint Victor, *Microcosmus,* ed. Philippe Delehaye (Lille, 1951), 73–74.

42. The date of composition is disputed. See L. Amoros, "Escritos de San Buenaventura," in *Obras de san Buenaventura*, 2d ed. (Madrid, 1955), 1.47; also *De reductione artium ad theologiam*, ed. Sister Emma Therese Healy, in *The Works of Saint Bonaventure* (St. Bonaventure, N.Y., 1955), 1.14. References to the *De reductione* are to the latter edition. For Bonaventure's classification, see 1.40; for his relationship to Hugh of Saint Victor, see Bonaventure Hindwood, O.F.M., "The Division of Human Knowledge in the Writings of Saint Bonaventure," *Franciscan Studies* 38 (1978), 233–234.

43. Bonaventure, *De reductione*, 1.29.

44. "Primum igitur lumen, quod illuminat ad figuras artificiales, quae quasi exterius sunt et propter supplendam corporis indigentiam repertae, dicitur lumen artis mechanicae," *De reductione*, 2.20.

45. "Per hoc modum [whereby sense perception was understood] est reperire in illuminatione artis mechanicae, cuius tota intentio versatur circa artificialium productionem. In qua ista tria possumus intueri, scilicet Verbi generationem et incaranationem, vivendi ordinem et Dei et animae foederationem. Et hoc, si consideremus egressum, effectum et fructum; vel sic: artem operandi, qualitatem effecti artificii et utilitatem fructus eliciti." *De reductione*, 1.30.

46. See al-Farabi, *De scientiis*, ed. Manuel Alonso Alonso (Madrid, Granada, 1954). For *De ortu scientiarum*, see *Alfarabi, Über den Ursprung der Wissenschaften*, ed. C. Baumker, Beiträge zur Geschichte der Philosophie des Mittelalters 19.3 (Muenster, 1916).

47. Domingo Gundisalvo, *De divisione philosophiae*, ed. Ludwig Baur, Beiträge zur Geschichte der Philosophie des Mittlalters 4.2–3 (Muenster, 1903); all citations are from this edition. For Gundisalvo's sources, see Baur's notes. 164ff.

48. Al-Farabi, *De ortu scientiarum*, 20.

49. Ibid., 21.

50. Al-Farabi, *De scientiis*, 109.

51. Ibid., 111–112.

52. Domingo Gundisalvo, *De divisione philosophiae*, 14–17.

53. Ibid., 20: "Materia vero naturalis sciencie est corpus, non secundum quod est ens, nec secundum quod est substancia, nec secundum quod est compositum ex duobus principiis, que sunt materia et forma, sed secundum quod subiectum est motui et quieti et permutacioni."

54. Ibid., 32.

55. Ibid., 122: "Sciencia vero de ingeniis est sciencia excogitandi, qualiter quis faciat covenire omnia illa, quorum modi declarantur et demonstrantur in doctrinis."

56. The plumb-bob?

57. Domingo Gundisalvo, *De divisione philosophiae*, 35–36.

58. Hugh of Saint Victor, *Didascalicon*, 16: "Sunt etenim tria opera, id est,

opus Dei, opus naturae, opus artificis imitantis naturam." Hugh is here adapting Chalcidius's commentary on the *Timaeus;* see Taylor's note to this passage, 190–191, n. 59.

59. Domingo Gundisalvo, *De divisione philosophiae,* 123; also Bacon's *Opus maius,* 2.169, where Bacon writes of experience *per sensus exteriores,* which is carried out *per instrumenta.*

60. By the time of Robert Grosseteste and Roger Bacon, the view that the practical sciences contributed "instruments" to experimental science was well established. See A. C. Crombie, *Robert Grosseteste and the Origins of Experimental Science* (Oxford, 1953), 21 and 149–151.

61. Marie-Dominique Chenu, "The Masters of the Theological 'Science,' " in *Nature, Man, and Society in the Twelfth Century,* trans. Jerome Taylor and Lester K. Little (Chicago, 1968), 270–309.

62. Gillian Evans provides the background to this dispute in *From Old Arts to New Theology* (Oxford, 1981).

63. John of Salisbury, *Metalogicon libri IV,* ed. C.C.J. Webb (Oxford, 1929), 4; also PL 199, col. 825.

64. Ibid., 7; in PL, col. 827.

65. Ibid., 21; in PL, col. 833.

66. Ibid., 58; in PL, col. 856.

67. Ibid., 28–29; in PL, col. 838.

68. Ibid., 31; in Pl, col. 839.

69. Weisheipl, "Classification of the Sciences," 67.

70. See Crombie, *Robert Grosseteste;* also Guy Beaujouan, "The Transformation of the Quadrivium," in *Renaissance and Renewal in the Twelfth Century,* ed. Robert L. Benson, Giles Constable, and Carol D. Lanham, (Cambridge, Mass., 1982), 463–487.

71. Vincent of Beauvais, *Speculum doctrinale* (Douai, 1624), bk. 1, chap. 16, 398ff.

72. Michael Scot, *De divisione philosophiae,* in Vincent of Beauvais, *Speculum doctrinale,* 398.

73. Ibid., 399.

74. See Serge Lusignan, "Préface au 'Speculum maius' de Vincent de Beauvais: Refraction et diffraction," *Cahiers d'études médiévales* 5 (1979), 98–107.

75. Robert Kilwardby, *De ortu scientiarum,* ed. Albert G. Judy (Oxford, 1976); all references are to this edition. See too Weisheipl, "Classification of the Sciences," 75–78.

76. Kilwardby, *De ortu,* 11–14; see also D. E. Sharpe, "The *De ortu scientiarum* of Robert Kilwardby," *The New Scholasticism* 8 (1934), 2 for a view that stresses Kilwardby's independence from his sources.

77. Kilwardby, *De ortu*, 9: "Prima enim continet modum vivendi sine quo salus non est, et ideo est ad salutem necessaria."

78. Ibid., 10; Isidore of Seville, *Etymologiarum*, vol. 2, chap. 24.

79. Kilwardby, *De ortu*, 13; see also Crombie, *Robert Grosseteste*, 138–139, where Kilwardby is cited as having made "an important contribution to Oxford scientific thought" insofar as he stressed the relation between the theoretical sciences and the solutions to "particular, concrete problems encountered in attempting to satisfy the physical needs of the body."

80. Kilwardby, *De ortu*, 129–131.

81. Ibid., 131.

82. Ibid., 134; see also Sharpe, "The *De ortu*," 17–20.

83. Kilwardby, *De ortu*, 135; Judy provides Grosseteste's translations of the relevant passages from Eustratius of Nicaea's commentary on Aristotle's *Ethics* on 135, n. 2.

84. Aristotle, *Ethics*, 1140a1ff.

85. Kilwardby, *De ortu*, 133.

86. Ibid., 137.

87. Ibid., 139.

88. Weisheipl, "Classification of the Sciences," 86.

89. Thomas Aquinas, *Expositio super librum Boethii De trinitate*, ed. B. Decker (Leiden, 1955), q. 5, art. 3.

90. Ibid., q. 5, art. 1.

91. Ibid., q. 5, art. 4.

92. Thomas Aquinas, *Expositio in libros Ethicorum*, ed. A. M. Pirotta (Turin, 1934), vol. 1, lect. 1, 1.

93. Thomas Aquinas, *In Metaphysicam Aristotelis commentaria*, ed. M. R. Cathala (Turin, 1915), vol. 1, lect. 1, 1.

94. In *Expositio . . . Ethicorum*, lect. 7, nn. 1209–1211, Aquinas describes the program whereby boys are to be educated in the various sciences. He mentions logic, mathematics, natural science, moral science, and metaphysics. The mechanical sciences are not taught to those whose goal is the study of theology.

95. For Lull's career and an overview of his writings, see J. N. Hillgarth, *Ramon Lull and Lullism in Fourteenth-Century France* (Oxford, 1971) and two essays of Frances Yates, "The Art of Ramon Lull: An Approach to It Through Lull's Theory of the Elements" and "Ramon Lull and John Scotus Erigena," in *Collected Essays: Lull and Bruno* (London, 1982), 1.3–128.

96. Yates, "Art of Ramon Lull," 9–25.

97. Raymond Lull, *Arbor scientiae* (Lyons, 1637), 651–659.

98. Ibid., 660.

99. Ibid., 661, where Lull discusses the nature of work.

100. Throughout this chapter, my speculations on the classificatory system itself have been influenced by the work of Jack Goody, in *The Domestication of the Savage Mind* (Cambridge, 1977), 108–110.

5. THE SECULARIZATION OF LABOR

1. The complexities and importance of the twelfth century are well reflected in the recent book commemorating Charles Homer Haskins's *Renaissance of the Twelfth Century: Renaissance and Renewal in the Twelfth Century,* ed. Robert L. Benson, Giles Constable, and Carol D. Lanham (Cambridge, Mass., 1982).

2. Although I do not agree with all of his conclusions, Harold J. Berman, *Law and Revolution: The Formation of the Western Legal Tradition* (Cambridge, Mass., 1983) has been especially useful for illuminating the changes that occurred in twelfth-century legal thought (see 85–119); more specialized and equally useful is Paul R. Hyams, *Kings, Lords, and Peasants in Medieval England* (Oxford, 1980).

3. A summary of medieval agricultural history may be found in Georges Duby, "Medieval Agriculture," in *The Middle Ages,* ed. Carlo M. Cipolla, vol. 1 of *The Fontana Economic History of Europe* (New York, 1976), 175–220. In the pages that follow I have also used Georges Duby, *Rural Economy and Country Life in the Medieval West,* trans. Cynthia Postan (Columbia, S.C.: 1968); *The Cambridge Economic History of Europe,* vol. 1, *The Agrarian Life of the Middle Ages,* ed. M. M. Postan, 2d ed. (Cambridge, 1966); and David Herlihy, "The Agrarian Revolution in Southern France and Italy, 801–1150," *Speculum* 33 (1958), 23–41.

4. Described and documented by Lynn White, Jr., *Medieval Technology and Social Change* (Oxford, 1962), 57–69.

5. Georges Duby, *The Early Growth of the European Economy* (Ithaca, N.Y., 1974), 191. For the deforestation of Europe in the Middle Ages, see H. C. Darby, "The Clearing of the Woodland in Europe," in *Man's Role in Changing the Face of the Earth,* ed. William L. Thomas, 2 vols. (Chicago, 1956), 1.183–216.

6. Margaret T. Hodgen, "Domesday Water Mills," *Antiquity* 13 (1939), 261–279 cites 5,624, a figure that is "almost certainly too low" according to Reginald Lennard, *Rural England: 1066–1135* (Oxford, 1959), 278–287. Essential is Marc Bloch, "The Advent and Triumph of the Watermill," in *Land and Work in Medieval England,* trans. J. E. Anderson (Berkeley, 1967), 136–168.

7. See Robert J. Forbes, "Power," in *A History of Technology,* ed. Charles Singer et al., 8 vols. (Oxford, 1954–1984), 2.609.

8. Forbes, "Power," 2.610.

9. See Majorie N. Boyer, "Water Mills: A problem for the Bridges and Boats of Medieval France," *History of Technology* 7 (1982), 1–22.

10. Terry S. Reynolds, *Stronger Than a Hundred Men: A History of the Vertical Water Wheel* (Baltimore, 1983), 92 gives evidence from Augsburg city records of

1351 as the earliest evidence of a water-powered wire mill. Forbes, "Power," 643 discusses hammer forges. On water mills in monastic establishments see David Luckhurst, *Monastic Watermills: A Study of the Mills Within English Monastic Precincts* (London, n.d.). For Italian mills see John Muendel, "The Distribution of Mills in the Florentine Countryside During the Late Middle Ages," in *Pathways to Medieval Peasants,* ed. J. A. Raftis (Toronto, 1981), 83–115.

11. Excellent illustrations are contained in Singer's *History of Technology* and Reynolds, *Stronger Than a Hundred Men.*

12. See E. M. Carus-Wilson, "An Industrial Revolution of the Thirteenth Century," *Economic History Review* 12 (1941), 39–60.

13. Georges Duby, *Early Growth,* 223: "as every extant survey of manorial profits testifies, the most substantial rents enjoyed by landlords came from the exploitation of bread-ovens, mills, and tithes." Also Bloch, "Advent and Triumph of the Watermill," 156–157.

14. See *Cambridge Economic History of Europe,* "Trade," 2.119ff.

15. An excellent recent survey of this international trade is Philip D. Curtin, *Cross-Cultural Trade in World History* (Cambridge, 1984), esp. 111–127.

16. M. M. Postan, *Medieval Economy and Society,* vol. 1 of *The Pelican Economic History of Britain* (London, 1972), 213–214.

17. R. D. Face, "Techniques of Business in the Trade Between the Fairs of Champagne and the South of Europe in the Twelfth and Thirteenth Centuries," *Economic History Review* 2d ser. 10 (1958), 437.

18. The best general study is E. Fournial, *Histoire monétaire de l'occident médiéval* (Paris, 1970); also, Carlo M. Cipolla, *Money, Prices, and Civilization in the Mediterranean World, Fifth to Seventeenth Century* (Princeton, 1956); the rationalization of the European economy is one subject of Alexander Murray, *Reason and Society in the Middle Ages* (Oxford, 1978), 50–58.

19. For the flow of Islamic capital into the West, see R. S. Lopez, "Aux origines du capitalisme génois," *Annales d'histoire économique et sociale* 9 (1937), 445–451.

20. See J. C. Russell, "Population in Europe 500–1500," in *The Middle Ages,* ed. Cipolla, 36.

21. Marc Bloch, "Natural Economy or Money Economy: A Pseudo-Dilemma," in *Land and Work,* 230.

22. For scutage, see J. O. Prestwick, "War and Finance in the Anglo-Norman State," *Transactions of the Royal Historical Society* 4 (1954), 453–487; for the transformation of feudal relations generally see Berman, *Law and Revolution,* 304–305, where he describes the "reification of rights" which "fostered the increased economic autonomy of the vassal."

23. See Lester K. Little, "Pride Goes Before Avarice: Social Change and the Vices in Latin Christendom," *American Historical Review* 76 (1971), 16–49.

24. For resistance to mechanization in the cloth industry, see Carus-Wilson, "An Industrial Revolution," 53–54. For a brief and lucid summary of the transition from "gift economy to profit economy," see Lester K. Little, *Religious Poverty and the Profit Economy in Medieval Europe* (Ithaca, N.Y., 1978), 3–18.

25. Joel Kaye of the University of Pennsylvania has analyzed money as a form of medieval technology in an unpublished paper to which I am indebted.

26. Little, *Religious Poverty*, 35; I have found Little's discussion very valuable.

27. For general background on the history of the Cistercians see Dom Ursmer Berliere, "Les origines de Cîteaux et l'ordre bénédictin du XIIe siècle," *Revue d'histoire ecclésiastique* 1 (1900), 448–471; J.-B. Mahn, *L'Ordre cistercien et son gouvernement* 2d ed. (Paris, 1951); and David Knowles, "The Primitive Cistercian Documents," in *Great Historical Enterprises and Problems in Monastic History* (London, 1963).

28. For the origins and growth of Cîteaux, see R. A. Donkin, "The Growth and Distribution of the Cistercian Order in Medieval Europe," *Studia monastica* 9 (1967); 275–286.

29. For St. Bernard's life as seen by a contemporary, see William of Saint Thierry, *Vita prima S. Bernardi*, PL 185, cols. 225–268; for the distribution of Cistercian monasteries generally, see Frederik van der Meer, *Atlas de l'ordre cistercien*, 2d ed. (Paris, 1965).

30. R. A. Donkin, "The Cistercian Settlement and the Royal Forests," *Cîteaux in de Nederlanden*, 10–11 (1959–1960), 39–55 and 117–132; for the ideal of monastic isolation as expressed by the Cistercians, see E. Hoffman, "Die Entwicklung der Wirtschaftsprinzipien im Cisterzensorden wahrend des 12. und 13. Jahrhunderts," *Historisches Jahrbuch* 30 (1910), 699–727.

31. Bernard of Clairvaux, *Apologia ad Guillelmum*, in *Opera*, ed. Jean Leclercq (Rome, 1957), 3.81–82.

32. As described by Peter the Venerable, *Letters*, ed. Giles Constable, 2 vols., Harvard Historical Studies 78 (Cambridge, Mass., 1967), vol. 1, epistle 1, 28; see also Joan Evans, *Monastic Life at Cluny, 910–1157* (Oxford, 1931), 114 for Peter's comments on copying manuscripts ("It is more noble to set one's hand to the pen than to the plough").

33. For the *conversi* see J. S. Donnelly, *The Decline of the Medieval Cistercian Lay Brotherhood*, Fordham University Studies, History Series 3 (New York, 1949), 4–19; and Richard Roehl, "Plan and Reality in a Medieval Monastic Economy: The Cistercians," *Studies in Medieval and Renaissance History* 9 (1972), 84–94.

34. The role of the *conversi* is specified in the *Usus conversorum*, edited in *Les monuments primitifs de la Règle cistercienne*, ed. P. Guignard, Analecta Divionensia (Dijon, 1878), 276–287.

35. Roehl, "Plan and Reality," 94.

36. For the purchase of serfs by Cistercians, see Coburn V. Graves, "The Economic Activities of the Cistercians in Medieval England," *Analecta Sacri Ordinis Cisterciensis* 13 (1957), 7. Also James S. Donnelly, "Changes in the Grange Economy of the English and Welsh Cistercian Abbeys, 1300–1500," *Traditio* 10 (1954), 414.

37. See Bennett D. Hill, *English Cistercian Monasteries and Their Patrons in the Twelfth Century* (Urbana, Ill., 1968), 151–153.

38. For Mapes's quarrels with the Cistercians, see Graves, "The Economic Activities," 48–49; also B. Griesser, "Walther Map und die Cistercienser," *Cistercienser-Chronik* 36 (1924), 137–141 (cited by Graves, 48).

39. See Hill, *English Cistercian Monasteries*, 29.

40. For the Cistercians and economic growth, see J. A. Raftis, "Western Monasticism and Economic Organization," *Comparative Studies in Society and History* 3 (1961), 452–469. Also Norman F. Cantor, "The Crisis of Western Monasticism," *American Historical Review* 46 (1960), 47–67; Cantor concludes that "it seems no exaggeration to say that the crisis of Western monasticism was the crisis of medieval civilization itself" (67). John Van Engen, " 'The Crisis of Cenobitism' Reconsidered: Benedictine Monasticism 1050–1150," *Speculum* 61 (1986), 269–304 came to my attention too late for inclusion here.

41. For what follows, I am indebted to Brian Stock, "Experience, Praxis, Work, and Planning in Bernard of Clairvaux: Observations on the *Sermones in Cantica*," in *The Cultural Context of Medieval Learning*, ed. John E. Murdoch and Edith Sylla, Boston Studies in the Philosophy of Science 26 (Dordrecht, 1975), 219–268.

42. Bernard of Clairvaux, *Sermones super Cantica canticorum*, ed. Jean Leclercq et al. in *S. Bernardi Opera* (Rome, 1957–1958), sermon 36; cited in Stock, "Experience, Praxis, Work," 230.

43. Bernard of Clairvaux, *Sermones*, sermon 26; Stock, "Experience, Praxis, Work," 249.

44. For a thorough discussion of Bernard's views, see Maurice Vignes, "Les doctrines économiques et morales de Saint Bernard sur la richesse et la travail," *Revue d'histoire économique et sociale* 16 (1928), 575–576.

45. In PL 184, cols, 849–870; see sect. 30.

46. See *Vita Norberti Archiepiscopi Magdeburgenis, Vita A,* ed. George Heind et al., Monumenta germaniae historica, Scriptores 12 (Hanover, 1826), 663–706; and also Vita B—*Vita S. Norberti,* PL 170, cols. 1253–1344.

47. For the early history of the order, see François Petit, *La Spiritualité des Premontrés aux XIIe et XIIIe siècles* (Paris, 1947).

48. For the life of Bruno, see *Vita S. Brunonis,* PL 152, cols. 481–492; 491–526; and 526–552; the *Consuetudines* are printed in PL 153, cols. 631–758.

49. Bruno of Cologne, *Consuetudines,* cols. 752–753.

50. Guibert of Nogent, *De vita sua,* PL 156, cols. 853–856.

51. See Little, *Religious Poverty*, 87.

52. Gerhoh of Reichersberg, *Liber de aedificio Dei*, PL 194, col. 1302.

53. For Idung, see R.B.C. Huygens, "Zu Idung von Prufening und seinen Schriften, 'Argumentum super quatuor questionibus' und 'Dialogus duorum monachorum,' " *Deutsches Archiv für Erforschung des Mittelalters* 2 (1971), 544–545; critical edition of *Dialogus duorum monachorum* also edited by Huygens in *Studi medievali* 3d ser. 13.1 (1972), 375–470; references and translations are from this edition and cited by section number.

54. For a balanced account of the issues, see David Knowles, "Cistercians and Cluniacs: The Controversy Between St. Bernard and Peter the Venerable," in *The Historian and Character* (Cambridge, 1963), 50–75.

55. Idung, *Dialogus*, 1.28.

56. Ibid., 1.53.

57. Ibid., 1.54.

58. Ibid., 2.4; see also Joan Evans, *Monastic Life at Cluny*, 87–88.

59. Idung, *Dialogus*, 2.31.

60. Ibid., 2.7; also 2.9 and 2.13.

61. Ibid., 2.22.

62. Ibid., 2.51.

63. Ibid., 2.52.

64. See Walter Daniel, *Vita Ailredi*, ed. and trans. Maurice Powicke (Oxford, 1978), 22.

65. Daniel, *Vita Ailredi*, 22–23.

66. Aelred of Rievaulx, *De institutione inclusarum*, in *Opera omnia: Opera ascetica*, Corpus christianorum, continuatio medievalis 1 (Turnhout, 1971), 637–682. For Aelred's injunction to live by the work of the hands, see sect. 4.

67. Aelred, *De institutione*, sect. 9.

68. William of Saint Thierry, *Speculum fidei*, PL 180, sect. 15.

69. Anselm of Havelberg, *Liber de ordine canonicorum regularum*, PL 188, cols. 1105–1107 for instructions regarding manual labor.

70. Adam of Dryburgh, *Soliloquia de instructione animae*, PL 198, col. 855; for the heightened expectations of those who hoped to live well in the monastery, see idem, *De ordine et habitu atque professione canonicorum regularum*, PL 198, col. 531.

71. Philip of Harvengt, *De institutione clericorum*, PL 203, col. 706.

72. *Libellus de diversis ordinibus et professionibus qui sunt in aecclesia*, ed. and trans. Giles Constable and B. Smith (Oxford, 1972), 95–97; their translation; emphasis added.

73. Robert of Bridlington, *The Bridlington Dialogue*, ed. and trans. "a religious of CSMV" (London, 1960), 152.

74. Ibid., 153.

75. "Tametsi quibusdam indignum et indecens uideatur, ut sacri alteris officio mancipati huiusmodi rusticanis operibus deputentur, et maxime messioni propter manuum periculum," ibid.

76. Amalaraius of Metz, *Institutio canonicorum,* PL 105, cols. 887–888.

77. See Peter Damian, *De perfectione monachorum,* PL 145, cols. 303–304.

78. Rupert of Deutz, *De vita vere apostolica,* PL 170, cols. 609–664.

79. Rupert of Deutz, *Super quaedam capitula regulae divi Benedicti abbatis,* PL 170, col. 513; the third book of this commentary on the Benedictine Rule is devoted to the question of manual labor; I am indebted here to Marie-Dominique Chenu, "Monks, Canons, and Laymen in Search of the Apostolic Life," in *Nature, Man, and Society in the Twelfth Century,* trans. Jerome Taylor and Lester K. Little (Chicago, 1968), 208–210.

80. Rupert of Deutz, *Super quaedam capitula regulae,* col. 517.

81. See John Moorman, *A History of the Franciscan Order from Its Origins to 1517* (Oxford, 1968), 17 and passim. For St. Francis's own views of manual labor, see *S. Francisci Opuscula,* Bibliotheca franciscana ascetica Medii Aevi (Quaracchi, 1904), 79, where Francis expresses the hope that the "brethren will work at some task that is honest."

82. See Chenu, "Monks, Canons, and Laymen," 224, n. 45.

83. Thomas Aquinas, *Summa theologiae,* ed. and trans. Fathers of the English Dominican Province, 60 vols. (New York, 1964–1976), pt. 1a, q. 108, art. 2; see Chenu, "Monks, Canons, and Laymen," 225.

84. Duby, *Early Growth,* 162–164.

85. Ibid., 164.

86. See *S. Bernardi Opera,* ed. Jean Leclercq et al., (Rome, 1963), 3.221: "ut pene dubitem quid potius censeam appellandos, monachos videlicet an milites, nisi quod utrumque forsan congruentius nominarim, quibus neutrum deesse cognoscitur, nec monachi mansuetudo, nec militis fortitudo."

87. Barbara Rosenwein and Lester K. Little, "Social Meaning in the Monastic and Mendicant Spiritualities," *Past and Present* 63 (1974), 8.

88. Bonaventure, *Quaestiones disputatae, De perfectione evangelica,* in *Opera omnia,* 10 vols. in 9 (Quaracchi, 1882–1902), 5.162: "nullus homo debet esse sine labore in hac vita . . . sed ex hoc non sequitur quod oportet occupari circa laborem manuum et maxime lucrativum."

89. See Aquinas, *Summa theologiae,* 2, q. 100, art. 3; also of value on Aquinas's view of the relative value of intellectual versus manual occupations is Gaines Post, Kimon Giocarinis, and Richard Kay, "The Medieval Heritage of a Humanistic Ideal: *Scientia donum Dei est, unde verdi non potest,*" *Traditio* 22 (1955), 195–234.

90. Aquinas, *In Metaphysicam Aristotelis commentaria,* ed. M. P. Cathala (Turin, 1915), bk. 1, sect. 30.

6. SILENT WORKERS

1. Fernand Braudel, *Civilization and Capitalism,* 3 vols.; see in particular, vol. 1, *The Structures of Everyday Life: The Limits of the Possible* (New York, 1979); also Eric Wolf, *Europe and the People Without History* (Berkeley, 1982).

2. The anecdote is from Gervase of Canterbury, *Historical Works,* ed. W. Stubbs, Rolls Series 73 (London, 1879), 1.3–5. For the changing role of the mechanical arts see Paolo Rossi, *Philosophy, Technology, and the Arts in the Early Modern Era,* trans. Salvator Attanasio (New York, 1970), 1–63; "Mechanical Arts and Philosophy in the Sixteenth Century."

3. Michael T. Clanchy, *From Memory to Written Record* (Cambridge, Mass., 1979), 188–191; also M. B. Parkes, "The Literacy of the Laity," in *The Medieval World,* ed. David Daiches and A. Thoslby (London, 1973), 555–577.

4. H. E. Bell, "The Price of Books in Medieval England," *The Library* 4th ser. 17 (1937), 330.

5. Cited by Clanchy, *From Memory,* 187.

6. Lon R. Shelby, "The Education of Medieval English Masons," *Medieval Studies* 33 (1970), 9–10.

7. For the dissemination of the *De architectura* of Vitruvius see Pamela O. Long, "The Contribution of Architectural Writers to a 'Scientific Outlook' in the Fifteenth and Sixteenth Centuries," *Journal of Medieval and Renaissance Studies* 15 (1985), 265–298.

8. Shelby, "Education of Medieval English Masons," 13.

9. Theophilus, *De diversis artibus,* ed. C. R. Dodwell (London, 1961) is the standard edition, and I have consulted it for the Latin text; translations here are from John G. Hawthorne and Cyril Stanley Smith, *Theophilus: On Diverse Arts* (Chicago, 1962; repr. New York, 1979) whose notes on the technology of Theophilus I have found valuable.

10. Lynn White, Jr., "Theophilus Redivivus," in *Medieval Religion and Technology* (Berkeley, 1978), 101.

11. Theophilus, *On Diverse Arts,* 47.

12. Ibid., 12.

13. Ibid., 47.

14. Ibid., 78–79.

15. *The Two Earliest Masonic Mas.,* ed. Douglas Knoop, G. P. Jones, and Douglas Hamer (Manchester, 1938); line numbers refer to the edition of the Cooke manuscript in this volume.

16. I have consulted the Index of Christian Art at Princeton University.

17. Guillaume de Lorris and Jean de Meun, *Roman de la Rose,* ed. Ernest Langlois, 5 vols. (Paris, 1914–1924), lines 3797–3875; see also 11407–11482.

18. Geoffrey Chaucer, *The Works of Geoffrey Chaucer*, ed. F. N. Robinson, 2d ed. (Boston, 1957); see the Parson's Tale, lines 248–251.

19. Chrétien de Troyes, *Erec et Enide*, in *Arthurian Romances*, ed. and trans. W. W. Comfort (London, 1970), lines 747ff. (10–11).

20. See Chrétien de Troyes, *Le Chevalier de la charrette (Lancelot)*, in *Arthurian Romances*, lines 230ff. (274–275).

21. Andreas Capellanus, *The Art of Courtly Love*, trans. John Jay Parry (New York, 1941), 149.

22. For the life of St. Bernwald, see Thangmar's *Vita Berwardi* in Monumenta germaniae historica, Scriptores 4 (Hanover, 1841), 754–786, esp. 769, sect. 23; also in PL 140, cols. 393–436.

23. For William of Hirschau, see Monumenta germaniae historica, Scriptores 12 (Hanover, 1856), 209–225.

24. For St. Philip Benizi, see *Acta sanctorum quotquot toto orbe coluntur* (Antwerp, 1643–), August, vol. 4.

25. *Pierce the Ploughman's Crede*, ed. W. W. Skeat, EETS o.s. 30 (London, 1873); line numbers are to this edition.

26. William Langland, *Piers Plowman*, ed. W. W. Skeat, 2 vols. (Oxford, 1886).

27. For the social message of Piers Plowman, see Morton W. Bloomfield, *Piers Plowman as a Fourteenth Century Apocalypse* (New Brunswick, N.J., 1962).

28. Jacqueline Jones, *Labor of Love, Labor of Sorrow: Black Women, Work, and the Family from Slavery to the Present* (New York, 1985).

29. Sarah Pomeroy, *Goddesses, Whores, Wives, and Slaves: Women in Classical Antiquity* (New York, 1975).

30. Ibid., 149–204.

31. Tacitus, *Germania*, ed. A. Dopsch et al. (Leipzig, 1930), chap. 8.

32. Discussed in Suzanne Wemple, *Women in Frankish Society: Marriage and the Cloister, 500–900* (Philadelphia, 1983), 9–25.

33. For the participation of women in the early church, see Wayne Meeks, *The First Urban Christians* (New Haven, Conn., 1983).

34. For insight into the psychology of antifeminism, I have consulted Karen Horney, "The Dread of Women," in *Feminine Psychology* (New York, 1967), 133–146.

35. On witchcraft, see Edward Peters, *The Magician, the Witch, and the Law* (Philadelphia, 1978); for the late medieval and early modern periods see Keith Thomas, *Religion and the Decline of Magic* (New York, 1971).

36. A. Kroymann's edition of *De cultu feminarum* is in CCSL 1 (Turnhout, 1954), 341–370. For the passages cited here see 343–344; 365; 370.

37. Samuel Laeuchli, *Power and Sexuality: The Emergence of Canon Law at the Synod of Elvira* (Philadelphia, 1972), 3.

38. Georges Duby, *The Knight, the Lady and the Priest,* trans. Barbara Bray (New York, 1983), 111–115.

39. See Pierre J. Payer, *Sex and the Penitentials* (Toronto, 1984), 24–28.

40. Ibid., 35–36.

41. David Herlihy, "Land, Family, and Women in Continental Europe, 701–1200," *Traditio* 18 (1962), 110.

42. David Herlihy, "Life Expectancies for Women in Medieval Society," in *The Role of Women in the Middle Ages,* ed. Rosemarie Morewedge (Albany, 1975), 9.

43. Christine Fell, *Women in Anglo-Saxon Society* (Bloomington, Ind., 1979), 43.

44. Wemple, *Women in Frankish Society,* 127.

45. Lina Eckenstein, *Women Under Monasticism* (Cambridge, 1896), 125–126.

46. Caesarius of Arles, *Sermones,* ed. D. G. Morin, CCSL 103, 2 vols. (Turnhout, 1953); 43, 3 (234).

47. Ibid., 44, 6 (240).

48. Ibid., 1, 12 (9–10).

49. Ibid., 6, 7 (34–35).

50. Caesarius of Arles, *Opera omnia,* ed. D. G. Morin, 2 vols. (Maredsous, 1937–1942), 2.101–127.

51. Ibid., ch. 36.

52. Ibid., ch. 66.

53. Gregory of Tours, *The History of the Franks,* trans. Lewis Thorpe (Harmondsworth, 1974), 535.

54. "The Life of St. Macrina," trans. V. W. Callahan, is included in *Medieval Women's Visionary Literature,* ed. Elizabeth A. Petroff (New York, 1986), 77–82.

55. See, for example, the documents edited by Toulmin Smith, *English Gilds,* EETS o.s. 40 (London, 1870, repr. 1963), 34 (which names "brethern and sistern" of the Tailors guild of Norwich); 160–161 (which mentions forty-three founders of the Guild of Corpus Christi in Kingston-upon-Hull, eighteen of whom were women); but for the evident exclusion of women from positions of authority within a guild, see 36.

56. Cited by Anthony Black, *Guilds and Civil Society in European Political Thought from the Twelfth Century to the Present* (Ithaca, N.Y., 1984), 78.

57. Ibid., 94–95.

58. Eileen Power, *Medieval Women* (Cambridge, 1924, repr. 1975), 59.

59. Shulamith Shahar, *The Fourth Estate: A History of Women in the Middle Ages* (London, 1983), 201.

60. Heath Dillard, *Daughters of the Reconquest: Women in Castilian Town Society, 1000–1300* (Cambridge, 1984), 152–159.

61. Ibid., 161.

62. B. H. Putnam, *The Enforcement of the Statute of Labourers 1349–1359* (New York, 1908).

63. David Herlihy, *Medieval and Renaissance Pistoia: The Social History of an Italian Town* (New Haven, Conn., 1967), 83–84.

64. Mary Bateson, "Origin and Early History of Double Monasteries," *Transactions of the Royal Historical Society* 2d ser. 13 (1899), 139–141.

65. Sally Thompson, "The Problem of the Cistercian Nuns in the Twelfth and Early Thirteenth Centuries," in *Medieval Women,* ed. Derek Baker (Oxford, 1978), 227.

66. Thompson, "Problem of the Cistercian Nuns," 232.

67. R. W. Southern, *Western Society and the Church in the Middle Ages,* vol. 2 of *The Pelican History of the Church* (Harmondsworth, 1970), 313.

68. Ibid., 314.

69. See E. W. McDonnell, *The Beguines and Beghards in Medieval Culture* (New Brunswick, N.J., 1954) for a detailed history of the movement.

70. Ibid., 5–6.

71. Hadewijch of Antwerp, "Letters to a Young Beguine," trans. Eric Colledge, in Petroff, *Medieval Women's Visionary Literature,* 189.

72. Lester K. Little, *Religious Poverty and the Profit Economy in Medieval Europe* (Ithaca, N.Y., 1978), 132.

73. "[T]he world between the fifteenth and eighteenth centuries consisted of one vast peasantry, where between 80% and 90% of people lived from the land and nothing else." Braudel, *Structures of Everyday Life,* 49.

74. For women as book owners, see Susan Groag Bell, "Medieval Women Book Owners: Arbiters of Lay Piety and Ambassadors of Culture," *Signs* 7 (1982), 742–767.

75. Hildegard of Bingen, *Liber divinorum operum simplicis hominis,* PL 197, col. 885.

76. See Caroline Walker Bynum, *Jesus as Mother: Studies in the Spirituality of the High Middle Ages* (Berkeley, 1982), the essay entitled "Jesus as Mother and Abbot as Mother: Some Themes in Twelfth-Century Cistercian Writing," esp. 129–134.

77. For an exploration of the cultural creation of gender roles from an anthropological point of view, see Peggy Reeves Sanday, *Female Power and Male Dominance* (Cambridge, 1981), esp. 15–51; for a psychoanalytic interpretation of women's mothering, see Nancy Chodorow, *The Reproduction of Mothering* (Berkeley, 1978), esp. 173–190.

78. Indeed, Christine de Pizan's *Book of the City of Ladies* was the first detailed attempt to refute the antifeminism of the age, specifically the antifeminism of the *Roman de la Rose.*

79. The relationship of gender and nature is poignantly expressed in Susan Griffin, *Woman and Nature* (New York, 1978). Carolyn Merchant's *The Death of Nature* (New York, 1980), 42–68 provides documentation and analysis of women's relations to nature and the exploitation of both by men. On the limitations of male power, see the analysis of Mary O'Brien, *The Politics of Reproduction* (London, 1979).

80. Peter Abelard's *Historia calamitatum*—the story of his misfortunes—captures the spirit of the "new man" effectively. While it may seem perverse to accuse Abelard of "disdaining" the physical, both the personal letters and the "letters of direction" show how central the rejection of sexuality was for him.

81. Alexander Murray, *Reason and Society in the Middle Ages* (Oxford, 1978), 87–90.

82. Mary Douglas, *Purity and Danger* (London, 1966), 140–158; cited and discussed by R. I. Moore, "Family, Community and Cult on the Eve of the Gregorian Reform," *Transactions of the Royal Historical Society* 30 (1980), 67–69.

83. "For, at the beginning of the eleventh century, amid the great turmoil from which new powers were emerging, the prelates' great preoccupation was to try to save the monopoly, privileges, and immunities of the servants of God. Their policy was based on the general belief that the men charged with sacrifice, the mediators who interceded with the unseen powers, must keep well away from women." Duby, *Knight, Lady, and Priest,* 116.

CONCLUSION

1. See Peter Brown, *Society and the Holy in Late Antiquity* (Berkeley, 1982), 305–306.

2. For the tools used by men and women, and, in particular, the relation of these tools to the social status of women, see Ivan Illich, *Gender* (New York, 1982).

3. For a lucid expression of the relations between women and nature, see Sherry Ortner, "Is Female to Male as Nature Is to Culture?" in *Women, Culture, and Society,* ed. Michelle Zimbalist Rosaldo and Louise Lamphere (Stanford, 1974), 67–88.

4. For biomechanically correct tools see Rudolfs J. Drillis, "Folk Norms and Biomechanics," *Human Factors* 5 (1963), 427–441; for an example of the late-medieval exploration of the rule of chance and reason, see Robert Holcot, O.P., *Exploring the Boundaries of Reason: Three Questions on the Nature of God,* ed. Hester Goodenough Gelber (Toronto, 1983).

Bibliography

ABBREVIATIONS

CCSL   Corpus christianorum, series latina. 176+ vols. Turnhout, 1953–.

CSEL   Corpus scriptorum ecclesiasticorum latinorum. 88+ vols. Vienna, 1866–

EETS   Early English Text Society. Original series and extra series. 286+ vols. London, 1867–.

PG   Patrologiae cursus completus, series graeca. 161 vols. Ed. J.-P. Migne. Paris, 1857–1904.

PL   Patrologiae cursus completus, series latina. 221 vols. Ed. J.-P. Migne. Paris, 1844–1866.

PRIMARY SOURCES

Abelard, Peter. *Expositio in Hexaemeron.* PL 178, cols. 731–784.

Adam of Dryburgh. *De ordine et habitu atque professione canonicorum regularum.* PL 198, cols. 439–610.

———. *Soliloquia de institutione animae.* PL 198, cols. 843–872.

Adelard of Bath. *Die Questiones naturales.* Ed. Martin Müller. Beiträge zur Geschichte der Philosophie des Mittelalters 31.2. Muenster: W. Aschendorff, 1934.

Aelred of Rievaulx. *Opera omnia: Opera ascetica.* Corpus christianorum, continuetio medievalis 1. Turnhout: Brepola, 1971.

Agrippa, H. C. *Of the Vanity and Uncertainty of Artes and Sciences.* London: Henry Wykes, 1569.

———. *Three Books of Occult Philosophy.* London: printed by R. W. for Gregory Moule, 1651.

Alan of Lille. *De planctu Naturae.* PL 210, cols. 429–482.

Alcuin of York. *Interrogationes et responsiones in Genesim.* PL 100, cols. 515–566.

Amalarius of Metz. *Instituto canonicorum.* PL 105, cols. 815–934.

Ambrose. *Epistolae.* PL 16, cols. 913–1342.

———. *Hexaemeron.* PL 14, cols. 133–288. Also in *Sancti Ambrosii Opera.* Ed. K. Schenkl. CSEL 32.1 (1897).

Ames, William. *Technometry.* Ed. and trans. Lee W. Gibbs. Philadelphia: University of Pennsylvania Press, 1979.

Anselm of Havelberg. *Liber de ordine canonicorum regularum.* PL 188, cols. 1093–1118.

Bibliography

Apophthegmata patrum. PG 65, cols. 71–440.

Aquinas, Thomas. *Expositio in libros Ethicorum*. Ed. A. M. Pirotta. Turin: Marietta, 1934.

———. *Expositio super librum Boethii De trinitate*. Ed. B. Decker. Leiden: Brill, 1955.

———. *In Metaphysiciam Aristotelis commentaria*. Ed. M. R. Cathala. Turin: Marietta, 1915.

———. *Opera omnia*. Ed. G. M. Allodi. 25 vols. Parma: Fiaccadoruo, 1852–1873.

———. *Summa theologica*. Ed. and trans. Fathers of the English Dominican Province. 60 vols. New York: McGraw-Hill, 1964–1976.

Aristotle. *The Basic Works of Aristotle*. Ed. Richard McKeon, New York: Random House, 1941.

———. *The Complete Works*. Ed. Jonathan Barnes. 2 vols. Princeton: Princeton University Press, 1984.

Arnobius. *Adversus nationes*. Ed. Augustus Reifferscheid. CSEL 4 (1875).

Arnold of Bonneval. *De operibus sex dierum*. PL 189, cols. 1507–1570.

Athanasius. *Vita Antonii*. PG 26, cols. 835–976.

Augustine. *The City of God*. Trans. Henry Bettenson. Harmondsworth: Penguin, 1972.

———. *Confessiones*. CCSL 27 (1981).

———. *De civitate Dei*. Ed. Bernard Dombart and Alphonse Kalb. CCSL 47–48 (1955).

———. *De doctrina christiana*. Ed. Joseph Martin. CCSL 32 (1962).

———. *De Genesi ad litteram libri duodecim*. Ed. Joseph Zycha. CSEL 28.1 (1894).

———. *De opere monachorum*. PL 40, cols. 547–582.

———. *Obiurgatio* [Epistle 211, 1–4]. PL 33, cols. 958–965.

———. *La règle de saint augustin*. Ed. Luc Verheijen. 2 vols. Paris: Études augustiniennes, 1967.

Bacon, Francis. *Works*. Ed. Basil Montagu. 3 vols. Philadelphia: Carey and Hart, 1842.

Bacon, Roger. *Epistola Fratria Rogerii Baconis, De secretis operibus artis et naturae, et De nullitate magiae*. In *Opera quaedem hactenus inedita*, ed. J. S. Brewer. 3 vols. London: Longman, Green, Longman and Roberts, 1859.

———. *Opus maius*. Ed. J. H. Bridges. 3 vols. Oxford: Oxford University Press, 1897–1900.

Basil of Caesarea. *The Ascetical Works of St. Basil*. Trans. W.K.L. Clarke. London, SPCK, 1925.

———. *Asceticon parvum*. Trans. Rufinus. PL 103 [*Codex regularum*], cols. 483–554.

————. *Homiliae in Hexaemeron.* PG 29, cols. 3–208.

————. *Regulae fusius tractatae.* PG 31, cols. 889–1052.

Bede. *Opera exegetica: Libri quatuor in principium Genesis.* Ed. C. W. Jones. CCSL 118A (1967).

————. *Hexaemeron.* PL 91, cols. 9–190.

Bernard of Clairvaux. *Apologia ad Guillelmum.* In *S. Bernardi Opera,* ed. Jean Leclercq, C. H. Talbot, and H. M. Rochais. 8 vols. to date. Rome: Editiones Cistercienses, 1957–, 3.81–108.

————. *Sermones super Cantica centicorum.* In *S. Bernardi Opera,* ed. Jean Leclercq, C. H. Talbot, and H. M. Rochais. 8 vols. to date. Rome: Editiones Cistercienses, 1957–, vols. 1–2.

Bernardus Silvestris. *Cosmographia.* Ed. Peter Dronke. Leiden: Brill, 1978.

Biblia sacra. Ed. Alberto Colunga and Laurentio Turrado. 5th ed. Madrid: Autores Cristianos, 1977.

Boethius. *De trinitate.* Ed. Samuel Brandt. CSEL 48 (1906).

————. *In Isagogen Porphyrii commenta.* Ed. Samuel Brandt. CSEL 48 (1906).

Bonaventure. *De reductione artium ad theologiam.* In *The Works of Saint Bonaventure,* ed. Sister Emma Therese Healy. Vol. 1. St. Bonaventure, N.Y.: Franciscan Institute, 1955.

————. *Quaestiones disputatae, De perfectione evangelica.* In *Opera omnia.* 10 vols. in 9. Quaracchi: S. Bonaventurae Collegium, 1882–1902, 5.1–198.

The Book of Jubilees or Little Genesis. Ed. and trans. R. H. Charles. London: Oxford University Press, 1902.

Boyle, Robert. *Of the Usefulness of Experimental Philosophy.* In *Works.* 6 vols. London: printed for J. and F. Rivington, 1772.

Bruno, Giordano. *Expulsion of the Triumphant Beast.* Ed. and trans. Arthur Imerti. New Brunswick, N.J.: Rutgers University Press, 1964.

Bruno of Cologne. *Consuetudines.* PL 153, cols. 631–758.

Caesarius of Arles. *Opera omnia.* Ed. D. G. Morin, 2 vols. Maredsous: Éditions de l'Abbaye, 1937–1942.

————. *Regula ad virgines.* PL 67, cols. 1103–1121.

————. *Regula monachorum.* PL 67, cols. 1099–1104.

————. *Sermones.* PL 67, cols. 1041–1090; also, ed. D. G. Morin, CCSL 103, 2 vols. (1953).

Capellenus, Andreas. *The Art of Courtly Love.* Trans. John Jay Parry. New York: Columbia University Press, 1941.

Cassian, John. *Conlationes.* Ed. Michael Petschenig. CSEL 13 (1886), 6–711.

————. *De institutis coenobiroum.* Ed. Michael Petschenig. CSEL 17 (1888), 3–231.

Cassiodorus. *Institutiones.* Ed. R.A.B. Mynors. Oxford: Oxford University Press, 1937.

Bibliography

Chaucer, Geoffrey. *The Works of Geoffrey Chaucer*. Ed. F. N. Robinson, 2d ed. Boston: Houghton Mifflin, 1957.

Chrétien de Troyes. *Arthurian Romances*. Ed. and trans. W. W. Comfort. London: Dent, 1970.

Clement of Alexandria. *Paedagogus*. PG 8, cols. 247–685.

———. *Stromata*. PG 8–9, cols. 685–(9)602.

Columbanus. *Opera*. Ed. G.S.M. Walker. Scriptores latini Hiberniae 2. Dublin: Institute for Advanced Study, 1957.

Condorcet, Marie Jean. *Esquisse d'un tableau historique des progrès de l'esprit humain*. Paris: Masson et Fils, 1822.

Consuetudines benedictinae variae. Ed. Giles Constable. Corpus consuetudinum monasticarum 6. Siegburg: Schmitt, 1975.

Conway, Anne. *The Principles of the Most Ancient and Modern Philosophy*. Ed. Peter Loptson. The Hague: Mouton, 1982.

Cudworth, Ralph. *True Intellectual System of the Universe*. Excerpted in *The Cambridge Platonists*, ed. C. A. Patrides. Cambridge, Mass.: Harvard University Press, 1970.

Cyprian. *De habitu virginum*. PL 4, cols. 451–478.

———. *De opere et eleemosynia*. PL 4, cols. 625–646.

Daniel, Walter. *Vita Ailredi*. Ed. and trans. Maurice Powicke. Oxford: Oxford University Press, 1978.

Descartes. *The Philosophical Works*. Trans. Elizabeth S. Haldane and G.R.T. Ross. 2 vols. Cambridge: Cambridge University Press, 1911.

Didascalia et constitutiones Apostolorum. Ed. F. X. Funk. 2 vols. in 1. Paderborn: Ferdinand Schoeningh, 1905.

English Gilds. Ed. Toulmin Smith. EETS o.s. 40 (1870; repr. 1963).

Eusebius. *Historia ecclesiae*. PG 20, cols. 45–910.

———.*The History of the Church from Christ to Constantine*. Trans. G. A. Williamson. New York: New York University Press, 1966.

Evagrius of Pontus. *De oratione*. PG 79, cols. 1165–1200.

———. *Institutio ad monachos*. PG 79, cols. 1235–1240.

———. *The Praktikos; Chapters on Prayer*. Spencer, Mass.: Cistercian Publications, 1970.

Exordium parvum. Ed. P. Canisius. Analecta Sacri Ordinis Cisterciensis 6. Rome: Editiones Cistercienses, 1950.

Farabi, al-. *De ortu scientiarum*. In *Alfarabi, Über den Ursprung der Wissenschaften*, ed. Clemens Baumker. Beiträge zur Geschichte der Philosophie des Mittelalters 19.3. Muenster: W. Aschendorff, 1916.

———. *De scientiis*. Ed. Manuel Alonso Alonso. Madrid, Granada: Escuelas de Estudios Árabes de Madrid y Granada, 1954.

Bibliography

Francis of Assisi. *S. Francisci Opuscula.* Bibliotheca franciscana ascetica Medii Aevi. Quaracchi: S. Bonaventura Collegium, 1904.

Fulbert of Chartres. *Letters and Poems.* Ed. Frederick Behrends. Oxford: Oxford University Press, 1976.

Gerhoh of Reichersberg. *Liber de aedificio Dei.* PL 194, cols. 1187–1336.

Gervase of Canterbury. *Historical Works.* Ed. W. Stubbs. Rolls Series 73. London: Longman and Co., 1879.

Glanville, Joseph. *Plus ultra, or The Progress and Advancement of Knowledge Since the Days of Aristotle.* London, 1668; repr. Gainesville, Fla.: Scholars' Facsimiles and Reprints, 1958.

Godefroy of Saint Victor. *Microcosmus.* Ed. Philippe Delehaye. Lille: Gembloux, 1951.

Gregory the Great. *Dialogorum libri IV.* PL 77, cols. 149–430.

———. *Regula pastoralis.* PL 77, cols. 13–126.

Gregory of Nazianzus. *Orationes.* PG 35–36, cols. 395–(36)664.

Gregory of Nyssa. *De instituto Christiano.* PG 46, cols. 287–306.

———. *De virginitate.* PG 46, cols. 317–416.

Gregory of Tours. *Historia francorum.* Ed. W. Arndt and Bruno Krusch. Monumenta germaniae historica, Scriptores rerum Merovingicarum 1. Hanover: Hahn, 1884–1885; repr. 1961.

———. *The History of the Franks.* Trans. Lewis Thorpe. Harmondsworth: Penguin, 1974.

Grosseteste, Robert. *Hexaemeron.* Ed. Richard C. Dales and Servus Gieben. London: Oxford University Press, 1982.

Guibert of Nogent. *De vita sua.* PL 156, cols. 837–962.

Guillaume de Lorris and Jean de Meun. *Roman de la Rose.* Ed. Ernest Langlois. 5 vols. Paris: Firman-Didot, 1914–1924.

Gundisalvo, Domingo. *De divisione philosophiae.* Ed. Ludwig Baur. Beiträge zur Geschichte der Philosophie des Mittelalters 4.2–3. Muenster: W. Aschendorff, 1903.

Hildegard of Bingen. *Liber divinorum operum simplicis hominis.* PL 197, cols. 739–1038.

Historia monachorum in Aegypto. Trans. Rufinus. PL 21, cols. 387–462.

Honorius Augustodunensis. *Clavis physicae.* Ed. Paolo Lucentini. Rome: Edizioni di storia e letteratura, 1974.

———. *Hexaemeron.* PL 172, cols. 253–266.

Hugh of Saint Victor. *Adnotationes elucidatioriae in Pentateuchon.* PL 175, cols. 29–86.

———. *De arca Noe morali.* PL 176, cols. 619ff.

———. *Didascalicon de studio legendi: A Critical Text.* Ed. Charles Henry

Buttimer. *Studies in Medieval and Renaissance Latin* 10. Washington, D.C.: Catholic University of America Press, 1939.

———. *The Didascalicon of Hugh of Saint Victor.* Trans. Jerome Taylor. New York: Columbia University Press, 1961.

———. "*Epitome Dindimi in philosophiam:* Introduction, texte critique, et notes." Ed. Roger Baron. *Traditio* 11 (1955):91–148.

Idung. *Dialogus duorum monachorum.* Ed. R.B.C. Huygens. *Studi medievali,* 3d ser. 13.1 (1972):375–470.

Isidore of Seville. *Etymologiarum sive originum, libri xx.* Ed. W. M. Lindsay. 2 vols. Oxford: Oxford University Press, 1911.

Jerome. *Epistulae.* PL 22, cols. 325–1182; also CSEL 54–56 (1910–1918).

John of Salisbury. *Metalogicon libri IV.* Ed. C.C.J. Webb. Oxford: Clarendon, 1929.

———. *The Metalogicon of John of Salisbury.* Trans. D. D. McGarry. Berkeley: University of California Press, 1962.

John the Scot (Johannes Scottus Eriugena). *Periphyseon (De divisione naturae).* Ed. and trans. I. P. Sheldon-Williams. Scriptores latini Hiberniae 2. Dublin: Institute for Advanced Studies, 1981.

Kilwardby, Robert. *De ortu scientiarum.* Ed. Albert G. Judy. Oxford: Oxford University Press, 1976.

Kyeser, Konrad. *Bellifortis.* Ed. G. Quarg. 2 vols. Duesseldorf: VDI, 1967.

Lactantius. *Divinae institutiones.* In *Opera omnia,* ed. Samuel Brandt. CSEL 19 (1890).

Lanfranc of Bec. *The Monastic Constitutions.* Ed. and trans. David Knowles. London: Thomas Nelson, 1951.

Langland, William. *Piers Plowman.* Ed. W. W. Skeat. 2 vols. Oxford: Oxford University Press, 1886.

Libellus de diversis ordinibus et professionibus qui sunt in aecclesia. Ed. and trans. Giles Constable and B. Smith. Oxford: Oxford University Press, 1972.

Lull, Raymond. *Arbor scientiae.* Lyons: I. Pillehotte, 1637.

Martianus Capelle. *De nuptiis Philologiae et Mercurii.* Ed. Adolf Dick. Leipzig: Teubner, 1925.

———. *Martianus Capella and the Seven Liberal Arts.* Trans. William H. Stahl and Richard Johnson. New York: Columbia University Press, 1977.

Medieval Women's Visionary Literature. Ed. Elizabeth A. Petroff. New York: Oxford University Press, 1986.

Minucius Felix. *Octavius.* Ed. H. A. Holden. Cambridge: Cambridge University Press, 1853.

Norman, Robert. *The Newe Attractive . . . a Short Discourse of the Magnes or Lodenstone.* London: T. East for Richard Ballad, 1585.

Origen. *Homélies sur le Genèse.* Ed. L. Doutreleau. Sources chrétiennes 7. Paris: Éditions du Cerf, 1976.

———. *Homilien zum Hexateuch,* ed. W. A. Baehrens. In *Werke,* ed. Kirchen-väter-Commission der Könglichen Preussichen Akademie der Wissenschaften. 12 vols. to date. Leipzig: J. C. Hinrichs, 1899–, vol. 7.

Orosius, Paulus. *Historiarum adversus paganas, libri septem.* PL 31, cols. 665–1174.

Pachomiana latina. Ed. Amand Boon. Bibliothéque de la Revue d'histoire ecclésiastique 7. Louvain: Bureaux de la Revue, 1932.

Pachomius. *Pachomian Chronicles and Rules.* Trans. Armand Veilleux. Kalamazoo, Mich.: Cistercian Publications, 1981.

Palladius. *Historia Lausiaca.* PG 34, cols. 991–1278.

———. *The Lausiac History.* Ed. Dom Cuthbert Butler. Texts and Studies, Contributions to Biblical and Patristic Literature 6.1. 2 vols. Cambridge: Cambridge University Press, 1898–1904.

Peter Damian. *De perfectione monachorum.* PL 145, cols. 291–328.

Peter the Venerable. *Letters.* Ed. Giles Constable. 2 vols. Harvard Historical Studies 78. Cambridge, Mass.: Harvard University Press, 1967.

Philip of Harvengt. *De institutione clericorum.* PL 203, cols. 665–1206.

Philo Judaeus. *De vita contemplative.* In *Philonis Alexandrini Opera quae supersunt,* ed. L. Cohn. 7 vols. in 6. Berlin: George Reimer, 1896–1930, vol. 4.

———. "On the Creation of the World." In *Philo,* ed. F. H. Colson and G. H. Whitaker. 10 vols. Cambridge, Mass.: Harvard University Press, 1929–1962, 1.1–137.

Pierce the Ploughman's Crede. Ed. W. W. Skeat. EETS o.s. 30 (1873).

Plato. *Collected Dialogues.* Ed. Edith Hamilton and Huntington Cairns. New York: Random House, 1961.

Rabanus Maurus. *De universo.* PL 111, cols. 13–614.

Ray, John. *The Wisdom of God as Manifested in the Works of Creation.* London: S. Smith, 1691.

La Règle de saint Benoît. Ed. Adalbert de Vogüé. Sources chrétiennes 181–186. 6 vols. Paris: Éditions du Cerf, 1971–1972.

Le Règle du Maître. Ed. Adalbert de Vogüé. Sources chrétiennes 105–107. 3 vols. Paris: Éditions du Cerf, 1964–1965.

"Règle des IV pères et seconde Règle des pères." Ed. Jean Neufville, in *Revue bénédictine* 77 (1967):47–95.

Les Règles des saints pères. Ed. Adalbert de Vogüé. 2 vols. Paris: Éditions du Cerf, 1982.

"La *Regula orientalis.*" Ed. Adalbert de Vogüé. *Benedictina* 13 (1976):241–271.

Regularis concordia. Ed. Thomas Symons. London: Thomas Nelson, 1953.

Bibliography

Robert of Bridlington. *The Bridlington Dialogue.* Ed. and trans. by "a religious of CSMV." London: SPCK, 1960.

Rupert of Deutz. *De vita vere apostolica.* PL 170, cols. 609–664.

———. *Super quaedam capitula regulae divi Benedicti abbatis.* PL 170, cols. 477–538.

Sprat, Thomas. *History of the Royal Society.* Ed. Jackson I. Cope and Harold Whitmore Jones. St. Louis: Washington University Press, 1958; repr. of 1667 ed.

Sulpicius Severus. *Vita Sancti Martini.* Ed. C. Holm. CSEL 1 (1866).

Tacitus. *Germania.* Ed. A. Dopsch et al. Leipzig: Teubner, 1930.

Tertullian. *Apologeticum.* In *Opera,* ed. Georg Wissowa and August Reifferscheid. CSEL 20 (1890).

———. *De anima.* Ed. J. H. Waszink. Amsterdam: J. M. Meulenhoff, 1947.

———. *De cultu feminarum.* Ed. A. Kroymann. CCSL1 (1954).

———. *De idololatria.* In *Opera,* ed. Georg Wissowa and August Reifferscheid. CSEL 20 (1890):30–58.

———. *De testimonia animae.* In *Opera,* ed. Georg Wissowa and August Reifferscheid. CSEL 20 (1890):134–143.

Thongmar. *Vita Berwardi.* Monumenta germaniae historica, Scriptores 4. Hanover: Hahn, 1841, 754–786.

Theophilus. *De diversis artibus.* Ed. C. R. Dodwell. London: Thomas Nelson, 1961.

———. *On Diverse Arts.* Ed. and trans. John G. Hawthorne and Cyril Stanley Smith. Chicago: University of Chicago Press, 1963.

Thierry of Chartres. *De sex dierum operibus.* Ed. Nicholas M. Häring, in "The Creation and the Creator of the World According to Thierry of Chartres and Clarenbaldus of Arras." *Archives d'histoire doctrinale et littéraire du Moyen Âge* 22 (1955):137–216.

Turgot, Anne-Robert-Jacques. *On Progress, Sociology, and Economics.* Ed. and trans. Ronald L. Meek. Cambridge: Cambridge University Press, 1973.

The Two Earliest Masonic Mss. Ed. Douglas Knoop, G. P. Jones, and Douglas Hamer. Manchester: Manchester University Press, 1938.

Tyndall, John. *Advancement of Science.* New York: Asa Butts, 1874.

Usus conversorum. In *Les monuments primitifs de la Règle cistercienne,* ed. P. Guignard. Analecta divionensia. Dijon: J.-E. Rabutot, 1878.

Vincent of Beauvais. *Speculum doctrinale.* Douai: Baltazaris Belleri, 1624.

Vita Norberti Archiepiscopi Magdeburgensis, Vita A. Ed. George Heind et al. Monumenta germaniae historica, Scriptores 12. Hanover: Hahn, 1856:663–706.

Vita prima graeca: The Life of Pachomius. Ed. and trans. Apostolos N. Athanassakis. Missoula, Mont.: Scholars Press, 1975.

Bibliography

Vita S. Brunonis. PL 152, cols. 481–552.

Vita S. Norberti (Vita B). PL 170, cols. 1253–1344.

Vita S. Pachomii. Trans. Dionysius Exiguus. PL 73, cols. 227–282.

Walter of Henley. *Walter of Henley and Other Treatises on Estate Management and Accounting.* Ed. Dorothea Oschinsky. Oxford: Oxford University Press, 1971.

Whewell, William. *History of the Inductive Sciences.* 3d ed. 3 vols. London: Parker, 1857.

William of Conches. *Glossae super Platonem.* Ed. Edouard Jeauneau. Paris: Vrin 1965.

———. *Philosophia mundi.* PL 172.

William of Ockham. *Philosophical Writings.* Ed. and trans. Philotheus Boehner. London: Thomas Nelson, 1957.

William of Saint Thierry. *Speculum fidei.* PL 180, cols. 365–398.

———. *Vita prima S. Bernardi.* PL 185, cols. 225–268.

Wotton, William. *Reflections upon Ancient and Modern Learning.* London: J. Leake for P. Buck, 1694.

Secondary Sources

Abou-el-Haj, Barbara. "Bury St. Edmunds Abbey Between 1070 and 1124: A History of Property, Privilege, and Monastic Art Production." *Art History* 6 (1983):1–29.

Adelson, Howard L. *Medieval Commerce.* Princeton: Princeton University Press, 1962.

Alessio, Franco. "La filosofía e le 'artes mechanicae.' " *Studi medievali* 3d ser. 1.6 (1956):71–155.

Alverny, Marie-Thérèse d'. "Le Cosmos symbolique du XIIe siècle." *Archives d'histoire doctrinale et littéraire du Moyen Âge* 28 (1953):31–81.

Amand, David. *L'Ascese monastique de Saint Basile.* Liège: Éditions de l'Abbaye, 1948.

Amoros, L. "Escritos de San Buenaventura." In *Obras de San Buenaventura.* 2d ed. Madrid: Editorial Catolica, 1955.

Anderson, Nels. *Man's Work and Leisure.* Leiden: Brill, 1974.

Arendt, Hannah. *The Human Condition.* Chicago: University of Chicago Press, 1958.

Attfield, Robin. "Christian Attitudes Toward Nature." *Journal of the History of Ideas* 44 (1983):369–386.

———. *The Ethics of Environmental Concern.* New York: Columbia University Press, 1983.

Aymard, M. A. "Hierarchie du travail et autarchie individuelle dans le Grèce

Bibliography

archaïque." *Revue d'histoire de la philosophie et d'histoire générale de la civilisation* (1943):124–146.

———. "L'idée du travail dans la Grèce archaïque." *Journal de psychologie* (1948):29–45.

Bacht, H. "Antonius und Pachomius: Von der Anachorese zum Conobitentum." In *Antonius Magnus eremita*, ed. B. Steidle. Studia Anselmiana 38. Rome: Herder, 1956, 66–107.

———. "L'importance de l'idéal monastique de saint Pachôme pour l'histoire de monachisme Chrétien." *Revue d'ascétique et de mystique* 26 (1950):308–326.

Baker, Derek, ed. *Medieval Women*. Oxford: Oxford University Press, 1978.

Baldwin, J. W. *Masters, Princes, and Merchants: The Social Views of Peter the Chanter and His Circle*. 2 vols. Princeton: Princeton University Press, 1970.

Barley, M. W. "Cistercian Land Clearances in Nottinghamshire: Three Deserted Villages." *Nottingham Medieval Studies* 1 (1957):75–89.

Baron, Roger. *Science et sagesse chez Hughes de Saint-Victor*. Paris: Lethielleux, 1957.

Bateson, Mary. "Origin and Early History of Double Monasteries." *Transactions of the Royal Historical Society* 2d ser. 13 (1899):137–198.

Bautier, Robert H. *The Economic Development of Medieval Europe*. London: Thames and Hudson, 1971.

Beaujouan, Guy. *L'interdépendance entre la science scholastique et les techniques utilitaires (XIIᵉ, XIIIᵉ, XIVᵉ siècles)*. Les Conférences du Palais de la Découverte, ser. D, 46. Paris: Université de Paris, 1946.

Becker, Carl. *Progress and Power*. Stanford: Stanford University Press, 1936.

Bell, H. E. "The Price of Books in Medieval England." *The Library* 4th ser. 17 (1937):312–332.

Bell, Susan Groag. "Medieval Women Book Owners: Arbiters of Lay Piety and Ambassadors of Culture." *Signs* 7 (1982):742–767.

Benson, Robert L., Giles Constable, and Carol D. Lanham, eds. *Renaissance and Renewal in the Twelfth Century*. Cambridge, Mass.: Harvard University Press, 1982.

Benton, John F. "Trotula, Women's Problems, and the Professionalization of Medicine in the Middle Ages." *Bulletin of the History of Medicine* 59 (1985):30–53.

Benz, Ernst. "The Christian Expectation of the End of Time and the Idea of Technical Progress." In *Evolution and Christian Hope: Man's Concept of the Future from the Early Fathers to Teilhard de Chardin*. Garden City, N.Y.: Doubleday, 1966, 121–142.

———. "I fondamenti cristiani della tecnica occidentale." In *Tecnica e casistica*, Enrico Castelli, ed. Rome: Centro Internazionale di Studi Umanistici, 1964, 241–263.

Bibliography

Berlière, Dom Ursmer. "Les origines de Cîteaux et l'ordre bénédictin du XII siècle." *Revue d'histoire ecclésiastique* 1 (1900):448–471.

Berman, Harold J. *Law and Revolution: The Formation of the Western Legal Tradition.* Cambridge, Mass.: Harvard University Press, 1983.

Berthelot, M. "Pour l'histoire des arts mécaniques et de l'ortellerie vers la fin du Moyen Âge." *Annales de chimie et de physique* 6th ser. 24 (1891):433–521.

Black, Anthony. *Guilds and Civil Society in European Political Thought from the Twelfth Century to the Present.* Ithaca, N.Y.: Cornell University Press, 1984.

Bloch, Marc. *Land and Work in Medieval Europe: Selected Papers.* Trans. J. E. Anderson. Berkeley: University of California Press, 1967.

Bloomfield, Morton W. *Piers Plowman as a Fourteenth Century Apocalypse.* New Brunswick, N.J.: Rutgers University Press, 1962.

Blum, Jerome. "The European Village as Community: Origins and Functions." *Agricultural History* 45 (1971):157–178.

———. "The Internal Structure and Polity of the European Village Community from the Fifteenth to the Twentieth Century." *Journal of Modern History* 43 (1971):541–576.

Boissonnade, P. *Life and Work in Medieval Europe: Fifth to Fifteenth Centuries.* New York: Knopf, 1927.

Bolton, J. L. *The Medieval English Economy, 1150–1500.* London: Dent, 1980.

Bowler, Peter. *Evolution: The History of an Idea.* Berkeley: University of California Press, 1984.

Boyer, Marjorie N. "A Day's Journey in Medieval France." *Speculum* 26 (1951):597–608.

———. "Medieval Pivoted Axles." *Technology and Culture* 1 (1960):128–138.

———. "Water Mills: A Problem for the Bridges and Boats of Medieval France." *History of Technology* 7 (1982):1–22.

Braudel, Fernand. *The Structures of Everyday Life: The Limits of the Possible.* Vol. 1 of *Civilization and Capitalism, 15th–18th Century.* New York: Harper & Row, 1979.

Brown, Ernest W. et al. *The Development of the Sciences.* New Haven, Conn.: Yale University Press, 1923.

Brown, Peter. "The Rise and Function of the Holy Man in Late Antiquity." *Journal of Roman Studies* 61 (1971):80–101.

———. *Society and the Holy in Late Antiquity.* Berkeley: University of California Press, 1982.

Bullock, James. *Adam of Dryburgh.* London: SPCK, 1958.

Bullough, Vern L. "Status in Medieval Medicine." *Journal of Health and Human Behavior* 2 (1961):204–210.

Bibliography

Burford, Alison. *Craftsmen in Greek and Roman Society*. Ithaca, N.Y.: Cornell University Press, 1972.

Bury, J. B. *The Idea of Progress*. New York, 1920; repr. New York: Dover, 1932.

Bynum, Caroline Walker. *Jesus as Mother: Studies in the Spirituality of the High Middle Ages*. Berkeley: University of California Press, 1982.

Cantor, Norman F. "The Crisis of Western Monasticism." *American Historical Review* 46 (1960):47–67.

Carus-Wilson, E. M. "An Industrial Revolution of the Thirteenth Century." *Economic History Review* 12 (1941):39–60.

Charbonnel, N. "La condition des ouvriers dans les ateliers impériaux au ive et ve siècles." In *Aspects de l'Empire romain*. Paris: P.U.F., 1964, 61–93.

Cheney, Mary G. "The Decretal of Pope Celestine III on Tithes of Windmills, JL 17620." *Bulletin of Medieval Canon Law* 1 (1971):63–66.

Chenu, Marie-Dominique. "Civilisation urbaine et théologie." *Annales: Économies, Sociétés, Civilisations* 29 (1974):1253–1263.

———. *Nature, Man, and Society in the Twelfth Century*. Trans. Jerome Taylor and Lester K. Little. Chicago: University of Chicago Press, 1968.

Chitty, Dewas. *The Desert a City*. Oxford: Oxford University Press, 1964.

Chodorow, Nancy. *The Reproduction of Mothering*. Berkeley: University of California Press, 1978.

Cipolla, Carlo. *Before the Industrial Revolution*. 2d ed. New York: W. W. Norton, 1980.

———. *Guns and Sails in the Early Phase of European Expansion*. London: Collins, 1965.

———. *The Middle Ages*. Vol. 1 of *The Fontana Economic History of Europe*. New York: Barnes and Noble, 1976.

———. *Money, Prices, and Civilization in the Mediterranean World, Fifth to Seventeenth Century*. Princeton: Princeton University Press, 1956.

Clagett, Marshall. *The Science of Mechanics in the Middle Ages*. Madison: University of Wisconsin Press, 1961.

Clanchy, Michael T. *From Memory to Written Record*. Cambridge, Mass.: Harvard University Press, 1979.

Cohen, I. B. *Scientific Revolutions*. Cambridge, Mass.: Harvard University Press, 1980.

Coleman, Emily R. "Medieval Marriage Characteristics: A Neglected Factor in the History of Medieval Serfdom." *Journal of Interdisciplinary History* 2 (1971):205–219.

Coleman, William. "Providence, Capitalism, and Environmental Degradation— English Apologetics in an Era of Economic Revolution." *Journal of the History of Ideas* 37 (1976):27–44.

Collingwood, R. G. *The Idea of History*. Oxford, 1946; repr. New York: Oxford University Press, 1956.

Constable, Giles. "Twelfth-Century Spirituality and the Late Middle Ages." *Medieval and Renaissance Studies* 5 (1971):27–60.

Crane, R. S. "Anglican Apologetics of the Idea of Progress." *Modern Philology* 26 (1934):273–306.

Crombie, A. C. *Robert Grosseteste and the Origins of Experimental Science*. Oxford: Oxford University Press, 1953.

Cullmann, Oscar. *Christus und die Zeit*. Zurich: Evangelischer Verlag, 1946.

Curtin, Philip D. *Cross-Cultural Trade in World History*. Cambridge: Cambridge University Press, 1984.

David, M. "Les 'laboratores' jusqu'au renouveau économique des xie–xiie siècles." In *Études d'histoire du droit privé offertes à P. Petot*. Paris: Librairie générale de droit et de jurisprudence, 1959, 107–120.

Davis, J. C. *Utopia and the Ideal Society*. Cambridge: Cambridge University Press, 1981.

Delaruelle, E. "Le travail dans les règles monastiques occidentales du IVe au IXe siècle." *Journal de psychologie normale et pathologique* 41 (1948):51–64.

De Rijk, L. M. "Some Notes on the Twelfth-Century Topic of the Three (Four) Human Evils and of Science, Virtue, and Techniques as Their Remedies." *Vivarium* 5 (1967):8–15.

Devos, Paul. "Les nombres dans l'Historia Monachorum in Aegypto." *Analecta Bollandiana* 92 (1974):97–108.

Dick, Steven. *The Plurality of Worlds*. Cambridge: Cambridge University Press, 1982.

Dillard, Heath. *Daughters of the Reconquest: Women in Castilian Town Society, 1000–1300*. Cambridge: Cambridge University Press, 1984.

Dodds, E. R. *The Ancient Concept of Progress*. Oxford: Oxford University Press, 1973.

Donkin, R. A. "The Cistercian Settlement and the Royal Forests." *Cîteaux in de Nederlanden* 10–11 (1959–1960):39–55; 117–132.

———. "The Growth and Distribution of the Cistercian Order in England." *Studia monastica* 9 (1967):275–286.

Donnelly, James. "Changes in the Grange Economy of the English and Welsh Cistercian Abbeys, 1300–1500." *Traditio* 10 (1954):399–458.

———. *The Decline of the Medieval Cistercian Lay Brotherhood*. Fordham University Studies, History Series 3. New York: Fordham University Press, 1949.

Douglas, Mary. *Purity and Danger: An Analysis of the Concepts of Pollution and Taboo*. London: Routledge and Kegan Paul, 1966.

Bibliography

Drillis, Rudolfs J. "Folk Norms and Biomechanics." *Human Factors* 5 (1963): 427–441.

Drover, C. B. "A Medieval Monastic Water Clock." *Antiquarian Horology* 1 (1954):54–59.

Duby, Georges. *The Early Growth of the European Economy.* Trans. Howard B. Clarke. Ithaca, N.Y.: Cornell University Press, 1974.

———. *The Knight, the Lady, and the Priest: The Making of Modern Marriage in Medieval France.* Trans. Barbara Bray. New York: Pantheon, 1983.

———. *Rural Economy and Country Life in the Medieval West.* Trans. Cynthia Postan. Columbia: University of South Carolina Press, 1968.

———. *The Three Orders, or, Feudal Society Imagined.* Trans. Arthur Goldhammer. Chicago: University of Chicago Press, 1980.

Eamon, William. "Technology as Magic in the Late Middle Ages and the Renaissance." *Janus* 70 (1983):171–212.

Eckenstein, Lina. *Women Under Monasticism.* Cambridge: Cambridge University Press, 1896.

Edelstein, Ludwig. *The Idea of Progress in Classical Antiquity.* Baltimore: Johns Hopkins University Press, 1967.

Egbert, Virginia Wylie. *The Medieval Artist at Work.* Princeton: Princeton University Press, 1967.

Eisenstein, Elizabeth A. *The Printing Press as an Agent of Change.* 2 vols. in 1. Cambridge: Cambridge University Press, 1979.

Elvin, Mark. *The Pattern of the Chinese Past.* Stanford: Stanford University Press, 1973.

Evans, Gillian. *From Old Arts to New Theology.* Oxford: Oxford University Press, 1981.

Evans, Joan. *Monastic Life at Cluny, 910–1157.* Oxford: Oxford University Press, 1931.

Face, R. D. "Techniques of Business in the Trade Between the Fairs of Champagne and the South of Europe in the Twelfth and Thirteenth Centuries." *Economic History Review* 2d ser. 10 (1958):427–438.

Feingold, Mordechai. *The Mathematicians' Apprenticeship: Science, Universities and Society in England, 1560–1640.* Cambridge: Cambridge University Press, 1984.

Feldhaus, Franz M. *Die Technik der Antike und des Mittelalters.* Hildesheim: Olms, 1971 (orig. 1931).

Fell, Christine. *Women in Anglo-Saxon Society.* Bloomington: Indiana University Press, 1979.

Finley, M. I. "Technical Innovation and Economic Progress in the Ancient World." *Economic History Review* 2d ser. 18 (1965):29–45.

Bibliography

Fitchen, John. *The Construction of Gothic Cathedrals.* Chicago: University of Chicago Press, 1961.

Forbes, Robert James. *Man the Maker: A History of Technology and Engineering.* New York: Abelard-Schuman, 1958.

Fournial, E. *Histoire monétaire de l'occident médiéval.* Paris: F. Nathan, 1970.

Garin, E. "Gli umanisti e la scienza." *Rivista di filosofía* 52 (1961):259–278.

Geertz, Clifford. *The Interpretation of Cultures.* New York: Basic Books, 1973.

Geoghegan, A. T. *The Attitude Toward Labor in Early Christianity and Antique Culture.* Washington, D.C.: Catholic University Press, 1945.

Gilchrist, John Thomas. *The Church and Economic Activity in the Middle Ages.* London and New York: Macmillan and St. Martin's, 1969.

Gille, Bertrand. "Le machinisme au Moyen Âge." *Archives internationales de l'histoire de science* 23 (1953):281–286.

————. "Recherches sur les instruments du labor au Moyen Âge." *Bibliothèque de l'École des Chartes* 120 (1962):5–38.

Gillespie, Neal C. *Charles Darwin and the Problem of Creation.* Chicago: University of Chicago Press, 1979.

Gilson, Étienne. *History of Christian Philosophy in the Middle Ages.* New York: Random House, 1955.

Gimpel, Jean. *The Cathedral Builders.* Trans. Teresa Waugh. New York: Harper & Row, 1984.

————. *The Medieval Machine.* Harmondsworth: Penguin, 1976.

Glacken, Clarence. *Traces on the Rhodian Shore: Nature and Culture in Western Thought from Ancient Times to the End of the Eighteenth Century.* Berkeley: University of California Press, 1967.

Glotz, G. *Le travail dans la Grèce ancienne.* Paris: F. Alcan, 1920.

Goldstein, Thomas. *The Dawn of Modern Science.* New York: Houghton Mifflin, 1980.

Goodall, Jane. "Tool-Using and Aimed Throwing in a Community of Free-Living Chimpanzees." *Nature* 201 (28 March 1964):1264–1266.

Goodich, Michael. "Sodomy in Medieval Secular Law." *Journal of Homosexuality* 1 (1976):427–433.

Goody, Jack. *The Domestication of the Savage Mind.* Cambridge: Cambridge University Press, 1977.

————. *Technology, Tradition and the State in Africa.* Cambridge: Cambridge University Press, 1971.

Gordon, Walter M. "The Monastic Achievement and More's Utopian Dream." *Medievalia et humanistica* 9 (1979):199–214.

Graff, Harvey J., ed. *Literacy and Social Development in the West.* Cambridge: Cambridge University Press, 1981.

Gransden, Antonia. "Realistic Observation in Twelfth-Century England." *Speculum* 47 (1972):29–51.

Graves, Coburn V. "The Economic Activities of the Cistercians in Medieval England." *Analecta Sacri Ordinis Cisterciensis* 13 (1957):3–60.

Griesser, B. "Walther Map und die Cistercienser." *Cistercienser-Chronik* 36 (1924):137–141.

Griffin, Susan. *Woman and Nature*. New York: Harper & Row, 1978.

Gryglewicz, F. "La valeur morale du travail manuel dans la terminologie grecque de la Bible." *Biblica* 37 (1956):314–337.

Guitton, Jean. *Le temps et l'éternité chez Plotin et Augustin*. Paris: Boivin, 1933.

Hall, Bert S. and Delno C. West, eds. *On Pre-Modern Technology and Science: A Volume of Studies in Honor of Lynn White, Jr.*. Malibu, Calif.: Undena, 1976.

Hanawalt, Barbara A. "Childbearing Among the Lower Classes of Late Medieval England." *Journal of Interdisciplinary History* 8 (1977):1–22.

Hatcher, John. *English Tin Production and Trade Before 1550*. Oxford: Oxford University Press, 1973.

Heard, Gerald. *The Ascent of Humanity*. New York: Harcourt, Brace, 1929.

Heimann, A. "The Six Days of Creation in a Twelfth-Century Manuscript." *Journal of the Warburg and Courtauld Institutes* 1 (1937–1938):269–275.

Herlihy, David. "The Agrarian Revolution in Southern France and Italy, 801–1150." *Speculum* 33 (1958):23–41.

———. "Land, Family, and Women in Continental Europe, 701–1200." *Traditio* 18 (1962):89–120.

———. "Life Expectancies for Women in Medieval Society." In *The Role of Woman in the Middle Ages*, ed. Rosemarie Morewedge. Albany: State University of New York Press, 1975.

———. *Medieval and Renaissance Pistoia: The Social History of an Italian Town*. New Haven, Conn.: Yale University Press, 1967.

———. *Medieval Households*. Cambridge, Mass.: Harvard University Press, 1985.

Hewes, Gordon. "An Explicit Formulation of the Relationship Between Tool-Using, Tool-Making, and the Emergence of Language," *Visible Language* 7 (1973):101–127.

Hill, Bennett D. *English Cistercian Monasteries and Their Patrons in the Twelfth Century*. Urbana: University of Illinois Press, 1968.

Hillgarth, J. N. *Ramon Lull and Lullism in Fourteenth-Century France*. Oxford: Oxford University Press, 1971.

Hilton, Rodney. *Bond Men Made Free*. London: Methuen, 1973.

———and P. H. Sawyer. "Technical Determinism: The Stirrup and the Plough." *Past and Present* 24 (1963):90–100.

Bibliography

Hindwood, Bonaventure, O.F.M. "The Division of Human Knowledge in the Writings of Saint Bonaventure." *Franciscan Studies* 38 (1978):220–259.

Hodgen, Margaret T. "Domesday Water Mills." *Antiquity* 13 (1939):261–279.

Hoffman, E. "Die Entwicklung der Wirtschaftsprinzipien im Cisterzensorden wahrend des 12. und 13. Jahrhunderts." *Historisches Jahrbuch* 30 (1910):699–727.

Holcot, Robert, O.P. *Exploring the Boundaries of Reason: Three Questions on the Nature of God.* Ed. Hester Goodenough Gelbes. Toronto: University of Toronto Press, 1983.

Horn, Walter. "Water Power and the Plan of St. Gall." *Journal of Medieval History* 1 (1975):219–258.

———and Ernest Born. *The Plan of St. Gall.* 3 vols. Berkeley: University of California Press, 1979.

Horney, Karen. *Feminine Psychology.* New York: W. W. Norton, 1967.

Houllevigue, L. *The Evolution of the Sciences.* New York: Van Nostrand, 1910.

Hull, David. *Darwin and His Critics.* Chicago: University of Chicago Press, 1973.

Hunter, Michael. *Science and Society in Restoration England.* Cambridge: Cambridge University Press, 1981.

Huygens, R.B.C. "Zu Idung von Prufening und seinen Schriften, 'Argumentum super quatuor questionibus' und 'Dialogus duorum monachorum.' " *Deutsches Archiv für Erforschung des Millelalters* 2 (1971):544ff.

Hyams, Paul R. *Kings, Lords and Peasants in Medieval England.* Oxford: Oxford University Press, 1980.

Ibanes, Jean. *La doctrine de l'église et les réalités économiques au XIIIe siècle.* Paris: Presses universitaires de France, 1967.

Illich, Ivan. *Gender.* New York: Pantheon, 1982.

Jaccard, P. *Histoire sociale du travail de l'antiquité à nos jours.* Paris: Payot, 1960.

Jacobs, Margaret C. *The Radical Enlightenment: Pantheists, Freemasons, and Republicans.* London: Methuen, 1981.

Jaspert, B. *Regula Magistri, Regula Benedicti: Bibliographie ihrer Erforschung 1938–1970.* Subsidie monastica 1. Montserrat: Abadia de Montserrat, 1971.

Jones, E. L. *The European Miracle.* Cambridge: Cambridge University Press, 1981.

Jones, Jacqueline. *Labor of Love, Labor of Sorrow: Black Women, Work, and the Family from Slavery to the Present.* New York: Basic Books, 1985.

Jones, P. J. "A Tucson Monastic Lordship in the Later Middle Ages: Camaldoli." *Journal of Ecclesiastical History* 5 (1954):168–183.

Jones, Richard F. *Ancients and Moderns: A Study of the Rise of the Scientific Movement in Seventeenth Century England.* 2d ed. Saint Louis: Washington University Press, 1961.

Bibliography

Kellenbenz, H. "Industries rurales en occident de la fin du Moyen Âge au XVIIIe siècle." *Annales: Économies, sociétés, civilisations* 18 (1963):823–882.

Kelly, J.N.D. *Jerome*. New York: Harper & Row, 1975.

Kershaw, Ian. "The Great Famine and Agrarian Crisis in England, 1315–1322." *Past and Present* 59 (1973):3–50.

Kessler, H. *"Hic Homo Formatur:* The Genesis Frontispieces of the Carolingian Bibles," *Art Bulletin* 53 (1971):143–160.

Kitahara-Frisch, Jean. "Symbolizing Technology as a Key to Human Evolution." In *Symbol as Sense*. New York: Academic Press, 1980, 211–223.

Knowles, David. *Cistercians and Cluniacs*. London: Oxford University Press, 1955.

———. "Cistercians and Cluniacs: The Controversy Between St. Bernard and Peter the Venerable." In *The Historian and Character*. Cambridge: Cambridge University Press, 1963:50–75.

———. *Great Historical Enterprises and Problems in Monastic History*. London: Thomas Nelson, 1963.

———. *The Monastic Order in England*. Cambridge: Cambridge University Press, 1940.

———. *The Religious Orders in England*. Cambridge: Cambridge University Press, 1948.

Kramer, Stella. *The English Craft Guilds: Studies in Their Progress and Decline*. New York: Columbia University Press, 1927.

Ladner, Gerhart B. "Homo Viator: Medieval Ideas on Alienation and Order," *Speculum* 42 (1967):233–259.

———. *The Idea of Reform: Its Impact on Thought and Action in the Age of the Fathers*. Cambridge, Mass.: Harvard University Press, 1959.

Laeuchli, Samuel. *Power and Sexuality: The Emergence of Canon Law at the Synod of Elvira*. Philadelphia: Temple University Press, 1972.

Lancaster, Jane B. "On the Evolution of Tool-Using Behavior." *American Anthropologist* 70 (1968):56–66.

Landes, David. *The Unbound Prometheus*. Cambridge: Cambridge University Press, 1969.

Leclercq, Dom Jean. *Études sur le vocabulaire monastique du Moyen Âge*. Rome: Herder, 1961.

———. *The Love of Learning and the Desire for God: A Study of Monastic Culture*. Trans. Catharine Misrahi. 2d ed. New York: Fordham University Press, 1974.

———. *Otia monastica: Études sur le vocabulaire de la contemplation au Moyen Âge*. Studie Anselmiana 51. Rome: Herder, 1963.

———. *'Otium monasticum' as a Context for Artistic Creativity*. In *Monasticism and the Arts,* ed., Timothy Gregory Verdon. Syracuse, N.Y.: Syracuse University Press, 1984, 63–80.

Lee, Ronald. "Population in Pre-Industrial England: An Econometric Analysis." *Quarterly Journal of Economics* 87 (1973):581–607.

Le Goff, Jacques. *Time, Work, and Culture in the Middle Ages.* Trans. Arthur Goldhammer. Chicago: University of Chicago Press, 1980.

Leighton, Albert. *Transport and Communication in Early Medieval Europe.* Newton Abbot: David and Charles, 1972.

Leiss, William. *The Domination of Nature.* Boston: Beacon, 1972.

Lennard, Reginald. *Rural England: 1066–1135.* Oxford: Oxford University Press, 1959.

Levasseur, Émile. "Le Travail des moines dans les monastères." *Séances et travaux de l'Académie des sciences morales et politiques* 154, n.s. 60 (1900):449–470.

Lienhard, Joseph T. *Paulinus of Nola and Early Western Monasticism.* Cologne and Bonn: Heinstein, 1977.

Little, Lester K. "Pride Goes Before Avarice: Social Change and the Vices in Latin Christendom." *American Historical Review* 76 (1971):16–49.

———. *Religious Poverty and the Profit Economy in Medieval Europe.* Ithaca, N.Y.: Cornell University Press, 1978.

Lloyd, T. H. *The English Wool Trade in the Middle Ages.* Cambridge: Cambridge University Press, 1977.

Long, Pamela O. "The Contribution of Architectural Writers to a 'Scientific Outlook' in the Fifteenth and Sixteenth Centuries." *Journal of Medieval and Renaissance Studies* 15 (1985):265–298.

Lopez, R. S. "An Aristocracy of Money in the Early Middle Ages." *Speculum* 28 (1953):1–43.

———. "Aux origines du capitalisme génois." *Annales d'histoire économique et sociale* 9 (1937):445–451.

———. *The Commercial Revolution of the Middle Ages.* Englewood Cliffs, N.J.: Prentice-Hall, 1971.

———. "The Evolution of Land Transport in the Middle Ages." *Past and Present* 9 (1956):17–29.

Luckhurst, David. *Monastic Watermills: A Study of the Mills Within English Monastic Precincts.* London: Society for the Protection of Ancient Buildings, n.d.

Lusignan, Serge. "Préface au 'Speculum maius' de Vincent de Beauvais: Refraction et diffraction." *Cahiers d'études médiévales* 5 (1979):98–107.

Lutz, Cora E. "Remigius' Ideas on the Origin of the Seven Liberal Arts." *Medievalia et humanistica* 10 (1956):32–49.

Machlup, Fritz. *The Branches of Learning.* Vol. 2 of *Knowledge: Its Creation,*

Distribution, and Economic Significance. 3 vols. Princeton: Princeton University Press, 1982.

MacKenzie, Donald. "Marx and the Machine." *Technology and Culture* 25 (1984):473–502.

Mahn, J.-B. *L'Ordre cistercien et son gouvernement.* 2d ed. Paris: Boccard, 1951.

Maier, Anneliese. " 'Ergebnisse' der spatscholastischen Naturphilosophie." *Scholastik* 35 (1960):161–188.

Marrou, Henri. *A History of Education in Antiquity.* Trans. George Lamb. New York: Sheed and Werd, 1956.

Martin-Larber, O. "L'Exploitation d'une grange Cistercienne à la fin du XIVe et au debut du XVe siècle." *Annales Bourgogne* 29 (1957):161–180.

Marx, Karl. *Capital.* Trans. Ben Fowkes and David Fernbach. 3 vols. New York: Random House, 1977–1981.

———. *A Contribution to the Critique of Political Economy.* Trans. S. W. Ryazanskaya. Moscow: Progress Publishers, 1970.

———. *Early Writings.* Trans. Rodney Livingstone and Gregor Benton. New York: Random House, 1975.

———. *The Eighteenth Brumaire of Louis Bonaparte.* In *The Marx–Engels Reader,* ed. Robert C. Tucker. New York: W. W. Norton, 1972.

———. *Selected Writings.* Trans. David McLellan. Oxford: Oxford University Press, 1977.

Mayr, Otto. *Authority, Liberty, and Automatic Machinery in Early Modern Europe.* Baltimore: Johns Hopkins University Press, 1986.

Mazzaoui, Maureen F. *The Italian Cotton Industry in the Later Middle Ages, 1100–1600.* Cambridge: Cambridge University Press, 1981.

McDonnell, E. W. *The Beguines and Beghards in Medieval Culture.* New Brunswick, N.J.: Rutgers University Press, 1954.

McKirahan, Richard D., Jr. "Aristotle's Subordinate Sciences." *British Journal for the History of Science* 11 (1978):197–220.

Meeks, Wayne. *The First Urban Christians.* New Haven, Conn.: Yale University Press, 1983.

Meer, Frederik van der. *Atlas de l'ordre cistercien.* 2d ed. Paris: Elsevier, 1965.

Merchant, Carolyn. *The Death of Nature.* New York: Harper & Row, 1980.

Miller, Richard W. *Analyzing Marx.* Princeton: Princeton University Press, 1984.

Mitcham, Carl and Robert Mackey, eds. *Philosophy and Technology.* New York: Macmillan, 1972.

Mommsen, Theodor E. "St. Augustine and the Christian Idea of Progress: The Background of *City of God.*" In *Medieval and Renaissance Studies,* ed. Eugene F. Rice, Jr. Ithaca, N.Y.: Cornell University Press, 1959.

Moncrief, Lewis W. "The Cultural Basis for Our Environmental Crisis." *Science* 170 (1970):508–512.

Bibliography

Mondolfo, Rodolfo. *Alle origini della filosofía della cultura.* Bologna: L. Capelli, 1956.

Montealegre, Alberto. *Formation de la méthode experimentale et son utilisation en pédagogie.* Louvain: Nauwelaerts, 1959.

Moore, R. I. "Family, Community and Cult on the Eye of the Gregorian Reform." *Transactions of the Royal Historical Society* 30 (1980):49–69.

Moorman, John. *A History of the Franciscan Order from Its Origins to 1517.* Oxford: Oxford University Press, 1968.

Mumford, Lewis. *The Myth of the Machine,* vol. 1, *Technics and Human Development;* vol. 2, *The Pentagon of Power.* New York: Harcourt, Brace, and World, 1967–1970.

———. *Technics and Civilization.* New York: Harcourt, Brace, and World, 1934.

Mundo, Ansgar. *"Les Anciens synodes abbatiaux et les Regulae SS. Patrum.* Studia Anselmiana 44. Rome: Herder, 1966, 107–125.

Murdoch, John E. "The Development of a Critical Temper: New Approaches and Modes of Analysis in Fourteenth-Century Philosophy, Science, and Theology." In *Medieval and Renaissance Studies* 7, ed. Siegfried Wenzel. Chapel Hill: University of North Carolina Press, 1978, 51–79.

Murray, Alexander. *Reason and Society in the Middle Ages.* Oxford: Oxford University Press, 1978.

Nerf, Jeffrey. *Reactionary Modernism: Technology, Culture, and Politics in Weimar and the Third Reich.* Cambridge: Cambridge University Press, 1984.

Noble, David F. *Forces of Production.* New York: Knopf, 1984.

Noble, T. "The Monastic Ideal as a Model for Empire: The Case of Louis the Pious." *Revue bénédictine* 86 (1976):235–250.

North, J. D. *Richard of Wallingford.* Oxford: Oxford University Press, 1976.

O'Brien, Mary. *The Politics of Reproduction.* London: Routledge and Kegan Paul, 1979.

Ollman, Bertell. *Alienation: Marx's Conception of Man in a Capitalistic Society.* Cambridge: Cambridge University Press, 1971.

Olschki, Leonardo. *Geschichte der neusprachlichen wissenschaftlichen Literatur.* 3 vols. Heidelberg, Leipzig, Halle: C. Winter, M. Niemeyer, 1919–1927.

Ortega y Gasset, José. *Toward a Philosophy of History.* Trans. Helene Weyl. New York: W. W. Norton, 1941.

Ortner, Sherry. "Is Female to Male as Nature Is to Culture?" In *Women, Culture, and Society,* ed. Michelle Zimbalist Rosaldo and Louise Lamphere. Stanford: Stanford University Press, 1974.

Pacey, Arnold. *The Culture of Technology.* Cambridge, Mass.: M.I.T. Press, 1983.

———. *The Maze of Ingenuity.* Cambridge, Mass.: M.I.T. Press, 1976.

Bibliography

Pagels, Elaine. "What Became of God the Mother? Conflicting Images of God in Early Christianity." *Signs* 2 (1976):293–303.

———. "When Did Man Make God in His Image?" *The Scholar and the Feminist* 3 (1976):31–44.

Panofsky, Erwin. *Abbot Suger.* Princeton: Princeton University Press, 1946.

Parkes, M. B. "The Literacy of the Laity." In *The Medieval World,* ed. David Daiches and A. Thoslby. London: Aldus, 1973, 555–577.

Parkley, Kenneth Page. *Man the Tool-Maker.* Chicago: University of Chicago Press, 1976.

Passmore, John. *Man's Responsibility for Nature.* 2d ed. London: Duckworth, 1974.

Payer, Pierre. *Sex and the Penitentials.* Toronto: University of Toronto Press, 1984.

Penco, G. "La composizione sociale delle communità monastiche nei primi secoli." *Studia monastica* 4 (1962):257–281.

Peters, Edward. *The Magician, the Witch, and the Law.* Philadelphia: University of Pennsylvania Press, 1978.

Petit, François. *La spiritualité des Prémontrés aux XIIe et XIIIe siècles.* Paris: Vrin, 1947.

Pevsner, Nikolaus. "The Term 'Architect' in the Middle Ages." *Speculum* 17 (1942):549–562.

Pollard, Sidney. *The Idea of Progress.* New York: Basic Books, 1968.

Pomeroy, Sarah. *Goddesses, Whores, Wives, and Slaves: Women in Classical Antiquity.* New York: Schocken, 1975.

Post, Gaines, Kimon Giocarinis, and Richard Kay. "The Medieval Heritage of a Humanistic Ideal: *Scientia donum Dei est, unde verdi non potest.*" *Traditio* 22 (1955):195–234.

Postan, M. M. *Medieval Economy and Society,* vol. 1 of *The Pelican Economic History of Britain.* London: Pelican, 1972.

———. "Why Was Science Backward in the Middle Ages?" In *The History of Science: A Symposium.* Glencoe, Ill.: Free Press, 1951, 25–33.

Poulle, Emmanuelle. *Jean Fusoris, un constructeur des instruments astronomiques du XVe siècle.* Paris: Champion, 1963.

Power, Eileen. *Medieval English Nunneries.* Cambridge: Cambridge University Press, 1922.

———. *Medieval Women.* Cambridge: Cambridge University Press, 1924, repr. 1975.

Prestwick, J. O. "War and Finance in the Anglo-Norman State." *Transactions of the Royal Historical Society* 4 (1954):453–487.

Prinz, F. *Frühes Mönchtum im Frankenreich.* Munich: Oldenburg, 1965.

Bibliography

Putnam, B. H. *The Enforcement of the Statute of Labourers 1349–1359.* New York: n.p., 1908.

Radding, Charles M. "Superstition to Science: Nature, Fortune, and the Passing of the Medieval Ordeal." *American Historical Review* 84 (1979):956–974.

Raftis, J. A. *Warboys: Two Hundred Years in the Life of an English Medieval Village.* Toronto: Pontifical Institute of Medieval Studies, 1974.

———. "Western Monasticism and Economic Organization." *Comparative Studies in Society and History* 3 (1961):452–469.

———, ed. *Pathways to Mediaeval Peasants.* Toronto: Pontifical Institute of Medieval Studies, 1981.

Reynolds, Terry S. *Stronger Than a Hundred Men: A History of the Vertical Water Wheel.* Baltimore: Johns Hopkins University Press, 1983.

Ritschl, Friedrich. *Questiones Varronianae.* Bonn: n.p., 1845.

Robbins, Frank E. *The Hexaemeral Literature.* Chicago: University of Chicago Press, 1912.

Roberts, Lawrence D., ed. *Approaches to Nature in the Middle Ages.* Binghamton, N.Y.: Center for Medieval and Early Renaissance Studies, 1982.

Roehl, Richard. "Plan and Reality in a Medieval Monastic Economy: The Cistercians." *Studies in Medieval and Renaissance History* 9 (1972):83–113.

Roover, Raymond de. "The Concept of the Just Price: Theory and Economic Policy." *Journal of Economic History* 18 (1958):418–434.

Rosenwein, Barbara. "Rules and the *Rule* at Tenth-Century Cluny." *Studia monastica* 19 (1977):307–320.

———and Lester K. Little. "Social Meaning in the Monastic and Mendicant Spiritualities." *Past and Present* 63 (1974):4–32.

Rossi, Paolo. *The Dark Abyss of Time.* Trans. Lydia G. Cochrane. Chicago: University of Chicago Press, 1984.

———. *Francis Bacon: From Magic to Science.* Trans. Sacha Rabinovich. Chicago: University of Chicago Press, 1968.

———. *Philosophy, Technology, and the Arts in the Early Modern Era.* Trans. Salvator Attanasio. New York: Harper & Row, 1970.

Rousseau, Philip. "Cassian, Contemplation, and the Cenobitic Life." *Journal of Ecclestical History* 26 (1975):113–126.

Runciman, Steven. *The Medieval Manichee: A Study of the Christian Dualist Heresy.* Cambridge: Cambridge University Press, 1947.

Samuelsson, Kurt. *Religion and Economic Action.* New York: Basic Books, 1961.

Sanday, Peggy Reeves. *Female Power and Male Dominance.* Cambridge: Cambridge University Press, 1981.

Schluchter, Wolfgang. "Die Paradoxie der Rationalisierung: Zum Verhaltnis von 'Ethik' und 'Welt' bei Max Weber." *Zeitschrift für Soziologie* 5 (1976):256–284.

Bibliography

Schmitt, Charles B. *Aristotle and the Renaissance.* Cambridge, Mass.: Harvard University Press, 1983.

Sedgwick, W. T. and H. W. Tyler. *A Short History of Science,* rev. ed. by H. W. Tyler and R. P. Bigelow. New York, 1939; repr. New York: Macmillan, 1958.

Shahar, Shulamith. *The Fourth Estate: A History of Women in the Middle Ages.* London: Methuen, 1983.

Sharpe, D. E. "The *De ortu scientiarum* of Robert Kilwardby (d. 1279)." *The New Scholasticism* 8 (1934):1–30.

Shelby, Lon R. "The Education of Medieval English Masons." *Medieval Studies* 33 (1970):1–26.

Singer, Charles et al. *A History of Technology.* 8 vols. Oxford: Oxford University Press, 1954–1984.

Siraisi, Nancy G. *Taddeo Alderotti and His Pupils.* Princeton: Princeton University Press, 1981.

Snope, R. H. *English Monastic Finances in the Later Middle Ages.* New York: Barnes & Noble, 1968.

Southern, R. W. *Medieval Humanism and Other Studies.* Oxford: Blackwell, 1970.

———. *Western Society and the Church in the Middle Ages.* Vol. 2 of *The Pelican History of the Church.* Harmondsworth: Penguin, 1970.

Stahl, William H. *The Quadrivium of Martianus Capella.* New York: Columbia University Press, 1971.

Steenberghen, F. van. *Aristotle in the West.* Trans. Leonard Johnston. Louvain: Nauwelaerts, 1955.

Sternagel, Peter. *Die artes mechanicae im Mittelalter.* Kollmunz: Lassleben, 1966.

Steneck, Nicholas. "A Late Medieval *Arbor scientiarum.*" *Speculum* 50 (1975): 245–269.

Stephanson, C. "In Praise of Medieval Tinkerers." *Journal of Economic History* 8 (1948):26–42.

Stock, Brian. "Experience, Praxis, Work, and Planning in Bernard of Clairvaux: Observations on the *Sermones in Cantica.*" In *The Cultural Context of Medieval Learning,* ed. John E. Murdoch and Edith Sylla. Dordrecht: Reidel, 1975, 219–268.

Te Brake, William H. "Air Pollution and Fuel Crisis in Pre-Industrial London: 1250–1650." *Technology and Culture* 16 (1975):337–359.

Thomas, Keith. *Man and the Natural World.* New York: Pantheon, 1983.

———. *Religion and the Decline of Magic.* New York: Charles Scribner's Sons, 1971.

———. "Work and Leisure in Pre-Industrial Society." *Past and Present* 29 (1964):50–62.

Bibliography

Thomas, William L., ed. *Man's Role in Changing the Face of the Earth*. 2 vols. Chicago: University of Chicago Press, 1956.

Thomson, Thomas. *Sketch of the Progress of Physical Science*. New York: Greeley and McElrath, 1843.

Ucko, Peter, ed. *Domestication and Exploitation of Plants and Animals*. London: Duckworth, 1969.

Van der Meulen, J. "A Logos Creator at Chartres and Its Copy." *Journal of the Warburg and Courtauld Institutes* 29 (1966):82–100.

Van Doren, Charles. *The Idea of Progress*. New York: Praeger, 1967.

Vignes, Maurice. "Les doctrines économiques et morales de Saint Bernard sur la richesse et le travail." *Revue d'histoire économique et sociale* 16 (1928):547–585.

———. *Saint Bernard et son temps*. Dijon: Association Bourguignonne des sociétés savantes, 1928.

Vogüé, Adalbert de. "The Cenobitic Rules in the West." *Cistercian Studies* 12 (1977):175–183.

———. "Travail et alimentation dans les règles de saint Benoît et du Maître." *Revue bénédictine* 74 (1964):242–251.

Wallace, William. *Galileo and His Sources*. Princeton: Princeton University Press, 1984.

———. *Prelude to Galileo*. Dordrecht: Reidel, 1981.

Washburn, Sherwood L. "Tools in Human Evolution." *Scientific American* 203 (1962):63–75.

Watson, Andrew H. "The Arab Agricultural Revolution and Its Diffusion, 700–1100." *Journal of Economic History* 34 (1974):8–35.

Weber, Max. *Economy and Society*. Trans. E. Fischoff et al. Berkeley: University of California Press, 1968.

———. *General Economic History*. Trans. Frank Knight. New Brunswick, N.J.: Rutgers University Press, 1981.

———. *The Protestant Ethic and the Spirit of Capitalism*. Trans. Talcott Parsons. New York: Charles Scribner's Sons, 1958.

Weisheipl, James A. "Classification of the Sciences in Medieval Thought." *Medieval Studies* 27 (1965):54–90.

———. "The Nature, Scope, and Classification of the Sciences." In *Science in the Middle Ages*, ed. David C. Lindberg. Chicago: University of Chicago Press, 1978:461–482.

Welbourn, F. B. "Man's Dominion." *Theology* 78 (1975):561–568.

Wemple, Suzanne. *Women in Frankish Society: Marriage and the Cloister, 500–900*. Philadelphia: University of Pennsylvania Press, 1981.

White, Leslie. "On the Use of Tools by Primates." *Journal of Comparative Psychology* 34 (1942):369–374.

Bibliography

White, Lynn, Jr. "Cultural Climates and Technological Advance in the Middle Ages." *Viator* 2 (1971):171–201.

———. *Medieval Religion and Technology*. Berkeley: University of California Press, 1978.

———. *Medieval Technology and Social Change*. Oxford: Oxford University Press, 1962.

———. "The Study of Medieval Technology, 1924–1974: Personal Reflections." *Technology and Culture* 16 (1975):519–530.

———. "What Accelerated Technological Progress in the Western Middle Ages?" In *Scientific Change*, ed. A. C. Crombie. New York: Basic Books, 1963.

Williams, Raymond. *Marxism and Literature*. Oxford: Oxford University Press, 1977.

Winner, Langdon. *Autonomous Technology*. Cambridge, Mass.: M.I.T. Press, 1977.

Wolf, Eric. *Europe and the People Without History*. Berkeley: University of California Press, 1982.

Woolfson, Charles. *The Labour Theory of Culture*. London: Routledge and Kegan Paul, 1982.

Workman, Herbert. *The Evolution of the Monastic Ideal*. London: Kelly, 1913.

Yates, Frances. *Collected Essays: Lull and Bruno*. London: Routledge and Kegan Paul, 1982.

Zilsel, Edgar. "The Genesis of the Concept of Scientific Progress." *Journal of the History of Ideas* 6 (1945):325–349.

———. "The Sociological Roots of Science." *American Journal of Sociology* 47 (1942):544–562.

Index

Index